Design for
Passenger Transport

Based on the proceedings of the Conference held at the University of Nottingham in April 1978 and organised by the Construction Industry Conference Centre Limited in association with:-

Chartered Institute of Transport
Design Council
Society of Industrial Artists and Designers
Design and Industries Association
Institution of Mechanical Engineers

Design for Passenger Transport

Edited by

FRANK HEIGHT

and

ROY CRESSWELL

PERGAMON PRESS

OXFORD · NEW YORK · TORONTO · SYDNEY · PARIS · FRANKFURT

U.K.	Pergamon Press Ltd., Headington Hill Hall, Oxford OX3 0BW, England
U.S.A.	Pergamon Press Inc., Maxwell House, Fairview Park, Elmsford, New York 10523, U.S.A.
CANADA	Pergamon of Canada, Suite 104, 150 Consumers Road, Willowdale, Ontario M2J 1P9, Canada
AUSTRALIA	Pergamon Press (Aust.) Pty. Ltd., P.O. Box 544, Potts Point, N.S.W. 2011, Australia
FRANCE	Pergamon Press SARL, 24 rue des Ecoles, 75240 Paris, Cedex 05, France
FEDERAL REPUBLIC OF GERMANY	Pergamon Press GmbH, 6242 Kronberg-Taunus, Pferdstrasse 1, Federal Republic of Germany

First edition 1979

British Library Cataloguing in Publication Data

Design for Passenger Transport *(Conference), University of Nottingham, 1978*
Design for passenger transport.
1. Terminals (Transportation) - Great Britain - Design and construction - Congresses 2. Vehicles - Design and construction - Congresses
I. Height, Frank II. Cresswell, Roy
629.04   TA1225   78-41264
ISBN 0-08-023735-5

The opinions expressed in this book are the authors' and not necessarily those of the editors, publisher or the Construction Industry Conference Centre Limited.

Printed and bound at William Clowes & Sons Limited Beccles and London

Contributors

THOMAS BEAGLEY, CB, FCIT, President, Chartered Institute of Transport; Deputy Chief Executive II, Property Services Agency, Department of the Environment.

DAVID S. BURNICLE, BEng, CEng, MIMechE, Product Engineering Director, Leyland Vehicles Ltd.

H.G. CONWAY, CBE, Deputy Chairman, Engineering Design Advisory Committee, Design Council.

JAMES S. COUSINS, RIBA, FSIAD, FRSA, Director of Industrial Design, British Railways Board (Member of the Organising Committee).

ROY CRESSWELL, BA, PhD, FRTPI, MCIT, AMBIM, Senior Lecturer, Department of Town Planning, University of Wales Institute of Science and Technology, Cardiff (Member of the Organising Committee).

RICHARD DEIGHTON, MA, MSc, Operational Research Manager, British Airports Authority.

I.C. DOWNS, Dipl.Arch., Dipl.TP, RIBA, MRTPI, Assistant County Architect, West Midlands County Council.

P.R. EVANS, MA, Chief Marketing Executive, Greater Manchester Transport.

PROFESSOR SIR HUGH FORD, DSc, PhD, CEng, FIMechE, FRS, President, The Institution of Mechanical Engineers; Head of Department of Mechanical Engineering, Imperial College of Science and Technology, University of London.

M. HEATH, Supervisor, Passenger Vehicle Division, Leyland Vehicles Ltd.

PROFESSOR FRANK HEIGHT, Des RCA, CEng, MIMechE, FSIAD, School of Industrial Design, Royal College of Art (Chairman of the Organising Committee).

GERRY MOLONY, CEng, MRAeS, Manager, Interior Requirements, British Airways Engineering Base.

DICK NEGUS, FSIAD, FSTD, President, Society of Industrial Artists and Designers; Partner Negus and Negus, London.

RAYMOND PLUMMER, TD, MCAM, Honorary Director, Design and Industries Association; Principal, Raymond Plummer Ltd., Publicity Consultants.

M.G. POLLARD, BSc, PhD, CEng, MIMechE, Research and Development Division, British Railways Board.

EIRLYS R.C. ROBERTS, CBE, BA (Hons) Cantab, Director-General, Office of European Consumer Organisations.

THE RT. HON. KENNETH ROBINSON, FCIT, Chairman London Transport.

JULES RONDEPIERRE, BS Ind.Des., Director, Corporate Design, TWA, New York.

WILLIAM SHULTZ, BA(Maths), AIAA, AAS, SETP, IHS, MTAI, NDTA, Director of Sales, Boeing Marine Systems.

RACHEL WATERHOUSE, MA, PhD, Chairman, Institute for Consumer Ergonomics, Loughborough University of Technology.

ALFRED A. WOOD, Dipl.Arch., Dipl.TP, FRIBA, FRTPI, FRSA, County Planner Architect, West Midlands County Council.

Conference Organising Committee

Professor Frank Height, Des RCA, CEng, MIMechE,
FSIAD, Chairman.

J.S. Cousins, RIBA, FSIAD, FRSA,
Representing The Society of Industrial Artists and Designers.

R.W. Cresswell, BA, PhD, FRTPI, MCIT, AMBIM,

M. Fetherstonough, FSIAD,
Representing The Design and Industries Association.

L.S. Higgins, MA, FCIT,
Representing The Chartered Institute of Transport.

W.H. Mayall, CEng, MRAeS,
Representing The Design Council.

G. McKay, OBE, CEng, FIMechE, MIRTE,
Representing The Institution of Mechanical Engineers.

ACKNOWLEDGEMENTS

The Editors and the Organising Committee wish to thank all the people who have participated in the arrangements and operation of the Conference and in the production of these proceedings.

A particular word of thanks is given to Jean Stephens, Elizabeth Howe, Carol Murrell, Louise Nixon and their colleagues at the Construction Industry Conference Centre for their efficiency in the organisation and administration.

Preface

This book is based on the proceedings of the Conference 'Design for Passenger Transport' held at the University of Nottingham in 1978, and organised in association with five bodies concerned with this subject – the Chartered Institute of Transport, the Design Council, the Society of Industrial Artists and Designers, the Design and Industries Association and the Institution of Mechanical Engineers. The aim of the Conference was to explore ways in which the standards of design, particularly related to the environment, could be improved to enhance the psychological and physical well-being of both passengers and staff. Various aspects of design in the fields of air, rail, road and water passenger transport were studied. This wide coverage was a deliberate policy in the hope that the possibilities would be explored for the interchange of techniques between modes of transport. Perhaps the uniqueness of this Conference, and of great significance, was the involvement of consumers' interests.

Parts One and Two deal with Passenger Handling Design, ranging from the design of interchanges and the needs of individual passengers to the sophistication of Corporate Design programmes for large transport undertakings. Parts Three and Four examine various forms of Vehicle Design with an emphasis on passenger comfort.

The wide range of operators', manufacturers' and consumers' interests represented at the Conference indicate the need for a continual exchange of ideas, and the fostering of a mutual understanding between them, which could lead to the attainment of higher standards of design for passenger transport.

Frank Height
Roy Cresswell

November 1978

Contents

Introduction :

Good Design in Transport

The Rt. Hon. Kenneth Robinson

For anyone who cares about design, and particularly design in industry, it must be all too obvious that in this context a special obligation falls upon those who operate passenger transport. As head of London Transport I tend inevitably to see this problem in the context of urban public transport, and it is here that the problem – and the challenge – can be seen in sharpest focus. Ubiquitous, obtrusive and inescapable, public transport is an integral and intimate part of the everyday life of city dwellers everywhere. The design standards set by public transport – in the widest senses of the word 'design' – will become a not insignificant part of the local culture, whether by acceptance or by rejection, and its basic notions will rub off, often perhaps unconsciously, on millions who would never give a construct-ive thought to the concept of design as such nor to aesthetic or functional considerations in general.

The same considerations may be said to apply, in a slightly different sense, to the other two principal areas of mass passenger transport, railways and air transport. Here the impact on the public and the environment is less concentrated though more widespread than in the case of urban public transport, with a third dimension added in the case of air travel. I believe therefore that what I have to say in the course of this introduction will, though essentially based on my London Transport experience, be found to be relevant in the wider context of passenger transport generally – "people moving" as our American friends so pertinently call it.

The range of impact which urban public transport makes on the city environment is considerable; the exterior and interior design of bus and train rolling stock, the design of stations above and below ground, of bus garages, train depots and interchanges, down to the relatively small change of street furniture associated with bus transport; posters, signs and graphics in general; the totality of all these can result in a discernible, satisfying and even exciting house style which marries function with visual satisfaction; or it can produce visual clutter, according to the success or failure of the undertaking's attention to design.

To return then to the area of my own experience. We in the London Transport Executive are the inheritors of a great tradition in design which goes back half a century and more, and which will forever be associated with the name of Frank Pick. In the nineteen-twenties and thirties Pick was one of a very small group of far-sighted men in industry and public service who thought long and hard about design in industry and, what is more, put their thinking into practice. The names I would place alongside that of Frank Pick, are Sir Stephen Tallents of the Post Office and Jack Beddington of Shell; and of these I would unhesitatingly place Pick as primus inter pares. He was a founder of the organisation Design in Industry and few men have talked so intelligently and lucidly about the nature of design.

Perhaps the best short definition of design is "fitness for purpose", though design embodies rather more than just that. In Frank Pick's words "If art may be put aside as something given by grace, design is integral in appearance values. Design means something purposed, fit for its function, economical of material and labour, sound in form and construction. That we must seek everywhere if appearance values are to be realised. Design is intelligence made visible". Even earlier, indeed during World War I, he had made the same point in a remarkable series of aphorisms, as apt today as 60 years ago. "First, fitness for use; second, quality for price; third, honesty in workmanship. Let nothing pretend to be what it is not .... The test of the goodness of a thing is its fitness for use. If it fails this first test no amount of ornamentation or finish will make it any better; it will only make it more expensive, more foolish."

The message therefore is clear. Design and function must be inter-related. Appearance and visual satisfaction need not, indeed should not, conflict with purpose. Good design is integral with function, and never a concealment or even a mere embellishment of function. All these lessons Frank Pick learned and taught. In the very different conditions of today, we in London Transport strive to put them into practice. How far we succeed is for our passengers and the general public to judge. But I can assure you that in LT good design is never regarded as a frill, to be discarded when the economic winds blow cold. Good design is adopted to the best of our ability because we believe it will enable us to perform our basic task of moving people more efficiently, because it is right in itself, and because experience has taught us that, far from being a costly luxury, good design is in itself good business.

Perhaps I can enlarge rather more fully on the elements of design, starting with the functional concept – fitness for purpose – which as I have said I regard as basic. This idea comprehends both correct and economical engineering design together with a calculated appraisal to ensure that the needs of the human consumer and user are properly met – what engineers, psychologists, and doctors now call the "ergonomic" approach. Design to meet operational needs to the fullest extent is, or should be, fundamental to the approach of any engineer, architect, printer, tailor, or anyone else designing for production and use. As an essential preliminary, it calls for understanding of what the purpose is, and for this to be defined in the clearest possible specification. By specification here I do not mean a manufacturing specification – that is the technician's affair; I mean a specification for use, defining with the utmost clarity what the product must perform and what constraints must be observed. Such a specification is difficult to write, because it demands hard logical thinking; and this is an employment which some may regard as a time-wasting luxury. In any event, the writing of the specification should never be left to the designer alone: he may, as a human being, have his own ideas about what he wants in the product, but he is unlikely to possess all the skills and experience to know what to specify in every respect as to the kinds of use the product may have to undergo, the forms of wear it may have to suffer, the maintenance requirements, and so forth. A slipshod specification will inevitably result in a less than satisfactory design. It might be going too far to say that there are no bad designs, only bad specifications; but it is near enough to the truth to be uncomfortable - at least for the clients. If managements fail to make clear exactly what they need, they will get products which fall short of the best they could have got through taking sufficient preliminary thought.

Since we are discussing design in the context of passenger transport, let us look at this problem of function in the simplest of terms, in terms of something which affects all transport operators, the seat.

Most transport undertakings aim to provide seats for most of their passengers - peak-hour commuters perhaps excepted. Seats in vehicles are therefore an element of critical importance. An almost endless list of considerations must be taken into account in drawing up the specification for and subsequently designing a seat. A seat should be reasonably comfortable to sit on and must therefore have regard to the dimensions of the average human frame and the normal human seated posture. It must also cater to a very limited degree for the larger than average, but such tolerance will need to be balanced against the prime economic consideration, namely the need to maximise carrying capacity in terms of passenger numbers. The degree of seating comfort will probably vary with the likely length of journey; a seat in a long-distance aircraft or train may well have to approximate more nearly to the comfort of an armchair than the seat on a city bus. Springing and upholstery will doubtless take into account and as far as possible compensate for the movement of the vehicle itself. The seat covering must be durable but need not be hard or abrasive; it should pay regard to the costs of maintenance and therefore be capable of being easily cleaned. The design of the covering material offers a wide scope to the designer but should at least harmonise with the colour scheme of the vehicle interior. Doubtless there are other factors I have failed to mention, but what I have sought to show is that a well-designed vehicle seat is unlikely to emerge at the end of the process unless proper attention has been given to the initial specification. And if it is well-designed from a functional standpoint, the odds are that it will look good in visual and aesthetic terms.

Good design in the visual sense, it seems to me, has so often in the past emerged as an almost incidental by-product of sensible planning for a defined purpose - planning of a building or a machine or some other artefact to perform efficiently the task assigned to it. The bridges of Telford and Brunel, the China clippers, the Victorian warehouse and the Georgian dwelling-house - these did their job well and generally looked good into the bargain. In our own century the minimisation of wind resistance on moving objects began to be scientifically calculated in the interests of fuel and energy,

economy and increased speed. The aesthetic satisfactions of stream-lined design were again a by-product. And so by process of reason one reaches, as so often, the obvious conclusion - design and function are inter-related.

I mentioned earlier the visual impact which an urban passenger transport undertaking like London Transport inevitably makes upon the cityscape with its ubiquitous buses, its stations, its trains, not to mention ephemera like tickets, maps and posters. It seems to me that a design-conscious undertaking will wish to capitalise on its ubiquity by developing a "house-style", a readily recognisable set of identification signals. Through such a medium the travelling public - indeed the public at large - are continuously reminded of the undertaking's presence in their midst.

More than sixty years ago, when few if any concerns had any conscious design policy, the London Underground group of companies developed a "house-style", an instantly recognisable trade mark or device - the "bar and circle", "bull's eye" or "roundel" which, slightly refined in shape in recent years, has remained the symbol in London that means: "here is transport"; or "here you can find out about transport". Whether it first symbolised a wheel and a beam, or whether it was derived from a railway station name board given emphasis by a splash of colour behind it, does not now matter; the symbol is of elementary geometrical simplicity and harmonious proportion, doing its duty equally well as a name-sign for a station, a simple outline device on vehicles denoting ownership, in outline again on letter-paper, crockery, uniforms, or publicity to indicate their origin. All this long antedated the now almost universal and indispensable 'logo', which we see in such variety all around us.

But this was only the start. In 1916 a distinguished calligrapher, Edward Johnston, was commissioned by the Underground to design a display sans-serif typeface to be used throughout the whole system on signboards, maps, notices, destination boards and blinds, and printed material of an official and semi-permanent kind (as distinct from ephemeral publicity, which can rightly be allowed a more modish presentation). The type face thus designed, possessing characteristics of the utmost clarity and authority and displayed with a proper regard for right spacing and contrast of letters and surround, proved to have the essential quality of a classic design in any field: it has worn well. It was conceived as a large-size display type, and there have been some difficulties in using it in smaller sizes; but recent studies by distinguished typographers have been unanimous in recommending that it should be retained, with only minor modifications, and its range extended.

On the firm basis of the symbol and the Johnston type, the problems of presenting London Transport's multiple impact on its passengers, staff, neighbours, and passers-by in acceptable and harmonious visual forms were tackled vigorously under the guidance and with the authority of Frank Pick who was by then the Managing Director. Attention in great detail was devoted to rolling stock, buildings, publicity and other printed material, tickets, uniforms, station equipment, street furniture, catering equipment, and so forth. Pick relied, with the architects and designers he commissioned, on classic forms of basic geometrical simplicity to make a coherent and satisfactory visual impact - and he had the skill and shrewdness to introduce, under highly sensitive control, some minor elements of visual "shock" which were effective in preventing boredom. Pick was not a professional designer; he was that equally, if not more, important being, a completely enlightened patron, wielding the authority and possessing the resources needed to ensure that his policies were carried into effect.

There has proved to be about London Transport's house-style and basic design policy an element of timelessness. As I have said, there have been of course modifications over the years, but if a London Rip Van Winkle of, say, the 1920's or 30's were to re-emerge in the London of today he would have little or no difficulty in recognising the transport services and their adjuncts. This, I suggest, is mainly due to the fact that Pick and those he commissioned concentrated on basic good design - fitness for purpose - and eschewed the modish and merely fashionable.

I think it is fair to compare London Transport's record in this respect with that of the Paris Metro, which during its principal development period made such extensive use of Art Nouveau. Today we appreciate this style as possessing a beauty and charm - but it is a beauty which is antique and slightly bizarre. It may be relevant to mention that an Art Nouveau wrought-iron portico from a Paris Metro station stands in the sculpture courtyard of the Museum of Modern Art in New York, a gift from France, and wonderful it looks. But for more than forty years the style was regarded as outmoded and eccentric. For the Metro to attempt to repeat it today would be to indulge in historical pastiche.

If there is a moral here it is that the transport designer must remember that much of what he designs is destined for a fairly long life - up to forty years for an underground train, for instance, and even longer for stations. In the course of such a period fashion will change many times, but the basic purpose of his end-product will remain constant. As long as he concentrates on fitness for purpose as his main objective, his work should stand the test of time.

It used to be thought that mass production tended to be the enemy of good design. Such misconception probably arises from a confusion about different aspects of efficiency, from a failure to distinguish between the process of production and the function of the product. This distinction was stressed with typical clarity of thought by Frank Pick. Speaking some sixty years ago, in the midst of a world war, he said: "The end is always commercial, that is, the largest and cheapest output. And while there is nothing wrong in it, it is not all: it is just a partial aim. It is just as important, just as deserving of thought and care, that there should be efficiency in the product as well as efficiency in production. Efficiency in production is the side of industry. There must be efficiency in the product: that is the side of design.

The two must depend together".

Perhaps I should conclude by summarising what I have been trying to say. This book discusses various aspects of design. Rightly or wrongly I have seen my function in these opening comments as that of dealing, however, inadequately, with the nature of design itself, its relevance to public transport and the central role it has to perform in today's world.

The transport operator's task in this regard is crucial. Control of design in any large and multi-faceted organisation is not easy to achieve. But this makes it all the more important that such an organisation, particularly if it lies in the public sector, should have a policy of design control that is comprehensive, consistent and coherent. Such a policy should be seen, not as an exotic activity, but as a completely normal part of the job of those who direct and run the business. They in their turn must recognise that good design contributes to a product of high quality, that attention to design enhances the corporate efficiency of the undertaking and, as I said earlier, that good design is good business. They must learn to ask the right questions: not "Can we afford good design?" but "How much are we losing by bad design?" Finally, good design, in detail as well as in broad conception, underlines, I suggest, the importance of the consumer. And in the end no public provider, however strong his monopoly, can flourish or even survive without the goodwill of the consumer and at least the tolerance of the public at large.

Part 1
Passenger Handling Design

Chapter 1:

Airports, Railway Stations and People

Eirlys R. C. Roberts

Not for anything you could offer me would I have the job of managing Heathrow Airport – or, for that matter, King's Cross or Paddington Station. So I speak with sympathy for, if not sufficient understanding of the difficulties of those who design or run airports and stations. All the same, I believe that the people who use them need sympathy also, and it is on their behalf that I am going to speak.

My own experience of airports starts with Heathrow, Gatwick, Southend, Newcastle, Glasgow, Edinburgh and Inverness and goes via Dublin to Brussels, Antwerp, Paris, Bordeaux, Oslo, Copenhagen, Stockholm, Amsterdam, Luxembourg, Rome, Venice, Milan, Cologne, Kennedy, Washington, Birmingham Alabama, Delhi and Katmandu. So some of my comments will be personal, and I shall try to label them so. Most of what I shall say comes from the reports of Airports and Transport Consumer Consultative Committees, reports on railway stations and duty-free goods in 'Which?', and reports of local railway stations in the magazines of the Sutton, Birmingham, Oxford, Bexley, Cheltenham, Southampton and Bromley consumer groups. Other sources are a study in depth of Dutch railway signs carried out at Utrecht University, and a large number of thoughtful articles in design and engineering publications. Finally, I have used a survey kindly organised by the 'Which?' Survey Unit for this conference. In it they asked a sample of people what they thought about airports and stations, which they liked and which they disliked, and what changes in them they would like to see.

AIRPORTS

Let us start with airports and with the easiest opinions to establish – people's dislikes about the airports they know.

RETRIEVING LUGGAGE The length of time people have to wait to retrieve their luggage at the end of their journey is the chief complaint. It comes highest on the list both in the British Airports Authority's surveys and in the Heathrow and Gatwick Consultative Committees' reports.

Last year, at Terminal 3 in Heathrow, it was said that the average time from landing to retrieval of the last piece of luggage was 48 minutes; similar delays were common in Terminals 1 and 2. The British Airports Authority's aim is an average of 40 minutes.

People mind about a long wait, particularly, I believe, because they are already tired. First, they, and their luggage, had to get to the air terminal, then to the airport, then to check in, then through passport control, then through security, then to a long walk, then to a wait in the departure lounge, then on to the aircraft and the flight, usually cramped, then off the aircraft, then a long walk, then through passport

control and by the time they get to the luggage reclaim, they've about had it; a wait of over half an hour at that stage is almost intolerable.

The first suggestion from us passengers must be for the airlines to reduce the delay, since responsibility lies with them and not with the airport. If it is really impossible to retrieve luggage faster, then the airport (which inevitably receives the complaints) should tell us why, on a large poster. We will have plenty of time to read it.

My own second suggestion is that – if the waiting time is really inevitable – Heathrow and Gatwick should have comfortable chairs, small tables and, if nothing more, a mobile canteen in the luggage reclaim area, so that our wait could be made tolerable and even agreeable.

It is not only tiredness that some people feel when they are waiting for their luggage, there is also anxiety. In Terminals 1 and 2 (but not 3) you have no idea, for some time, at which carousel your luggage will arrive, and you prowl anxiously around, wondering if you have missed it and it has been whisked off somewhere. And when the notice does go up, it gives the flight number but not where the plane comes from. Everyone knows where they came from, while most people forget their flight number, have thrown away the boarding card which gives it and cannot read it on their ticket because the carbon is so faint. Altogether, they do not mind being given the flight number but they positively want to know which place the luggage comes from.

The rounded luggage retrieval carousels at Heathrow Terminals 1 and 2, are, in my view, an abomination compared with the flat conveyor belts you get elsewhere. They throw your luggage around, it can be quite a strain for the not-so-agile to get their luggage off them, and they have to be manned. I have to state this as a personal view because I find no comments about them in the surveys or reports, but it is a strong view.

Trolleys for taking luggage from one part of the airport to the other are a problem about which passengers have been vocal for as long as I can remember. There are never enough, and they are not where you want them to be. The airport authorities have taken this complaint seriously and, both at Heathrow and Gatwick, there are now many more trolleys than hitherto, and they are more conveniently stationed. A complaint now is that they are heavy and difficult to manoeuvre, and I think they are – oddly so, because they must be very expensive.

BEING TOLD I remember once being stranded at Schipol Airport in the middle of the night with the plane not leaving, with nowhere to go and no one to tell us what was happening. A British television crew, braver than I, practically broke the place up in their rage and frustration and I still remember my feeling of impotent fury, simply because we didn't know what was going to happen to us and no one would tell us. I also remember, on the other hand, the gratitude (at least mine) when a Belgian pilot took ten minutes to explain to us why we were being held up for half an hour on a Brussels runway.

Lack of information, poor signposting and inaudible announcements have always been a worry to passengers in airports; however, managers and designers seem to have taken the problem seriously and, with time, made many improvements. But I sometimes wonder if they get far enough inside our skins.

A motorist driving from London to Heathrow, is guided off the motorway in plenty of time, with very clear, large signs telling him how to get to Terminal 1, 2 or 3. This is splendid if he knows which Terminal he wants. But he doesn't. He knows his destination (say Paris) and hopefully, by which airline he is travelling. But he cannot be expected to know that if he is going to Paris by British Airways he wants Terminal 1, whereas if he is going to Paris by Air France, he wants Terminal 2. So I should add something like this to the directions to:-

TERMINAL 1 - "All British, Irish and Cyprus
airline flights within Europe"
and to the directions to:-
TERMINAL 2 - "All non-British airline flights
within Europe"
and to:-
TERMINAL 3 - "All flights outside Europe"

Then you just have to hope the motorist knows that Paris is in Europe.

But this is a subject about which no one can ever afford to be complacent. It is true that international symbols - such as those for lavatories - are a help. But symbols have their disadvantages too. The symbols for MEN and WOMEN, for instance, are singularly prudish in their attempt to iron out all sex differences. I once saw a most distinguished lady coming hastily, and with heightened colour, out of the MEN at Heathrow. Again, almost everyone who uses airports knows now that there is a tube link to London and would instantly recognise the red London Transport sign. But directions at the "Way Out" of at least one Terminal merely include the word "Trains" in black among your other choices of Buses, Airline coaches and so on. It's a lost opportunity for real clarity.

Last week at Gatwick I saw a young businessman running breathlessly back along a forward-moving travelator which was clearly marked "Gates 19 - 28" having obviously missed the diversion to the left for "Gate 18" for Brussels.

I give these examples simply to illustrate what I believe is the main job in information for managements and designers - that they must never let their imaginations go to sleep. Passengers, on the whole, are not more stupid than managements and designers. But they are necessarily more ignorant about the airport; they may be nervous, not concentrating properly, distracted or encumbered with children, and possibly trying to cope with a foreign language.

Designers have to imagine all this. And managers have to remember that many people do not take in information from print or written signs nearly as well as they do from a nice friendly person who is talking to them in their own language. So it is disheartening to find in airports all over the world, that the INFORMATION desk is so often unmanned - or so inadequately manned that the queue is forbiddingly long.

FOOD One has to move delicately here because passengers come in all sorts, and what one person finds quite good, another will find inedible. But about some things they are agreed. A survey in 1976 of 4,700 passengers at Heathrow, Gatwick, Edinburgh and Glasgow airports found the catering at the buffets either adequate (42%) or positively good (51%). But the passengers criticised specific points. They thought prices were high, seats not comfortable, and the surroundings dirty - floors and tables should be cleaned more often.

The criticism about cleanliness is particularly interesting because it is made strongly by foreigners. Clearly, half the fault lies with us passengers - we leave litter and mess - but the other half rests with the airport. They need more cleaners, going around more often. In fact it is all part of a larger problem. Most English people would probably be shocked to discover that other European nations consider us dirty, but many of them do; compared with most northern Europeans we certainly are. British airports cannot be expected to solve the national problem. But with more cleaners in the buffets and some firm notices they might lead the way.

WALKING, WAITING AND QUEUEING I have an ambivalent feeling about the long walks necessary at all major airports, wherever they are. I don't say that I enjoy them, but they are the only exercise I am likely to get that day, so I know they're good for me. And that goes for businessmen with briefcases. But it does not go for travellers with heavy handluggage or mothers with children or the old or rheumaticky. Passengers in general do not like these long walks (57% of those who answered a British Airports Authority questionnaire on Heathrow).

Travelators (when they are working) help, and so do sufficient trolleys. Gatwick promises shorter walks in future in their sympathetic notices to trudging passengers, but I have seen no suggestions that any of the other big airports are going to shorten theirs.

Waiting, even when sitting down, let alone standing in a queue, is something most passengers find very wearisome and it is - obviously - particularly wearisome when planes are late and the waiting is unexpected. You worry helplessly about the people waiting to meet you, equally helpless, at the other end.

Manchester Airport once solved the last problem by having a service which would get a message to the people waiting for you, wherever they were. Manchester no longer has the service and I know of no other airport which does this.

For normal routine waits, between check-in and boarding, conditions at most of the airports I know are not bad. The airports were obviously able to plan for them. But long waits for transit passengers are normal enough and so, unfortunately, are those for passengers whose planes have been delayed. No one seems to have planned for them.

It is better to be delayed in some airports than others. Brussels on a hot summer's day, with the sun pouring in through the great glass wall of the concourse, is as good as a Southern beach. Amsterdam and Copenhagen have superb shops. Dublin has Pay-television fixed to the chair rests. But it has always puzzled me that no entertainment (which could be charged for) is provided for these normal, if unplanned, waiting times.

Consider children, for instance. There is a play area for children on the Queen's Building in Heathrow, but it is a long trek to get there and, in any case, once there you cannot hear the flight announcements. So what mother in her senses, waiting for a delayed plane , is going to take her children there? I do not know of any other airport which has a play area for children - certainly I have never seen announcements about them. If there were one, even if it provided no more than a large colour television, it would take some of the misery out of parental waiting, to say nothing of the children.

For the people in this audience I suppose a few hours' waiting is not unbearable. We can always read or do some work. But thousands of people don't choose to pass their time that way. Why couldn't they have, within the departure area, a television room, or a small news cinema or even advertising colour slides? Heathrow, certainly, would cry out about lack of space, but everything could be charged for and most airports could find room for something that would make money as well as adding so greatly to the amenities.

DUTY FREE In this country, duty on a £4 - £5 bottle of whisky is about 75%. The price difference between airport and U.K. off-licence is about £1.25, or about 33%. This is nothing like the full 75% duty. The savings on cigarettes are greater. Sherry, incidentally, except in Amsterdam and Madrid, is actually dearer in foreign airport shops than it is as home. "Duty-free" is therefore, a misleading expression, to say the least, and it deceives some people, but not all. In answer to the Consumers' Association questionnaire, only 5% thought you saved all the duty on alcohol, 9% all the duty on tobacco. On scent, you save very little, if anything, because scent carries little duty. And on other goods you may save only VAT and import duty - soon cancelled out if prices in the country in which you are buying are higher than those at home.

Large areas of most of the departure lounges of the airports I know are taken up by these "duty-free" shops and the proprietors (and, through them, the airports) are said to make a handsome profit. Customs officers point out that the shops arose only by transference, as it were - ship's crews were allowed duty-free liquor, couldn't drink all their allowance on board and so were allowed to take it ashore.

They see them as an untidy anachronism, of no great benefit to passengers. However, people like them and no one is likely to suggest abolishing this minor pleasure of an often wearisome journey.

However, passengers are well advised to know the prices in the shops at home and do the necessary arithmetic, or alternatively refer to the 'Which?' report.

THE DISABLED My impression is that the British Airports Authority pays much attention to severely disabled passengers, providing special lavatories and wheelchairs where required. I do not know what the disabled think, but my suspicion is that the long walks and scarcity of trolleys are hard on those who have some intermediate disability.

GETTING TO THE AIRPORT There is no doubt whatever that the tube link from Heathrow to Central London is an enormous advantage. It does not seem to be much quicker than the airport bus together with whatever transport you need to get to the West London Air Terminal. But certainly for anyone who uses the Piccadilly, District or Metropolitan line it is much more convenient. I know that when I reach Heathrow late in the evening it is a relief to know that there is only one stage left before getting to King's Cross. It's as convenient as the little train that lands you in the middle of Brussels and much more convenient than the one from Charles de Gaulle which deposits you on the outskirts of Paris.

But there are criticisms. The rolling stock is new and the bays at the end of each compartment are larger than normal to accommodate luggage. But people don't put their luggage there, presumably because they cannot see it and are afraid it might be stolen. Why not install wired cages like they have on some airport buses on the Continent, and a glass wall between them and the passengers? What people do at the moment is to put their suitcases in front of them, over-lapping their neighbour's feet and making them exceedingly uncomfortable.

More serious is the comment that the airport tube train is most convenient only for the Piccadilly and District lines. Anyone who wants to go to Victoria, Waterloo, Paddington, Euston or Liverpool Street is out of luck and has to change. This is in line, incidentally, with the general gap in London's railway planning. In Paris, buses link all the main railway stations. We have no such service. No doubt it's good for taxis; it's bad for passengers.

CONSULTATIVE COMMITTEES All seven British Airports Authority airports have Consumer Consultative Committees, whose job it is to consult with the airport authorities on all matters concerning the interests of the users of the aero-drome and the people living around it. The members of these Committees are predominantly representatives of the local authorities in the area. The Heathrow and Gatwick Committees have one representative each from Consumers' Association and from a local environmentalist group. The Heathrow Committee also has 4 members of the general public, chosen from 400 volunteers who offered to serve. In the circumstances, it is scarcely surprising that the Committee should have concentrated on the problem of the aircraft noise which is such a hardship to people living near, and to have paid little attention, in comparison, to passengers. The consumer members must feel frustrated sometimes because the Committee's role is only an advisory one and the management is not obliged to take action on their recommendations. But both Committees have now set up a Passenger Services Sub-Committee, on which the Consumers' Association and the independent representatives sit, and they mention a few small ways in which the Sub-Committee have been successful. Heathrow also mentions one in which it was not successful, when the Committee suggested to London Transport that to call the airport tube station Heathrow Central is confusing, especially for foreigners, when there is no Heathrow North, South, East or West. London Transport has taken no notice.

One can only be glad that the Consultative Committees exist, be grateful to the members who serve on them, and hope for more success for them in the future.

RAILWAY STATIONS

Airports are a rarity in most people's lives, railway stations so common they scarcely think about them. But, like airports, they are places where people have to wait - waiting for the train is an essential part of travelling by it. And we are entitled to wonder whether the people who plan the splendid new trains think quite so hard about the not quite so splendid stations.

WAITING FOR THE TRAIN Last year 'Which?' reported on 80 British railway stations and found the few waiting rooms on the main London stations (except for Euston) grim, uncomfortable and unfriendly. Outside London, waiting was slightly pleasanter - more waiting rooms and more seats on the platforms. But the waiting rooms themselves were no more inviting.

Comments from local consumer groups in the past have not been more complimentary and my own experience - for what it's worth - is of wind-swept shelterless platforms in East Anglian winters, and equally wind-swept and shelterless platforms in Belgium, Denmark, Southern Ireland and almost anywhere else in Northern Europe that I happen to have visited.

Unlike airports, railway stations clearly can't afford heating.

INFORMATION One cannot expect that innumerable small stations, scattered over Europe, shall have information systems as elaborate and precise as those of airports. Nor, on the whole, are they needed. But in major stations you need to know from which platform your train is leaving (usually the notices are clear), and on which platform your friends are arriving (clear in London, not always in the provinces). A smaller station should always have its name frequently and clearly marked in large letters so that there

is no danger of passengers missing it - or having to worry about possibly missing it - even on the wettest, darkest winter night. On the Continent, I have usually found the stations so marked. In this country I have not. However, all is not well on the Continent either, in this matter of station information. Six years ago, Utrecht University studied the signs used in stations by the Netherlands railways. The systems of signs and pictograms was designed so as to be comprehensible, both to native Dutch and to foreigners.

The University found - not surprisingly - that the more frequently people travelled and the younger they were, the better they understood the signs. So the younger, frequent travellers identified 77% of the signs correctly, the older, less frequent travellers, only 53%. This was discouraging enough. Even more discouraging was that 29% of all the passengers thought the exit sign meant entrance, and 24%, that the entrance sign meant exit.

LUGGAGE As with airports, the problem is worst for the old, for the not very strong and for mothers already encumbered with children. And again, as with airports, the 'Which?' station survey found that there were too few trolleys and even they were often in the wrong places. In any case, even in a modern station like Euston, there are so often stairs to be negotiated that the trolleys are only half-useful.

FOOD There was a time, just after the war, when British railway buffets seemed to make a great effort, especially with the coffee. Last year, 'Which?' reported on the buffets unenthusiastically, mentioning the erratic opening hours, rarely any hot food except heated-up pies, and sandwiches worse than those on trains. They preferred buffets on the Continent.

The Central Transport Consultative Committee, on the other hand, reporting in 1976, was favourably impressed with the catering at railway stations. They considered it immensely improved since 1973 and said that it often compared favourably with that obtainable outside, especially on the motorways. They pointed out, however, that standards of service had not improved as much as the standard of the food, and thought that special attention should be paid to this and to the question of more buffets being open on Sundays. They mentioned that, on some stations, prices are increased on Sundays to cover increased costs. This seemed reasonable to me, but not to the Consultative Committee.

TRANSPORT CONSULTATIVE COMMITTEES There are twelve Transport Consultative Committees in the U.K., including the Central Committee. They have the same consultative and advisory role with British Rail as the Airports Consultative Committees have with the British Airports Authority. Their composition is similar - mainly representatives of local authorities - but they usually have a few more representatives from women's groups and other local associations. Where they have reported, the Consultative Committees have generally taken a milder tone than Consumers' Association in its magazine 'Which?' or than local consumer groups in theirs. Perhaps, like the airports

Consultative Committees, they are more aware, than 'Which?' or the local consumer groups can be, of the difficulties faced by British Rail and so more inclined to be lenient, which is good or bad, depending on your point of view.

However that may be, this country is the only one, as far as I know, which has transport consultative committees at all and, as with the airport committees, we must be glad they exist, grateful to their members and hope that they get a stronger influence.

CONCLUSIONS

Airports and railway stations are an important part of public transport, a public service. So they should be designed and run primarily for the efficient serving, the safety, the comfort, the convenience and even - why not? - the positive pleasure of the people who use them.

The designers and the managers have to remember that the waiting time spent at airports and railway stations is not accidental but as essential a part of the system as the time spent in the plane or on the train; it deserves just as careful planning. This waiting time is not merely the waiting planned by the system but the accidental waiting caused by fog, strikes, late planes and late trains.

They also have to remember, with airports, as I'm sure they do, that many of the people waiting are bewildered by the newness of the experience or, however illogically, frightened.

From all the evidence I have been able to collect, it would seem that passengers are reasonably satisfied with Heathrow and Gatwick, finding them on the whole, modern, convenient and clean. But from everyone else's experience, and my own, I should like to suggest some improvements.

The airports have already been designed, and cannot be radically changed, and Heathrow, at least, is short of space and likely to remain so. If the long, broken-up progress from check-in to plane cannot be shortened, it could be at least relieved by more travelators (which don't break down) and by a successful attack on the trolley problem. The radical solution would be the one Arthur Hailey suggested in 'Airport' - that passengers should be packaged in a single container at the check-in and delivered 'in toto' to the air-craft. I don't think that they would mind in the least.

In the meantime, there is the normal problem of waiting for luggage and the unscheduled, but to-be-expected, waits for delayed planes, fog and strikes. This is where the airports need to provide positive entertainment, for grown-ups and children, with television, films (advertising or otherwise) and any other way they can devise for relieving the distress and frustration of people helplessly marooned through no fault of their own.

Information is the designer's greatest challenge and can be his greatest failure. On the whole, the information systems in British airports are good, and the passengers move like zombies from check-in to plane without mistakes. But any

new symbol may be misunderstood; the 29% of passengers who mistook the entrance sign in Dutch railway stations for the exit and the 24% who thought the exit sign was the entrance, must be taken as an awful warning.

Messy tables in the buffet areas and litter on the floors are the passengers' fault, as much as the airport's. But they affect the airport's reputation. If more cleaners would be too expensive, the right kind of notice and somewhere very easy for us to return trays and crockery would improve our habits.

Passengers are more critical of railway stations than they are of airports, because they are less modern, on the whole, and dirtier and less comfortable. The written information is worse than it is at airports but the staff (though not always well-informed) are much more friendly in the way they give it.

I have never heard it suggested that anyone should actually enjoy themselves in an airport or on a railway station, but I cannot see why not. On every flight, the pilot hopes you have enjoyed it, and airlines provide very pretty girls to help the idea along. The Trans-Europe expresses are a positive pleasure to ride in and so are our Inter-City trains. Heathrow makes a beginning with its plants in embrasures at one end of the long walk and murals, such as the frieze of blue doves, beside a travelator. Brussels has great green plants growing up great glass walls in the main concourse, and posters which make you want to visit the country as well as being pleasant to look at while you're waiting.

All this is tentative but perhaps it shows that, now and again, the seeds are there. The designers' job for the future - in my view - is to see that the seeds grow, and give us airports and stations that are not merely clean and efficient, but blossom with colour and life.

REFERENCES

Airline Users' Committee Annual Reports 1973/4, 1974/5, 1975/6

Heathrow Airport Consultative Committee Annual Report 1975/6

Gatwick Airport Consultative Committee Annual Reports 1973, 1974, 1976

'Which?' November 1977.   'Which?' Puts Trains to the Test

Holiday 'Which?'   May 1977

Consumer Group Magazines
Vigilant May 1968 (Sutton and District)
STATION WAITING ROOMS

The Birmingham Consumer Summer 1969, Spring 1970
NEW STREET STATION

The Oxford Consumer December 1965, September 1970
THE RAILWAY STATION

The Merry Ferret December 1965 (Bexley Consumer Group)
RAILWAY STATIONS

Consuming Interest November, December 1976
(Southampton and District)

Where in Cheltenham Spring 1976, Christmas 1976

Watchdog Spring and Winter 1969 (Bromley and District)

Special 'Which?' survey (unpublished) 1978
AIRPORTS AND RAILWAY STATIONS

Chapter 2:

Interchange Design

Alfred A. Wood and I. C. Downs

INTRODUCTION

This chapter defines three interrelated elements in design briefs for transport interchanges, namely: care and comfort of passenger movement, the needs of operators and thirdly, the exploitation of the commercial potential arising from a concentration of passengers. The complex inter-play of these factors is considered in detail using the design of a new Birmingham Airport, linked to road and rail proposals and the National Exhibition Centre, as a case study.

The designer's primary task in interchange design is to ensure that the passenger is able to transfer from one mode of transport to another in safety and comfort, and as smoothly as possible. To do this the designer must know and understand the needs of the type of transport and co-ordinate the various interests of the transport managements. All too often, particularly in the U.K., the transport authorities tend to develop each terminus individually in spite of often being adjacent to other forms of transport. It seems tragic that the individual development of terminals connected by indeterminate corridors, footpaths or other routes mean that the passenger often finds himself confused and lost as he leaves one building to seek his next connection.

Figure 2.1. Preferred site of new Birmingham Airport Terminal.

It is essential therefore that the designer produces a unified design approach to the interchange so that the travel weary, possibly jet lagged, passenger, can collect his baggage, gather information, rest and feed when he wishes and proceed to the next stage of his journey without undue concern as to where he is, or how he is to make the next stage of his journey. The detailed demand on the designer within buildings is discussed later in this chapter but recent preliminary work on the development of Birmingham Airport to connect with the recently completed British Rail International Station and the National Exhibition Centre forms an interesting case study.

The designer's task in accommodating and reconciling all these demands in the interest of the passenger is a complex one. It also must be remembered that whilst the passenger must always remain the designer's primary concern, the architect must also fully consider the operational needs of those responsible for the day to day running of the transport and the management of the terminal buildings.

A third element of direct concern to designer and operator is the potential commercial advantage of providing facilities for the traveller. Recent examples show how commercial and environmental advantages can benefit all concerned, if the designer appreciates the financial wisdom of providing well designed accommodation for concessionaires. Modern airports have made a great deal of use of duty free shops, and other concessions, as a means of boosting revenue. Rail and bus stations have been less alive to this valuable potential or have tended to provide the concessions in a very down-market manner: e.g. any London rail terminal.

These three elements are: clear passenger circulation in comfort and safety; fulfilling the needs of operators and management and thirdly, by using the commercial potential of high passenger flow and large numbers of waiting passengers to further the first two objectives.

The objective of clear cut passenger circulation in comfort, management function, and commercial potential must form part of the architect's approach to interchange design, and are currently being studied in the preliminary design stages for the development of a new airport at Birmingham to link with British Rail International Station and National Exhibition Centre.

BIRMINGHAM AIRPORT

When the West Midlands County Council assumed responsibility for Birmingham Airport in 1974, it inherited a development scheme for resiting the terminal close to the National Exhibition Centre, and needed little persuasion that such a project would be necessary to develop the proper potential of the airport. Shortly after the takeover the Department of Trade informed the County Council that it would like to see a formal proposal for the development of a new passenger terminal on the National Exhibition side of the airfield. The airport has regular and convenient services to major cities in Europe and obviously has great economic importance for the West Midlands region. The existing terminal building has reached the limit of modernisation without a radical change by way of a major expansion. At peak periods there is severe congestion and the facilities will be completely overloaded by the summer traffic of the late 1970's.

PLANNING BACKGROUND

The development of the airport creates a unique opportunity to link it closely to the new National Exhibition Centre (opened in 1976), a new British Rail station (Birmingham International), close to the point where two major motorways (M6 and M42) meet. The local plan for the area will be concerned with the strategic impacts of these three factors and their effect on the green belt (between Birmingham and Coventry) surrounding the National Exhibition Centre/Airport Complex. The local plan is now at the "general issues" stage and it is clear that there will be several effects following completion of the new airport:-

a) EMPLOYMENT   - It is estimated that at natural growth level (3m passengers by 1990) on-site employment will grow from approximately 2,300 to between 3,200 and 4,000 by 1990. In addition there would be 2,000 - 3,000 jobs generated in the wider West Midlands region.

b) SERVICE INDUSTRIES- There will be a significant increase of demand for service industries. The scale of demand will depend on the type of passenger traffic and number of scheduled flights.

c) TRANSPORTATION   - Airport expansion will generate increased traffic flows which the District Plan will consider, including the increased use of Birmingham International Station.

d) ENVIRONMENT   - Whilst more flights may mean longer periods of continuous noise, the actual noise "footprint" may eventually decrease as newer and quieter aircraft are introduced. Other considerations which the local plan will examine will be indirect pressures placed on adjacent areas by the airport expansion.

RELATIONSHIP WITH THE NATIONAL EXHIBITION CENTRE

The interrelationship between the Airport and the National Exhibition Centre will develop as more trade exhibitions with greater numbers of overseas visitors create increased travel demands. The new role of the airport could improve trade accessibility, especially to the potential markets of the E.E.C. Birmingham Airport is clearly a vital part of the National Exhibition Centre's attractiveness to the business visitor; indeed the Government's Consultation Document sees the National Exhibition Centre as a major influence in attracting the projected 3m passengers by 1990. Experience gained so far tends to confirm this. Passenger traffic through the air terminal during 1976 was 1.16m, an increase of 27,500 over the previous year, despite a decline in package tour travel and there has also been an increase in general aviation traffic directly related to National Exhibition Centre exhibitions. Special event charter flights from the continent are becoming established as a regular feature of National Exhibition Centre shows. During 1976 extra traffic of the following amounts was generated on scheduled international services:-

During 1976 21% more people used the Paris service, 16% more travelled from Brussels and Frankfurt and there was a 6% increase on the Amsterdam route, at a time when other airports (except Heathrow) showed some decline.

National Exhibition Centre generated traffic has also tended to extend and smooth the annual summer peak associated with air travel. This has several advantages including

1. More effective use of terminal facilities.
2. Higher average bedspace occupancy in tourist accommodation.
3. More consistent demand for seasonal labour (e.g. tourism and catering).

RELATIONSHIP WITH BIRMINGHAM INTERNATIONAL STATION

For physical and locational reasons the existing terminal site has not developed strong links with the station; it seems unlikely that this situation could be changed unless the Airport terminal and Station become more closely connected.

The County has recognised that the situation at Birmingham

differs from that at Gatwick and it is not possible to be certain that rail could become the predominant access mode. However, clearly there is an opportunity to make better use of public transport and the national rail network, and British Rail has indicated it. intention to promote rail access for air passengers to the fullest extent. For this opportunity to be exploited properly, it would seem to be essential for the Airport terminal to be reasonably adjacent to the National Exhibition Centre Station.

AIRLINE AND TRAVEL INDUSTRY REQUIREMENTS
There is increasing emphasis on the use of regional airports by airlines and travel industry representatives recognise that the congestion of the London airports is an unsatisfactory

feature of the British travel scene. Birmingham Airport has three important attributes which suggest that it may be attractive, in the future, to those seeking a new access to the industrial heart of the United Kingdom:-

a)   A catchment area having excellent road communications and containing intense commercial and industrial activity.

b)   Excellent access to the Heart of England Tourist Region which contains many prime attractions.

c)   Convenient and rapid access to Central London (one hour to Euston at thirty minute intervals) via the Inter-City link.

The provision of scheduled services as well as charter flights has been an important aspect of the role of the Airport in the past. This has resulted in a broadly-based range of traffic with scheduled services increasing in importance over the years so that they now constitute over 50% of the

Figure 2.2. Diagrammatic model showing the proposed rapid transit link between Birmingham Airport and Birmingham International Railway Station, indicating how intermediate buildings could be served.

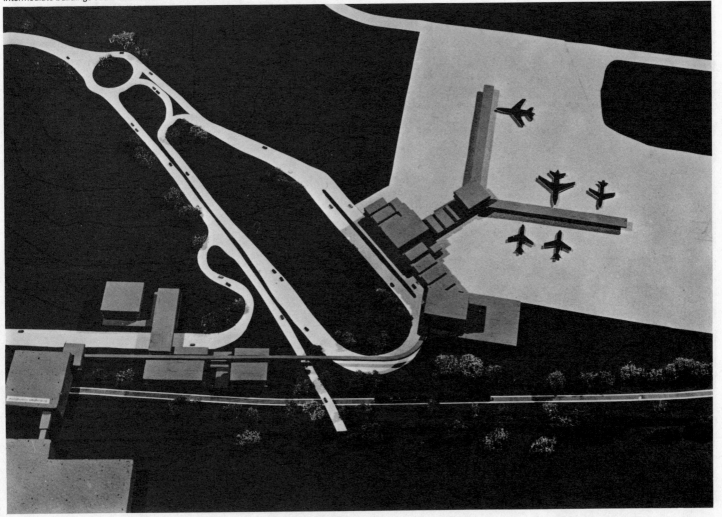

passenger throughput.   The attributes described previously are likely to encourage this trend and the West Midlands County Council supports the view that the Airport's most important role is to provide a good range of scheduled services to continental destinations.

The cramped conditions in the existing buildings do not allow the airlines either to offer their normal level of service to passengers or to provide adequate accommodation for their staff.   Airlines express the view that improved facilities must accompany any expansion of scheduled services.

TERMINAL LOCATION

Several locational options for the airport terminal were considered, ranging from expansion of the existing over-crowded terminal adjacent to the A45 to new locations on the railway side of the main runway.

Evaluation of the options led the County Council to choose a scheme which locates the main terminal building some 400 metres from the British Rail concourse.   This is some 200 metres further than one of the rejected options which had proposed a fixed bridge link incorporating a travelator connecting the rail concourse with the airport terminal passenger arrivals level.   Whilst this solution was appropriate to a terminal adjacent to the railway station, a similar link was not necessarily the most suitable means of access when the terminal to station distance increased beyond 200 metres.   It was considered both too costly and an unacceptable travel distance for passengers with luggage to have to walk further.

The alternative proposed is a small type of rapid transit "minitram" which carries up to 25 people plus their luggage on a fixed track.   Whilst there are several types of track

Figure 2.3. Airport and rail station linked to the National Exhibition Centre (top right).

and vehicles under consideration, research shows that working examples which can provide a good shuttle service also may be significantly cheaper than a fixed link bridge.

RAIL/TERMINAL LINK

The studies centred on four possible types of bridge link:-

1. Simple walkway.

2. Conventional travelator bridge.

3. Accelerating moving pavement.

4. Minitram.

The four options were measured against three possible distances (related to three terminal location options) at 200 metres, 400 metres and 700 metres. The results of projected journey times over 200 metres indicate that the conventional fixed link travelator gives a relatively long journey time (even if the passenger also walks) of over $1\frac{1}{2}$ minutes. The two vehicle minitrams gave the shortest journey time of 75 seconds compared with 85 seconds for the accelerating moving pavement.

For longer distances of 400 and 700 metres the fixed walking only bridge was not acceptable. The minitram continued to be faster than for a passenger to walk along a travelator.

On a capital cost basis the minitram proposal was approximately half the cost of the moving pavement and two thirds the cost of the fixed link. The minitram link of the preferred option will enable a proper integration to be achieved between the Airport and National Exhibition Centre/Station. The importance of this integration and the necessity of having an installed link are considered to be paramount. The vehicle based link lends itself to phasing as traffic builds up, an advantage not available with the travelator. It also allows greater flexibility of levels between Airport terminal and station concourse as gradient restrictions are less demanding than for a travelator bridge.

TERMINAL CONCEPT AND CAR PARKING

The preferred terminal concept provides for full pier service for up to 2.8 million passengers. Beyond this the proposed design is to be based on a throughput of 3 million passengers by 1990, either by using remote stands or by introducing a third pier. The landside space left to the East of the airport terminal building allows the designer to locate carparking in a convenient position for both long stay and short stay. Furthermore it is envisaged that use of separate rail car parks, as opposed to airport car parks, will be unnecessary if the design is right. It is extremely important to keep to a minimum the distances which passengers arriving by car or bus should have to walk, to reach either the railway station or airport terminal. The walk from car park to terminal for passengers leaving on a flight causes most problems. There is baggage to be carried (generous provision of convenient trolleys will of course help) and the passenger also has to contend with the British climate. It

follows that car parking must be provided in close proximity to the air terminal and the current recommendation of the International Air Transport Association (I.A.T.A.) is that the maximum walking distance should not exceed 300 metres unless some form of mechanical assistance is made available.

The design of the car parking should allow each arriving passenger to readily select a preferred parking zone (i.e. short, medium or long stay car parks) and also be able to reach all these zones after having driven up to the terminal to drop off passengers. Easily identified zones by the use of colour codes, symbols, or numbers will ensure quick identification on return to the car after the holiday or journey.

Passenger routes from car park to terminal and railway station should be identified by ground markings or a raised pavement which should follow a clear hierarchy of routes to the main entrances to buildings. These primary routes should be particularly well signed and lit.

There must also be space for coach parking, hire car parking, ample taxi ranks close to the terminal entrances and exits, and also space for petrol filling stations and a service/repair station.

The landside layout should also be arranged so that other users can be linked reasonably close to the terminal building. Opportunities for introducing hotel accommodation, some commercial offices and other ancilliary accommodation all related to the efficient and convenient functioning of the airport and railway station should be reserved as part of the landside use.

TERMINAL BUILDINGS

The airport terminal building itself is being designed on the principle of a vertically separated system of passenger circulation, illustrated by the cross section. This is, of course, relatively standard practice, and allows passengers arriving by car to approach the building along an elevated road to the main first floor concourse level, and to proceed at one level through the concourse to the piers and connect to the aeroplane itself by airbridges. The passengers' baggage meanwhile drops down to ground level, after the check-in, for loading at apron level into the body of the aircraft.

Flight arrival passengers proceed from the aircraft via the pier to the concourse through immigration control. The passengers are then brought down to ground level to be reunited with their baggage transferred from the aircraft at apron level. The passengers collect the luggage, proceed through Customs and leave the terminal at ground level.

Passengers travelling direct to the National Exhibition Centre will probably tend to be burdened only with hand luggage and thus can remain at first floor level before joining the minitram to travel to the railway station. Those with luggage to collect will, of course, have to return to first floor level. The minitram shuttle will bring passengers

Figure 2.4. Section through new Birmingham Airport Terminal building.

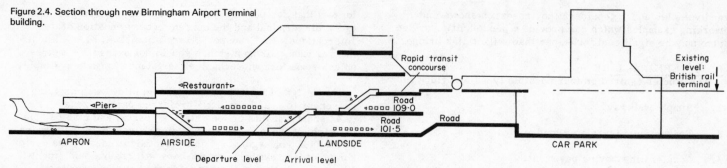

directly into the first floor station concourse prior to a short walk by covered bridge into the National Exhibition Centre. The minitram can also stop at certain points on the journey to connect with other buildings such as multi storey car parks, hotel and offices.

The Birmingham airport complex is as yet at briefing stage and the outline concepts described above will form the basis of design work to be undertaken over the next two or three years.

GENERAL DESIGN POINTS

Whilst the proposed airport/National Exhibition Centre and Railway Station is a unique example in the country of potentially close integration of different modes of travel, there are many factors in the design of any passenger facilities which demand careful consideration by the architect.

PASSENGER CIRCULATION - Should be clearly defined with the routes designed so that the passengers are visually conscious of the relative importance of the route. A clearly identifiable hierarchy of space and route is an essential way of ensuring that the traveller is not bewildered. Ideally, changes in level of the main routes should be avoided, though changes away from the main circulation can add visual interest. Passenger flows should not be impeded by cross flows or interrupted by concessionairy facilities. Escalators should be used where upward movement is involved as well as lifts, for use by passengers including the disabled. Designers should be alive to the task of satisfactorily designing major pedestrian ramps without sterilising large areas of wall and floor space. The disabled must be fully catered for in the design of doorways, ramps, lifts and special toilet provisions. As much as possible of the terminal should be accessible to the handicapped.

INFORMATION - Should be clearly and frequently stated so that the passenger can be aware of his exact location. Flight information and public address systems (which people can hear clearly) are, of course, normal and essential parts of any airport terminal building. Equally important in the case of transport interchanges are diagrammatic location plans and very clear route signs; direction and essential signs should be designed to distinguish them from information signs. Information kiosks are essential so that passengers may obtain help and advice quickly and conveniently. The value of consistent and well designed graphics cannot be over emphasised and the graphic designer should be a member of the design team.

FACILITIES - There must be adequate and agreeable waiting space for passengers and those meeting them. Concessions can provide entertainment and refreshment in these areas as well as revenue. Space should be provided not only for a range of catering facilities, but also for banks, bureaux de change, kiosks for books/newspapers, post office, general and specialised foods, and gifts/ souvenirs. Small shops offering services such as hairdressers and florists should also be considered. Special consideration must be given to spectators located away from the main pedestrian/passenger flows, so that they disrupt the working of the interchange as little as possible. Provision of comfortable seating areas is essential. Generous provision of public telephones and toilets is also necessary. It will also be sensible to provide a creche with an "aunt" to supervise play, and a place where mothers can look after small babies.

OFFICIAL PROCEDURES - Customs and immigration services all have mandatory systems to be adopted and therefore require adequate space. It should be remembered, however, that these procedures sometimes change and flexibility must be built in. Security procedures require a great deal of space and pose special management problems. Official space for medical checks and first aid should be provided with nursing staff in attendance. In designing generally the architect should endeavour to build into his scheme "natural" supervision from other members of the public, by avoiding 'dead ends' and blind corners.

LANDSCAPING - Should be an integral part of the early design studies, not only in treating the space outside all buildings - by for example breaking down the expanse of surface parking - but by using planting, especially trees, on both air and landsides to create an attractive impression on arrival. Landscaping within the building should be easily maintained and used to contrast with surface materials.

LIGHTING - Should be used imaginatively to highlight principal routes, softer lighting for sitting and waiting areas and restaurants.

ADVERTISING - Should be used sensibly so as not to cheapen the visual appearance, but it should be remembered that there is such a thing as "ghastly good taste". In many ways an airport is a town centre under one roof and the sort of liveliness and richness to be found in towns can be valuable as a means of making air travel rather less boring for the 'packaged' passenger.

FURNITURE – Should be comfortable, look well, and should be good quality and easily cleaned. Maintenance and cleaning must be of high standard. There should be a 'family' design relationship between all elements of furniture extending to telephone kiosk design, light fittings and ashtrays.

MATERIALS – Must be of very high quality and should be selected to provide a strong unifying image, be durable and easily cleaned to withstand the current vogue for paint aerosols and felt tips. All surfaces should be at least wipe-clean and preferably will withstand washing down.

CONCLUSION

Any successful design for an interchange must resolve the fundamental problems of passenger circulation to and from each mode of transport but also between them. A bold solution is required creating a unified approach not only at the conceptual stage of design but a solution which follows through to every detail of the project. The designer must be constantly aware that for many people air travel can involve a high degree of stress, and at the same time acute boredom, and the atmosphere and character of the space can have a marked effect on the attitude of any passenger passing through airports, stations and interchanges. An aggressive, fussy or (at the other end of the scale) a sterile environment has to be avoided both to clarify the location and route for the passenger and to minimise the frustrations of delay which inevitably occur. Operators and managements of transport undertakings and interchanges are experienced in these problems and the designer must produce spaces which make any delay at least comfortable and tolerable for the passenger. It is important for the designer to also appreciate the special problems which travel brings – catering for the disabled, the young family or the elderly, or for the child travelling alone. All these form part of the general travelling public who require perhaps extra reassurance and help during a distressing journey. It is here that colour, texture, and "environmental comfort" can make a considerable contribution.

Flying can be a tiring and a deeply boring business, and the primary requirement for the designer to bear in mind is that he must produce decent and civilised surroundings that work well and perhaps enable the traveller to recapture some of the magic of travel still to be found in some of the world's great railway stations and ports, but which still seems to elude us in the buildings created for air travel.

Part 1 Discussion:
Passenger Handling Design

Chairman: Raymond Plummer

RICHARD DEIGHTON (British Airports Authority) I agree with Eirlys Roberts; passengers do wait long times for their baggage and information signs are inadequate. There does seem to have been bad design, a lack of fitness for the purpose.

Air transport is expanding considerably and is subject to almost continuous change. The introduction of the wide-bodied aircraft, i.e. Boeing 747, took place virtually in a three-year period. Within three years airports had to cope with a situation where aircraft were suddenly three times as big as they had been previously. Obviously if an airport, designed to handle passengers and baggage of flight loads up to 100 at a time, then has to handle 350 to 400, and sometimes 500, it is not surprising that problems occur. Another example worth mentioning is the recent introduction of low fare flights such as Skytrain. These created an almost entirely new class of air passengers and we did not know what sort of facilities we should make for these passengers. This happended virtually overnight.

The problem we face in airport planning and design is that our lead time for producing new terminals is much longer than that of the airlines for changing their fleet mix or fare structure. Our lead time is in the range of four to eight years if we are talking about a new air terminal or modifications to old ones. For a completely new airport the lead time would be in the region of twelve years, so we are in the unfortunate position of having lead times of anything between four and twelve years. This means that it is virtually impossible for us to produce an airport which is tailor made for the kind of traffic that is going through it because we just do not know in advance what sort of traffic we are going to have. Therefore all planning is tied to a flexible approach. We now realise that it is much better to adopt a planning approach in which an airport is capable of being modified quickly to cope with different situations as they arise. It is much better to do that than to make a forecast of what type of aircraft are going to be around and then build an inflexible airport to fit, because nine times out of ten it will not happen that way.

I think really the answer is that planning and design suitably carried out will give long term solutions; actually making it work on the day is much more a question of management. It depends on the goodwill, the competence of the various managers, airport authorities, airlines and concessionaires. All these people have got to be able to carry out their business in the best possible way and if there is goodwill you can, most of the time, make a reasonable job of getting the passenger through the airport. The question of management, I think, is very important. In fact if you have an inadequate airport and good management, you will make it work; if you have a very well-designed airport, plenty of space, plenty of facilities, and bad management, you stand no chance on earth that it will ever work properly.

KENNETH ROBINSON (London Transport) Eirlys Roberts was very kind about the Heathrow tube link. She had two criticisms; the first was that it only went direct to one main line station. An underground extension is a pretty major investment and most of the underground investment took place long before Heathrow was even thought of; and it happened that the Piccadilly Line was the one most conveniently placed to go to Heathrow, thereby forming the first link between a major international airport and the underground system of a capital city anywhere in the world. This provides easy connections with all the other main-line rail stations from the airport with only one change, which is not too bad. The other criticism related to space for baggage. In the design stage we talked long and hard about how best we could accommodate airline passengers and their baggage and we decided we could only cater for the passenger with hand baggage; we designed special car interiors in order to do this. There is no room within the narrow confines of a tube train, which is itself limited by the size of the tube tunnel, to put luggage racks; you can only place it on the floor. On the Heathrow trains there is extra space for this. One trouble is that the Heathrow Extension has been so successful that people are travelling with more than just hand luggage simply because it is so convenient. Perhaps I can take up the point about sign-posting which is really for my colleague from British Airports Authority. We did try very hard to persuade BAA not to use the word "trains" on the airport signs, but they would not listen; now they are listening and I believe the change to the London Transport symbols is being made shortly.

MIRIAM HOWITT (Architect and Designer) There have been many helpful comments about passenger handling, but may I make one plea in favour of those meeting people in railway stations and airports. Frequently they are not considered at all. At railway stations, such as Euston, there is a marvellous concourse with about six seats in the middle; and it is a great trial if you try to meet someone at Heathrow Terminal 3. Incoming passengers file through a single door from the customs hall and, if you don't get there half an hour before, there is such a barrier of people (about five rows deep) that it is quite possible to miss the person you are meeting entirely. I think this business of meeting people should be considered seriously in the design of airports and stations.

EIRLYS ROBERTS (Office of European Consumer Organisations) During the Assistant Air Traffic Controllers' strike, I came back one night from Brussels and saw the ranks of people waiting to meet friends from flights that had been delayed one hour, three hours or five hours. I had never seen a more pathetic sight than the faces of those people who had been waiting for hours and who did not know how much longer they would have to wait. This problem (at airports much more than at railway stations) is something that has to be designed for and I think that airports should provide entertainment – some area where you could pay to see a film or slides, or even advertisements, or some other way of passing the time pleasantly. That would solve the problem not only for people who have to wait to go on to their flight but for people who have to wait to meet arrivals on incoming flights. Could I say one thing to Mr. Deighton. On the whole we do understand the problem of the fast development of aircraft and of the long time an airport takes to be designed. We know that things must go wrong and it is there that information comes in. What the airports should not do is to take a defensive attitude or appear to be ashamed of what is going on. We are quite ready to believe that it is not their fault, but when we are told that luggage is delayed "because of an industrial dispute" people seem to be hiding behind the words "industrial dispute". We know perfectly well it is a strike. Why not call it a strike? Then you are communicating with people. If you say there is half an hour's delay in the departure to Copenhagen "owing to a technical fault", that does not tell us anything. If you mean the wing's fallen off, then let us know. There is no need for a defensive attitude. On the whole, you have nothing of which to be ashamed and plenty to be proud about.

T. GLASGOW The U.S.A. Federal Aid for Bus Companies provides for hydraulic lifts so that people in wheelchairs can get into their buses. I was wondering why all British buses do not have the number of the route on the back. It is so easy to get on the wrong bus when approaching from the back.

I would like to mention a point about ships. Could not the 2" step in ships be done away with. I know of one Professor who, every time he uses a DFDS vessel has got to take two wheelchairs with him. He takes one along the companion way and then erects the other one inside his cabin. It is a difficult enough task getting one wheelchair into a car never mind two, so what does he do when he takes his wife and family on a trip like this – does he have to take two cars? Could we have more accessible telephones in ports and in bus and rail stations?

KENNETH ROBINSON (London Transport) I have a great deal of sympathy about the number on the back of the bus. There used to be numbers on the backs of all the London Transport buses. The argument, whenever I took this up with the bus operators was that people ought not to run for buses from behind. They ought to be waiting at the bus stop and would see the number on the front. I was never altogether convinced by that argument.

The American Federal Agency which subsidises bus purchase is now proposing only to do this if the buses are adapted to carry the disabled. This is an area where there is inevitably a conflict between economics on the one hand and humanity and psychology on the other. The disabled person very naturally and understandably wants to be treated like any other human being, having the same transport facilities and wants them to be adapted so that he can use them. The fact is that to design a transport system which the most severely disabled can use is quite inordinately expensive, and on economic grounds totally unacceptable.

It would be far, far cheaper to pay for taxis to carry severely handicapped people around than to adapt buses to do the job. These are the brutal economic facts. As always happens, one seeks some kind of compromise and we try in London Transport, and I think even greater efforts have been made in Paris, to carry disabled people with a certain degree of disablement, but we do not set out to carry the most disabled. Maybe in an ideal world, were there is all the money in the world and all the capital available to us, we would take a different view, but at the moment we have to compromise. On the Underground, we had great arguments over the Heathrow extension as to whether there should be lifts, and we had to argue to a number of people, disabled organisations and their sympathisers that it is no good getting somebody down onto the platforms at Heathrow in a wheelchair by means of a lift, because there is only one station on the whole of the London Underground system where there is a lift from platform level to street level. It is hopeless to try and get somebody into the system if you cannot get them out. Speaking from London Transport's point of view, and I should think that of all other transport operators, there is deep sympathy and a desire to help, but I think fundamentally there is a realisation that you cannot go the whole way and make a public transport system available to the most severely handicapped.

S. HARDY (London Transport) In response to Mr. Glasgow, at the recent "Transport for the Elderly and Handicapped" Conference at Cambridge, Professor Sven-Olof Brattgård of the Department of Handicap Research, University of Gotüborg, made reference to the provision for wheelchairs on the new Townsend Thoresen ships, where this problem has been dealt with.

DR. R.W. CRESSWELL (University of Wales Institute of Science and Technology) On the question of destination indicators, twenty-five years ago the majority of British buses had intermediate stop indicators on the front, together with further indicators on the rear or side. Now, on many buses the display is reduced merely to the route number and the ultimate destination, which may be the name of some obscure point in the suburbs, and there is no indication of the intermediate points passed by the bus. However, by contrast, if you get on a bus in London it may be going ultimately to, say, Shepherds Bush, but the route will be clearly shown in the intermediate indicator, e.g. Holborn, Oxford Circus, Marble Arch, etc. I would like to know from the bus operators and also from the bus manufacturers why this situation has come about. Many operators have actually panelled over intermediate destination indicators on the front of their buses, together with side and rear number indicators.

When the bus grants were first given at the rate of 25% under the Transport Act 1968, it was hoped that this grant would be used to provide improved buses, with perhaps improved information systems. Now the grant seems to have been absorbed as a subsidy. Although the situation has improved in the case of some urban bus operators, for others there has been a marked decline. As an example only the word "Service" appears in the final destination indicators on some buses. Surely there must be an enormous loss of potential custom when there is no way for the visitor or first-time passenger to know where a particular bus is going to, or which bus he needs for his journey.

F.R.F. EVANS (Midland Red Bus Company) As far as rear route numbers are concerned, the general feeling amongst drivers of one-man-operated buses is that they are afraid to leave the money at the front of the bus while they go to the back of the bus to alter the number. Understandably, the reason why route numbers are being deleted from the backs of buses is because of the changeover to one-man operation. I am doing a project at present at Wigston College in which I want to include the remote control of destination blinds. I feel that the public would appreciate numbers on the buses at the back. Any intending bus passenger running for a bus will have a lessening of his or her anxieties simply to see the number on the back of the bus which they have just missed. If they cannot see the number on the departing bus, they are inclined to fret a little. Everyone excepting farmworkers seems to live at a fast pace these days, with strains and stresses building up against them not infrequently. Therefore, anything which we can do, even in such a small way, e.g., having numbers on the rear end of buses, helps people to put aside some of those anxieties.

S.S. WIJSENBEEK (Netherlands Railways) We have just designed a new standard bus which is equipped with an electronic indicator system with which you can change numbers on the back, front and sides, together with the route indicators. There is also an inside route indicator which gives all the stops of the bus, which is operated by the driver/conductor by push buttons, but it is an electronic gadget and is therefore liable to faults and is also very expensive. That is really the whole problem – we bought just one and it is not completely what we want.

P.A. HAMILTON (Bicknell and Hamilton, London) Similar information systems are already working successfully and I am sure that most of you know that the Paris buses all have a route map inside. This map shows prominent buildings and intersections, fare stages and the position of stops. The name of the stop is indicated on the route map and on most bus stop signs. The information is even clearer than on the London Underground. In addition, external indicator boards are hung by the bus entrance. Since most buses remain on the same route the indicator boards and route maps have not to be changed often. I do not know why London Transport buses, for example, do not have such a facility. This type of information should be designed to serve all potential users including tourists.

A.A. WOOD (West Midlands County Council) They also have an external board on the side of the Paris buses which gives an indication of the stops that each bus will pass.

A. GURLEY (National Bus Company, London) Mr. Wijsenbeek touched on the point, but only from the European point of view, and that is the cost. It may not be appreciated that in Britain, buses enjoy a subsidy, in total, including the grant towards the cost of a new vehicle, and some rebate of fuel tax, etc., which is less than 20%. We have just carried out a survey of Continental operations and the vehicles there are subsidised, and I am talking in terms of the cost of operation, to a level as high as 87%. In other words we live in an entirely different financial world from our Continental friends. The other point is that we can have all these systems, but remember that they have to be maintained, and that too is an ongoing cost as well as the initial purchase cost and some of these devices have quite unpredictable lives. If you ask for a simple mechanical repeat thirty-six or forty feet away from the front blinds, you will very often find that you have got a number 13 on the front and a number 12 on the back. Mr. Robinson did not mention the argument as to why we delete the number with a one-man vehicle. There are two rather heavy things between the rear of the bus and the door that the passenger might get entangled with – they are called wheels. If a passenger gets a foot or leg under one of the wheels in his efforts to get up to the front once the bus has begun to move, he can suffer very severe injury.

P. LeBLOND (British Airports Authority) I would like to refer to Mr. Wood's comment about planting. Despite the fact that there are a number of very highly paid designers here, I think we would have to admit that nature is really the best designer. We take to heart very much the idea of planting at our airports and I think if you go to Gatwick, and to some extent Edinburgh, you will see that we have made a tremendous effort to try and keep as many trees and grass banks as we can. Mr. Wood's comment was actually about planting on the air side but there is a slight problem there in that trees tend to attract birds, and birds and jet engines do not mix very well, unfortunately. In fact, a few years ago we decided as an economy measure to stop cutting the grass all around our runways and we found as a side effect that this discouraged certain feeding birds who used to walk around on the short cut grass. When the grass was allowed to grow longer they could not feed and we got rid of part of our bird problem, but we certainly take to heart very much the idea of planting to make the place look a little more attractive.

A.A. WOOD (West Midlands County Council) I take Mr. LeBlond's point about having trees on the air side at airports. The problem of birds, of course, applies probably more when you are getting further away from the airport buildings towards the runway. The area I was talking about was immediately on the air side of the terminal where one really wants to make surroundings a little more agreeable than the sea of concrete that we provide at the moment. The question of birds when aircraft engines are being run-up, is perhaps not quite the same as the birds going into the intake of the jet engine when the aircraft is actually at the end of the runway and about to take off. I doubt if aircraft have fallen out of the sky near Berlin as a result of having trees on the air side of that airport.

RAYMOND PLUMMER (Design and Industries Association) I must say I got a little worried at one stage lest the passengers who ought to be able to see the vehicles they are going to travel in shouldn't be able to see the planes for the trees.

P.J. BROWNING (National Bus Company, Peterborough) I have got two comments on Eirlys Roberts' paper and then a short one on Alfred Wood's. Both my comments to Eirlys Roberts refer to her comments on railway stations. The first one suggests that stations are places where people have to wait. I do not think that is necessarily the case. I was reading recently that in China, where railway stations are considered to be military installations, nobody is allowed on to the station until five minutes before the train is due. I think if Major Cooke who I see is present here from the Ministry of Defence, could make a takeover bid for our stations, then many of the problems we are talking about would go overnight! But, more seriously, in that same paragraph, Eirlys Roberts says that airports are a rarity in most peoples lives, railway stations so common that they scarcely think about them. I think this is the kind of comment that comes from London and the South East where railway stations are common, and so is the use of them. Sometimes one hears, when there is a threatened one-day rail strike, a commentator say that there will be "chaos on Wednesday". Well there will be a certain amount of disruption in London and the South-East but in the rest of the country people will not notice at all, and I think this difference leads to the kind of comment that Eirlys Roberts actually made, that information on railway stations is less important than it is at airports. If you take the country lad from Gainsborough, say, making a journey to Exeter via London; when he arrives at Paddington Station and tries to find his train to Exeter I am not at all sure that his information requirements are any less significant than are those of people making a journey to Delhi or Singapore.

I had a slight feeling of disappointment at the end of Alfred Wood's contribution. I suggest that it might be partly summed up by what I consider is a fallacy when he said the primary task of an interchange is to enable passengers to transfer from one mode of transport to another. I cannot help thinking that somewhere there is a case for transfers between the same mode. He also talked principally about physical construction of interchanges. I would like to have heard just a little more about interchanging between bus and rail at New Street station or even more, perhaps, the problems of interchanging at a bus/bus connection on some windswept Yorkshire moor.

A.A. WOOD (West Midlands County Council) I take Mr. Browning's elegant rebuke, because I think he is absolutely right. I was of course, just talking about the single problem of interchange from one mode to another; but what he says is absolutely right because it is crucial that we must consider that people have got to change from one bus to another in the middle of our cities or indeed as he said on windswept moors. That is something which in a sense relates to the urban designers' brief in how we handle traffic and particularly public transport in our towns and in the country. Now this is a very wide area indeed and I would be delighted to bore you on some other occasion with thoughts about that.

It seems to me that with the recent developments of taking public transport right into the hearts of our otherwise traffic free areas in say part of the centre of Birmingham or in Oxford there are one or two critical factors that emerge. Where there are buses running up and down Cornmarket in Oxford there is a great temptation for the driver to see what his 0 - 30 m.p.h. acceleration time can be with a full load on board: it breeds some very very active pedestrians in Cornmarket I can tell you. The plain fact is that there is some thought needed in the field of interchanges in general.

EIRLYS ROBERTS (Office of European Consumer Organisations) I am delighted to answer the question that Mr. Browning put to me and indeed his comment because it made me feel totally at home. I can assure you there is nothing that we who live in London and the South-East of England are more accustomed to than statements from people in the North about how out-of-touch, altogether ignorant, unrealistic, decadent and absolutely deplorable people we are, so I am happy to hear it again as I have been so accustomed to in the past. But I am sure that Mr. Browning must agree with me, that even in the very very advanced and up-to-date and modern north of England people are much more accustomed to railway stations - they have known them for a much longer part of their life - they have grown up with them from childhood –they do not approach them in the same state of mind of slight worry, sometimes fear, often confusion, that they do at airports. Even "Which?" members, who are supposed to be comparatively well off and get around a lot, do not go to airports very often but commute by train a great deal.

RAYMOND PLUMMER (Design and Industries Association) Have you had many complaints about the indicators on buses?

EIRLYS ROBERTS (Office of European Consumer Organisations) We have not asked our members. We have not done a survey about indicators on buses. I agree with the comments very much myself as a bus user; but what our members are particularly worried about is the shortage of buses in rural areas.

N. TOWNEND (Greater Glasgow Passenger Transport Executive) We often get criticized in the bus industry about the fact that the Continentals do it a lot better than we do. Look at Continental destination screens whilst you are over there; they are virtually non-existent. On most of the services I know they rest on one simple, sensible fact, the service number, and I think this is a thing we ought to perhaps advertise more readily. You cannot really criticize the fact that a bus happens to have 'Service' on the destination blind if the correct destination blind setting is Kings Arms, if you have no idea whatsoever where the Kings Arms is. If it is Service 234 that is the thing you are probably looking for most, I would suggest.

Could I have some views from Mr. Wood on smaller interchanges that are going to become more and more necessary. The interchange where four local bus services meets an underground or suburban rail station. The small-scale where there is no scope for imaginative futurist architecture on a large scale or even for exotic trees.

A.A. WOOD (West Midlands County Council) Mr. Townend is quite right, of course. I would advise him to have a look at what Toronto does in the suburban areas where their tramway system meets some of the bus services. The West Midlands Passenger Transport Executive also has some old interchanges which it inherited: bus entrepot points really, where there is a need to provide shelter for people. There is sometimes the opportunity to provide a bookstall, a tobacconist and so forth. I can think of at least two of those which are historic examples in a sense, forty or fifty years old, which operate really quite well. I think there is a need to do this again and I believe the structure could be relatively modest and it should take a brief from the street. I was trying to suggest this morning that architecture and design generally are products which should take a brief from the area - they need not be necessarily "futuristic", which is the word that Mr. Townend used, but something that is really suited to the character and needs of the area. I think we are going to have to develop in this way in the future as more and more people will inevitably have to take to public transport as fuel becomes more and more expensive.

D.S. BURNICLE (Leyland Vehicles Ltd.) I represent a bus manufacturer to whom all things are possible at a price and I have been trying to remain neutral on this issue of whether buses should carry more destination indicators. Mr. Townend raised a couple of points which I feel I must reply to, not as a bus manufacturer but as a would-be passenger and he is tending to forget the would-be passengers. It is alright if you are a regular passenger and you know where the bus is going, but the motorist following behind the bus is subjected to subliminal advertising when he see a bus route number day in day out and it turns left at the traffic lights so he knows it goes past his office. The day his car will not start he thinks "Ah, I'll catch that 25 that goes right past my office". It has somehow just planted a little seed in his mind. The other point is that the number does not really need changing very often at all. I remember reading that in London in bygone days, they actually used to paint the buses different colours for different routes, now that is an excellent idea if you could see half a mile away which route each bus is on. Technically, as Mr. Wijsenbeek said, there is no reason why we cannot have electronic displays on buses very similar to the display boards in airports. At present the cost is enormous but I am sure with increased volume the cost would come down. I think most of these display units are designed for static use and being shaken about on a bus all day might really prove whether they were reliable or not - probably not.

DR. R.W. CRESSWELL (University of Wales Institute of Science and Technology) In the British context, I feel that the intermediate point indicators are perhaps more important than the rear number ones. However, it is the total information system which is really important. In Stockholm, for example, the buses only carry the route number, but excellent information is given at the stopping points and in the readily available leaflets. I think this is where we are sadly lacking in Britain, other than in a few cases such as London Transport and Greater Manchester Transport. Without this additional information, the provision of merely the ultimate destination and route number is very unhelpful to the visitor and first-time passenger on a particular route. It may not matter what information is given on the actual bus, provided that the total information system is well designed right through from the time-tables, the information in the interchange, on the bus stop and so on to the bus itself.

I think the same principles apply to rail transport and air transport. On inter-city trains until about ten or fifteen years ago there were boards fitted above the windows indicating the route, such as London - Leicester - Nottingham, or on the Western Region there were plates fixed below the windows of trains indicating the route. The new High-Speed Trains have destination indicators, but for some strange reason they are not at present used; the only information given on the trains are tatty pieces of paper stuck on the windows before they leave Paddington, indicating either Bristol or Swansea.

In an age when we have expensive suspension systems and heating or air conditioning systems in trains and buses, it is sad that more attention is not given to better information systems. It is to be hoped that transport operators will give more consideration to this important point when they are preparing specifications for new rolling stock.

J.A. LOWRIE (City of Nottingham Transport) The majority of passengers, interested in route and destination displays, board buses not at a terminus where the bus is stationary, but along the route where the bus approaches at speed. Consequently, passengers have to read the route or destination indicator quickly and ergonomics suggest that it is much easier to read a large numeral than to read a large destination display with intermediate place names. It is easier therefore to direct people to the correct bus by reference to route numerals rather than place names.

R. THOMAS (Manchester Polytechnic) I was particularly interested in Mr. Wood's comments about fun in waiting and about shopping centres, because although I know very little about transport, I know quite a lot about covered shopping centres which were essentially developed, if not invented in the U.S.A. in the early 1960's. I had an opportunity at that time to talk to people like Victor Gruen who specialised in this field. What I discovered was that there was an immense scholarship in how shopping centres were arranged and in fact the palm trees in the Malls were not accidents but they came from marketing research and were carefully considered to meet commercial need. Now generally speaking in passenger interchanges that sort of pressure does not exist. They are normally funded by government or a local authority rather than by commerce. Shopping centres have moved quickly in terms of introducing a sense of fun. Very often their methods are quite corny but the kids love them. Now because I was interested in this link between what both Eirlys Roberts and Kenneth Robinson said, perhaps there is some way we can move towards entertainment and fun during long waiting periods. Perhaps we can learn from what has happened on the shopping centre scene and how the sort of pressure that existed there could be of some assistance to us. Finally, I wonder whether Alfred Wood has thoughts about this and perhaps has a comment on it.

A.A. WOOD (West Midlands County Council) Well Mr. Thomas of course, has put his finger on really a lot of things. The development of traffic-free areas, for example - Germany was the first country to convert existing shopping streets into traffic-free areas; that started in Essen originally in 1927 and then subsequently again after the war and that was long before anything was done in this country. The pressures there, most interestingly, came from an organisation called the 'Werbegemeinschaft' (a shopping publicity organisation devoted to making Essen the main shopping centre of the Ruhr). The shopkeepers were the ones who thought it would be sensible to remove traffic from the streets and make them more agreeable for people to shop in, provided that they could park their cars fairly close to the centre, and provided also, and this is very important in a big conurbation, that there was good public transport access as well. This was, of course, by the tramway system which is partly underground in the city. So I think one does start to see the needs of commerce perhaps leading to better design and for more sensitive surroundings to be created for people. That is why I tried to stress that the needs of commerce ought to be met not just by providing stalls for concessions but by introducing the commercial considerations - I use that word in the widest sense - into the design of, in this case the airport building. But I am not sure the same thing could apply to bus stations, to small bus interchanges, such as those in relatively suburban areas. There the need for the kiosk, etc., can be something that will set the tone for the design of the whole thing.

Incidentally, might I just make one comment, I am getting slightly tired of numbers. I know I am not numerate and that has been one of my great disadvantages in life. Are we going to breed a generation that can only recognise those lavatory signs and all the other signs that we have now, and cannot actually read words? I think it is nice to know that a bus is going to go via Shaftsbury Avenue or via Oxford Circus or via Cowcaddens, in whatever city one is talking about. I think this can be done without too much difficulty. We tend as a nation to try and make things complicated when they can be a good deal simpler. What nation but the British could have produced the Pelican crossing? You know, where there is a flashing amber light where neither the motorist nor the pedestrian really understands who has the right of way? I suspect we do it because we are a sporting nation. I go to Germany quite a bit, and I travel not just on the Rhinegold or the TEE trains but on the local trains as well, the 'Bummelzugen' as they call them. There is a little plate on the side of the carriage which carries starting place and the destination. Well, the passenger knows roughly which way he is going and the staff do not have to change the plates at the end of the journey: they just leave them there, and the passenger knows that the train travels between say Bamberg and Nuremberg. It seems to me that that sort of relatively simple device could be copied without too much expense, and

without the need for staff to get out of their bus and change the signs every few minutes.

S. HARDY (London Transport) I am not sure what sort of fun Alfred Wood visualises in the Underground; perhaps a tunnel of love! Responding more seriously to his point, I must agree that some of our Underground passages and platforms are visually boring. It will be of interest to know that London Transport is doing something to improve the situation in the modernisation of its older stations. I have commissioned one eminent designer to prepare what I believe will be very exciting designs for two platform walls at Charing Cross underground station and another designer to prepare designs for two more platform walls at the same station.

PROFESSOR SIR HUGH FORD (President, The Institution of Mechanical Engineers) I am only sorry that we have spent so much of the time talking about route signs and notices on buses and the like and not enough, I think, considering some of the more important problems, for example getting people from A to B. At airports I do not like waiting around and while it may help to pass away the time to have something in an airport that you can look at, I think the important question we have to address ourselves to is how to move people without delays at interchange points - I think this is much more important. Good design, particularly in access to airports and railway stations, could help enormously in reducing the "uncertainty allowance" most of us feel we have to make to be sure of checking in by the official time.

KENNETH ROBINSON (London Transport) I think the only point I would like to make is a very trivial one. Eirlys Roberts did ask "Why Heathrow Central?" The answer is because we are led to believe that there will be a Heathrow East and Heathrow West before many years and by the time the airport is finally completed.

EIRLYS ROBERTS (Office of European Consumer Organisations) I am of course tremendously encouraged by all that Alfred Wood said and by the reactions of some of the audience to the plea for having much more fun and much more entertainment in airports and railway stations. I think we should be realistic about the long time it will take to solve the technical problems, so, with life as it is, let us make the waiting times as gay as we can. From a consumer you may think it sounds odd, but I am entirely behind Alfred Wood in his idea that the fun and entertainment can be commercial - we can be made to pay - we can use our instincts for buying things, and enjoying buying things, and looking at good advertising. So I am very encouraged.

A.A. WOOD (West Midlands County Council) I think it is very significant that we have been talking about bus indicators and so on. This is really all to do with information, about knowing what is happening; that really is the crucial thing. Sir Hugh said "well wouldn't it be better if we got people there without delay". Yes, absolutely right, but on the other hand Eirlys Roberts and I know that Murphy's law occurs - you know Murphy's law which

says when you drop a piece of bread and butter it will fall
butter side down – and it seems to me quite obvious that one
has got to work on the basis that people are going to be
delayed for some time when changing from one mode of travel
to another or indeed between two versions of the same mode.

Part 2
Case Studies — Passenger Handling Design

Chapter 3:

Design Policy for Greater Manchester Transport

P. R. Evans

PRINCIPLES AND OBJECTIVES

To all but the very regular and blasé air passenger, travel by aeroplane is still exciting, still a little prestigious; the airline and airport staff still intend to make (and often succeed in making) the customer feel important. The airport has its many facilities: the duty-free shops, the restaurants and the bars. Boat travel too has always been relatively romantic and even the best known in this country - the channel ferries - are comfortable, efficient and have good eating and drinking facilities. Inter-City trains have their restaurants and bars; the night trains have their bedrooms which (again with the exception perhaps for the hardened and blasé regular traveller) can have their favourable associations: shades of James Bond, for example, or of adventures on the Orient Express.

With all these types of travel there is (at least for some of the people, some of the time) an element of fun or pleasure. In "Up the Organisation" Townsend said that an undertaking would sooner or later founder if both profit and fun are not present. On this definition (and on both counts) urban public transport, providing commuter travel, should have followed the dodo some time ago. As an industry, commuter passenger transport can rarely be accused of profiteering; and the consumption of the product it sells is not really a rave-up for the customer. The fact that it has not become extinct is the result of its indispensability rather than of any plethora of intrinsic virtues in the market place.

Commuter travel such as is provided in the large conurbations like London and Greater Manchester is different from

Figure 3.1. Greater Manchester Transport logo and examples of typefaces.

the other types of travel both in the objective of the traveller and in the physical nature of his travel. It is purely functional and contains almost none of the pleasurable activity associated with air, boat, going for a spin in the car or out for the day on an excursion by train, where the actual travel itself is part of the fun – a fact exploited by British Rail in its Inter-City advertising with slogans like: "Your freedom starts the moment you board the train" and "Getting there is half the pleasure".

Urban transport serves mainly to get people from one place to another by mechanical means. It is an unwanted means to an end where the end itself, the objective, is not the seaside or holiday resort of rail or boat travel, or the sun-kissed distant shores of air travel. Most of the time it is not even the football match or bingo hall. The end is usually the office, the factory, the school, the job: the occupational environment rather than the pleasure environment. In economic terms therefore the buying of a commuter trip is usually a "derived" purchase, made not for the product in its own right; and in marketing terms it is also what I call a "distress" purchase, namely something which the purchaser would really rather not have to buy. In this respect it is comparable to the purchase of petrol for a motorist. Unlike the case with many motoring purchases, the need to stop (an interruption of his main purpose) to buy fuel (a product he virtually never sees and would certainly prefer to do without) is for the motorist one of the less pleasant aspects of his sport.

If the aim of the urban traveller is therefore different, so also are the means by which he travels. Many types of transport vehicle are more than mere people-carriers. In terms of comfort and facilities, the ship, the aeroplane and the Inter-City train are well equipped. But urban buses, and indeed urban commuter trains, are mere basic transporters. Their prime function, which in turn determines the main objective of their design, must be to carry as many people as possible as quickly and as economically as possible; in most cases their facilities don't extend as far as the "smallest room". The extent of peak demand, moreover, means that many passengers do not even get a chair.

In all these circumstances, the seller's overall strategy must be to combine the main objective (maximum capacity and speed at least possible cost) with that of lessening for the buyer the "distress" element of the purchase. In general terms, this objective dictates a constant effort to improve service specification, bus reliability, bus speed, fares and fare ticket systems and the whole seller/customer relationship. In design terms, it has dictated a priority for improvement aimed both at making the passenger's lot a less unhappy one, and at making public transport less uncompetitive with, for example, the private car, in three main areas which form something of a logical customer sequence in the sales transaction and which also determine the extent of customer satisfaction in the product and therefore its perceived success:

1. The informational publicity, both "advance" and at the point of sale.

2. The place at which the product is bought: the bus station and the bus stop.

3. The bus itself, on which the product is "consumed".

The importance of design, both basic and decorative, in these areas has never been fully recognised in the bus operating industry. No operator, for example, has gone to the extent of British Rail in making Design in its own right a Board appointment. British Rail's success over the past 15 years, particularly in corporate image terms (and in telling contrast with its previous image), is the palpable result of British Rail's getting its priorities right in this case. An unco-ordinated, disparate image will give the impression to the public of unco-ordinated and fragmented thinking and operations, even though the service standards might be good. An achievement of order and a high standard of design will improve the perceived quality of even a mediocre service.

The first of the three areas is that of Publicity.

INFORMATIONAL PUBLICITY
The main objectives determining the design of publicity are the obvious one of actually imparting information, both statutory and promotional, and also the one of making it easier for the passenger firstly to find the services he wants and then reassuring him as often as possible that he has found them; these last two points are geared to the "lessening of distress" theme. Complementary to the main objectives are the ones applying to all the transport operator's activities: the achievement of a corporate image and the maintenance of a high design standard. This has to be done, since we are operating in the public sector with public money, at the lowest possible cost.

In design terms these objectives dictate that the publicity must be "bespoke". In other words the information conveyed must be what the customer wants and where he wants it and it must not be either too much for him or what hundreds of other travellers want. It must be conveniently packaged, accessible and intelligible.

The design of our timetables therefore has been changed from the comprehensive conurbation-wide books (of which the set for Greater Manchester would weigh something like 10 lbs.) to individual bus guide leaflets (Figure 3.2.) covering a single route or a small group of routes; the vast majority of passengers require information for only a few routes. Because the passenger is likely to refer to the leaflets often, and perhaps while travelling, they are designed for easy carrying in the pocket and their typeface is standard throughout the range (a combination of Univers and Helvetica medium) and as large as possible. Standard paper sizes are used, printing being onto A4 which is bound into A5 pages which are themselves folded into leaflets measuring 21 cms. by 7.5 cms., convenient for pocket and handbag and also for the distribution racks which are designed to take up little wall or counter space and to allow clear identification of the subject matter of the leaflets. The racks are designed in modules of 5 compartments (Figure 3.3.).

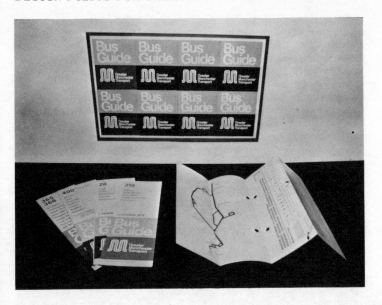

Figure 3.2. Bus guide leaflets.

Figure 3.3. Leaflet rack.

As can be seen in Figure 3.2. the corporate image is created across the range of leaflets by a relatively rigid adherence to cover layout and overall format, although a range of colours (itself strictly laid down as approved ink specifications) is used to indicate such as separate types of service, a new leaflet replacing an out-dated one, etc. The leaflet format does, of course, lead to economy in that it is the single guide rather than a whole book which is out of date at a service change.

Leaflets giving other information (maps, for example, or details of season tickets, concessionary fares and special promotions) are printed to the same format and with compatible design characteristics. An A5 binder has been produced to hold a series of guides for the use of libraries, hotels, information offices and the like.

At the point of sale (bus station, bus stop and even the bus itself) the corporate identity is maintained in the form of the bus stop sign and the information frame on the bus stop. As well as giving first-time information to the passenger who has not already been directed to the particular stop, the inform-ation there is also the first stage of reassurance for a passenger that he is in fact at the right stop, and that his bus will (we hope) arrive at a certain time. The reassurance is effected by both the repeat of the information on the bus guide leaflet and, less directly, by the use of the same type-faces and symbols as on the printed publicity.

The second stage of reassurance is the bus itself (Figure 3.4. - see overleaf) whose destination blind carries, in the same type-face, the destinations and number given on the leaflet and on the bus stop. The success of the publicity design depends very much on the degree of:-

(a) its relevance to what the passengers want to know.

(b) the extent to which it reassures and thus lessens the "distress" element of travel.

(c) its stressing of the positive (e.g. "This is where the 93 will stop "rather than the negative e.g. "The 94 does not stop here").

(d) its visual clarity.

(e) its simplicity: it is not too much so as to confuse but it is enough to communicate and/or reassure.

(f) its design uniformity (of type-face, layout, etc.) not only within the item itself or at the particular location but also from item to item and from location to location.

THE POINT OF SALE

The design principles and objectives for the point at which the product (the basic bus service) is sold and bought are as above: maximum capacity and speed; lowest cost; continuous reassurance; and the highest possible degree of "distress" lessening. At a bus/rail interchange (which we shall take as our example of point of sale design implementation) the last entails more of course than at a simple bus stop, partly because of the numbers of passengers involved, partly because of the more complex network of routes (and modes: bus, rail, taxi and car) in question and partly because when we built, for example, the Altrincham bus/rail Interchange we wanted to seize the opportunity of upgrading the normal down-market image of public bus transport and its attendant facilities.

Important extra design considerations are therefore the recognition factor: the degree to which intending passengers are able to find their way quickly around both the basic travel areas and the ancillary facilities, being reassured as they go; the ancillary facilities themselves; and the general comfort levels both for passengers and, since the organisations's overall image is ultimately dependent on staff attitudes to and treatment of customers, for Greater Manchester Transport staff.

Figure 3.4. Standard Greater Manchester Transport double deck bus. Leyland Atlantean with Northern Counties body.

As well as making it easy for passengers to get on the buses, we also have to ensure that buses and pedestrians are kept apart in that adequate, safe routes avoiding vehicle movements need to be provided for passengers travelling to and from Interchange on foot. There should be no conflict between the private car, the bus and the taxi: the design should cater for all, both in terms of traffic flow and of waiting space such as taxi rank and car park. Provision has to be made also for handicapped persons, for whom lifts may be necessary.

For overall control (i.e. the regulating and communication of bus and train arrivals and departures) public address equipment is necessary and closed-circuit televis·on desire-

able. Television becomes necessary if the location of the control unit does not command a view of bus stands and rail platforms.

In terms of corporate identity there should be no conflict between the bus and rail operators and harmonisation must be achieved of external appearance, signs and facilities: in fact of all "visible manifestations".

Approaching it as a potential passenger and looking at it with a passenger's eyes, we see that the Altrincham Interchange (Figure 3.5.) achieves many but not all of the aims. Access to it is from two sides. The first side leads to both buses and trains and the facilities are therefore prominently defined by a large neon-lit double sign (Figure 3.6., overleaf)

which shows the British Rail logo and the "M-blem" of Greater Manchester Transport which appears on all buses. (The double logo also appears on some of the trains which use the Interchange). The station name appears in the British Rail alphabet (virtually identical to the Helvetica Medium of our publicity), which is used for all the directional and inform-ational signs on the Interchange. On the first side there is also a Kiss 'n Ride facility and a taxi rank. On the second side is the Park 'n Ride facility (the parked cars can be seen on the left of Figure 3.7., overleaf) as well as a Kiss 'n Ride; the sign here is merely the Rail emblem since (and this is one of the design faults of the Interchange) there is no direct access to the buses except via the rail station and the cost of a platform ticket.

Starting with the bus/rail or rail identification sign, the flow through the Interchange and the information system which assists the flow are sequential. On the first side, for example, the passenger next meets a display board (big enough for 3 double royal poster size notices) which shows a plan of

Figure 3.5. Plan of Altrincham Interchange.

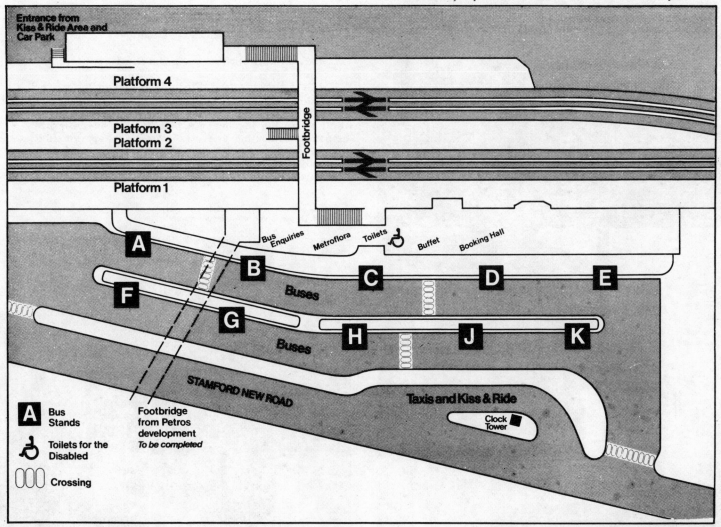

the Interchange with all its facilities and a list of all destinations (bus and rail) reached from the Interchange (Figure
3.8.). Each destination is coded with the bus stand or rail
platform number and all stands and platforms are sign-posted
from the display board. All the signs are in accordance with
British Rail corporate identity standards, with the exception
that an orange arrow points to a bus facility and a blue one to
a rail facility. At the bus stand itself the passenger sees the
confirmatory sign which reassures him that he has reached

Figure 3.6. Approach to Altrincham Interchange showing joint British Rail/Greater
Manchester Transport sign.

the right stand, together with confirmation of destination and
bus number and with detailed information (on a panel identical
to that which appears on bus stops along the routes) of the bus
routes (in stylised map form), timings, etc. The information
is in the same form as appears in the printed bus guides and
the destination and service number, again in the same type-
face, are repeated on the bus itself.

The sequence is therefore:-

1. Identification of mode of travel.

2. General information of all routes from Interchange and
all facilities (toilets, information office, refreshments,
sales kiosks, etc.).

3. Identification of specific access point required.

4. Signing to specific access point required.

5. Reassurance at access point.

6. Relation of bus number and destination.

7. Detailed information on route and times.

The first display board (Figure 3.8.) giving the general
information is at every access point to the Interchange and
also at bus/rail and rail/bus intermediate access points.
At all stages the design aim is both to guide and reassure:
the pattern is continuous from distant visual appreciation
through to the main buildings and to the attendant facilities
and finally to when the passenger joins his chosen mode of
transport.

Figure 3.8. Display board at Altrincham Interchange.

Figure 3.7. Aerial view of Altrincham Interchange.

Figure 3.9. Bus stands at Altrincham Interchange.

The first sign, the display board, consists of black anodised aluminium rectangular section frames with the logo on the top fascia panel. The three individual displays within the sign are covered by transparent Makrolon with key operated opening frames. The confirmatory sign at the bus stand is a sandwich constructed, black illuminated fascia mounted box sign. The sandwich comprises a rear perspex diffuser, interchangeable slats and a clear Makrolon front face. The further information panel is a non-illuminated, black anodised aluminium framed unit approximately 1200mm. wide by approximately 900mm. high. Within it is a Makrolon covered opening section with positions to receive two printed standard information sheets giving timetable, fare and route information for buses departing from each individual stand. Adjacent to

the covered section is a formica faced panel to receive special or emergency notices.   The whole sign is hinged to allow maintenance.

On the bus side, the customer facilities start with the bus stands themselves (Figure 3.9., see previous page).   Like all the main accommodation buildings and pedestrian areas of the Interchange they are fully covered and glazed with attractive tinted glass, held in gasket glazed black acrylic painted, aluminium frames which in turn are supported by acrylic finished, hollow mild steel structural members.   They incorporate metal suspended ceilings which provide void space for services such as the concealed Tannoy system linked to the central control.   The ceilings harmonise with the black rubber flooring panels which in turn give a feeling of quietness and sophistication to the public and pedestrian areas which is far preferable to the hard concrete finishes normally provided. Lighting, bright but diffused, is provided by horizontal bands across the covered areas.   The general standard of enclosure deliberately aims at lessening the passenger's discomfort prior to the arrival or departure of his bus.   The modular, gasket glazed shelter has been designed to allow ease of maintenance should vandal or vehicular damage occur.

The ancillary customer facilities (news kiosks, snack bar, etc.) are grouped between the bus and rail boarding points and all conform to the overall corporate identity standards of the Interchange.   A fault is the inadequacy of the customer information point which is to be enlarged.

At the bus bays, operational signing is also included so that the bus driver can recognise his parking position relative to the service route he provides.   Our general policy is to adopt a "saw tooth" parking arrangement which allows buses to park in adjacent stands more efficiently than the normal, linear procedure.   Such is being incorporated in several bus stations at present under construction, but in the case of Altrincham Interchange the site restraints prevented other than the linear scheme which can be seen in Figures 3.5. and 3.7.

THE BUS

The double-decker bus itself (and we shall restrict our-selves to the double-decker, which makes up 80% of the fleet) is the most basic of people transporters.   Within the limits of technical possibility, the interiors of aeroplanes, ships and trains can be made (at least for the premium-paying passenger) reasonably luxurious.   The bus has remained a stranger to such luxury, partly because it is socially and economically a more down-market form of transport, and partly because of the constraints on its design.   These constraints - most of them outside the designer's control - are firstly those of economy and space and thereafter a whole range of physical parameters.   For example, the "within walls" turning circle of 21.64m. (71 ft.) limits the front over-hang to around 2.3m. (7.5 ft.).   A gangway inside the bus of 0.91m. (3 ft.) is required between the exit and bottom of the stairs to the upper saloon.   The minimum seat pitch is legally stated and rigorously checked before the vehicle is licensed as also are upper and lower saloon interior heights.   An

overall maximum width is also legally specified, as are the strict maximum ground loads (gross vehicle weight 16260 kg.; rear axle 10120 kg.) which must be observed.   These load levels can easily modify seating capacity since the heavy engine transmission unit, whether it is at front or back, has a severe effect on one axle only, presenting problems to the uniform load which a bus full of normal passengers repres-ents.   Our passenger will quite justifiably take a dim view of being herded to one end of the bus just because the law demands it: axle overloading is not important to him on a wet, cold night.   All the preceding requirements dictate a normal bus height of between 4.32m. (14 ft. 2 ins.) and 4.42m. (14 ft. 6 ins.).   Special low height buses of around 4.17m. (13 ft. 8 ins.) are also built but they have even more problems, particularly where the lower saloon floor has humps and boxes to cater for chassis parts that do not fit in the reduced-height underfloor area.

So far, therefore, the interior design envelope and the minimum seat pitch have been virtually decided.   The actual inside volume depends now on the construction method used by the chosen body-builder, but the objective of minimum possible cost makes it necessary for the operator both to accept a number of standard features designed by the body-builder and also to use proprietary items which have been carried over from other vehicles in his own fleet or which are generally used throughout the industry.   There are furthermore certain localised external constraints such as local traffic area regulations (because of unsuitable roads, for example) on size of vehicles, and internal constraints dictated by previous operating practice (for example, one-man operation) or by current and proposed policies (for example on fare collection, "Self-service" cancellation of pre-purchased tickets, etc.) which will certainly affect the entrance and driving areas.

Despite the constraints and the objectives of speed and economy, the aim of lessening the passenger's "distress" has resulted in certain design features whose purpose is to increase passenger safety and comfort:-

1. The bus has a single door, allowing the driver a direct view of the single exit/entrance at all times (Figure 3.4.).

2. The staircase faces forward so that in the event of heavy braking, any ascending or descending passenger will be thrown onto the stairs rather than away and consequently down (Figure 3.10.)

3. Side facing seats are kept to a minimum (only one in the latest standard double-decker) since passengers are more subject to the effects of lateral accelerations when in this postion (Figure 3.10.).

4. The interior decor (Figure 3.10.) is both serviceable and aesthetically pleasing.   Formica is widely used: white crystal-pattern for the ceiling, black crystal-pattern (to reduce the incidence of graffiti) for the sides and rosewood on the backs of the seats and on some interior panels.   The seat upholstery in the lower saloon is a

toning moquette with hide cheek panels. The upper saloon's upholstery is vinyl, partly for historical reasons (the worker in perhaps oily overalls tended to use the upstairs shiny seats) and partly because vandalism when it happens is usually on the top deck: vinyl is cheaper than moquette.

5. There is an abundance of handholds, all easily reached by the less able-bodied passenger. On the back of every seat there is a double top-rail (Figure 3.10.). There are seven vertical stanchions upstairs, arranged alternately down the bus, and six downstairs plus a single vertical rail at the bus entrance with an extra half-rail. The driver's cab has hand-rails in front of it for the passenger to steady himself as he is paying his fare and there are further rails around the luggage rack and at the bottom of the stairs. The holds do not obstruct access and are not a safety hazard in the case of an accident. In fact, there are no sharp edges in the bus interior.

6. Seats are easy to enter and leave. We think a fair balance has been struck between the seating capacity (75 passengers) and the need to allow obstruction-free floor space (on which 20 standing passengers can be accommodated).

7. Access to mechanical components from within the saloon has been kept to a minimum to protect the seat upholstery from the ravages of the workshop.

8. Advertising and information space is provided for in the coving panels so that stickers do not need to be affixed to the windows and thus obscure passengers' vision.

Figure 3.10. Interior of lower saloon of standard Greater Manchester Transport double deck bus.

The exterior design, decor and graphics of the bus are more important environmentally than both public and operators believe: in Greater Manchester, with its complement of over 3,000 buses, the bus is virtually a permanent feature of the urban landscape. We are pleased with the design of our destination blinds (Figure 3.4.) with their clear, quick and easy-to-read typography which conforms to the standard type-face used in all our signs. We have avoided the desire shown by many operators to put up a multiplicity of destination messages, often in differing typefaces, which serve usually to confuse the passenger. We are still managing to confuse (and this is a fault we have to put right) with the excess of interior messages within the bus.

The outside decor of the double-decker bus (Figure 3.4.) is bright and "different", but has many "unnatural breaks" such as wheel arches, window lines, trim lines and panel breaks, etc. and this design disadvantage is exaggerated by the orange/white/orange/white/orange series of colour changes. So far we have succeeded in design terms only with (a) our dual-purpose bus/coach single-decker (Figure 3.11.), which is mainly orange with white roof and with our name and logo appearing white out of orange; and (b) with the coaches of our separate travel units (Figure 3.12.), where we achieve a family corporate decor through use of a coaching "M-blem", a common "Starsky and Hutch" livery design and common type-face (futura bold italic) (Figure 3.1.). At the same time, but without losing this family look and identity, we have retained the separate trading colours of the individual Divisions.

As with Henry Ford's assessment of advertising, it is difficult to measure the benefits – commercial, promotional, financial – of whatever progress we have made in design. On the publicity, we think we have created, by consistent use of standard design, colour, lettering and symbol elements, a good overall impression. At the Altrincham Interchange we have certainly succeeded in commercial as well as design terms: both bus and rail passengers have increased (contrary to the general trend) and incremental revenue has been higher than the incremental running costs of the whole project. On the bus it can be said that the absence of complaints about design is praise itself.

We have started therefore (but only started) along the road to a consistent design style. Our success or otherwise in the future depends of course on what the passengers think of us. What they think, the impression they get, depends on our providing good service, on our improving their lot and on our being – and looking – smart and efficient. One of the best ways of creating the right impression in a large organisation like ours is in the consistent use of the same distinguishing features of good design and decor wherever they are approp- riate. This gives a cumulative impact to what I would call the "visible and tangible manifestations" of the organisation, causes its facilities to be easily recognised and produces a corporate identity which reflects the unity of the organisation behind and the purpose of all our activities.

Figure 3.11. Dual - purpose bus/coach - Leyland Leopard with Eastern Coachworks body.

Figure 3.12. Coach for one of Greater Manchester Transport's separate travel units — Charterplan. Leyland Leopard with Duple body.

Figure 3.13. Since this chapter was written a modified double-deck livery has been introduced for the new Leyland Titan. This incorporates a greater area of orange and overcomes some of the aesthetic problems mentioned on page 36. The skirt panels are now dark brown and there is a single broad white band between the windows of the two decks.

Chapter 4:

Passenger Behaviour and Expectations at an Airport

Richard Deighton

INTRODUCTION

The British Airports Authority is responsible for running seven of Britain's major airports – Heathrow, Gatwick, Stansted, Aberdeen, Edinburgh, Glasgow and Prestwick. The BAA is responsible for the development, management and operation of these airports, which last year handled in excess of 34m air passengers – three-quarters of all air passengers travelling to, from and within the UK. The BAA is very conscious of its role as a service organisation whose main commodity is people, and therefore pays close attention to the needs and desires of its customers. Consequently, when providing new airport facilities and when running the existing ones, the BAA needs to know, firstly, what air passengers do when they pass through its airports, and, secondly, what kind of airport they would like us to provide them with. Armed with this knowledge of passenger behaviour and expectation the BAA can then set about providing airport facilities which are effective, economic and which are what the air passenger wants.

In this chapter I shall describe briefly two surveys we undertook to assess passenger behaviour and expectation. In the first survey we observed what passengers did while passing through an air terminal; in the second survey we asked passengers to tell us what they thought of the airport and what improvements they thought were necessary. I shall present the results of the surveys and point out the implications they have for airport planning and management.

THE SURVEY ON PASSENGER BEHAVIOUR

In the summer of 1973 we conducted an exercise at Heathrow airport to find out how long passengers spent in the terminal building, where in the building they spent their time, and how they were occupied. This we did by 'tailing' passengers around the building, recording where they went and how long they spent there. We observed some 400 passengers in all in the three International terminals. Passengers departing by air were observed, from entering the building and checking-in through to boarding the aircraft; passengers arriving by air were observed, from leaving the aircraft through to leaving the terminal building and boarding whatever vehicle was to transport them away from the terminal.

The results were as follows:

- Arriving passengers spent, on average, 27 minutes in the building. The shortest time spent was 10 minutes and the longest was 70 minutes.
- Departing passengers spent, on average, 60 minutes in the building. The shortest time spent was 10 minutes and the longest was 3 hours.

- Understandably, arriving passengers showed no great inclination to spend longer in the building than was strictly necessary. Their dwell time in the building breaks down as follows:

Activity	Minutes (average)
Moving from aircraft to Immigration	4.0
Queueing and being processed by Immigration	4.6
Waiting for luggage at Baggage Reclaim	9.1
Customs examination	0.8
In landside arrivals concourse area	5.9
Waiting for surface transport to depart	2.6
TOTAL	27.0 minutes

Thus arriving passengers spend 21 out of 27 minutes in what can be termed 'necessary' processing activity, and only 6 minutes in 'optional' activity in the concourse, such as visiting the airport bank, greeting friends, and so on.

- In contrast, departing passengers spend the majority of their time in 'optional' activity in the lounge areas of the terminal. The time they spend in the building breaks down as follows:

Activity	Minutes (average)
Queueing and being processed at Check-in	5.6
In landside departures concourse area	18.4
Queueing and being processed at Passport Control	2.3
In airside departures lounge area	23.7
Moving from lounge to boarding gate	2.5
Queueing and being processed at Security Check, and subsequently boarding the aircraft	8.0
TOTAL	60.5 minutes

After boarding the aircraft, passengers would have waited for about 10 minutes before the aircraft departed. This means that, because he would have checked in baggage up to about 30 minutes prior to departure of his aircraft, the average passenger arrived in the building some 40 minutes earlier than was theoretically necessary. This of course reflects the reality that passengers intentionally leave earlier than strictly necessary when travelling to the airport, so that if they are held up on the way they can still catch the flight. In most cases they are not held up as much as they have allowed for, and so they arrive at the airport well before the flight is due to depart.

- A significant proportion of passengers (particularly on departures) make use of facilities other than those directly concerned with the process of getting into or out of an aeroplane. For example, 49% of departing passengers visited the duty free shop, 27% used the airside catering facilities, and 28% visited the landside bookstall, and so on.

- When a comparison is made of the range of terminal facilities used respectively by arriving and departing facilities, the difference in motivation of arriving and departing passengers is again apparent. For example, 17% of departing passengers made use of the landside catering facilities - for an average time of 22 minutes - while only 2% of arriving passengers used the catering facilities, for an average time of 7 minutes (of course, facilities in the landside waiting areas, such as catering, are used not just by passengers but also by their friends and escorts).

More detailed survey results appear in Appendices 4.1. and 4.2.

We can therefore summarise the conclusions of the survey as follows. The behaviour of passengers arriving by air at the airport is almost entirely orientated towards reclaiming their baggage and getting away as soon as they can. In contrast, the behaviour of passengers departing by air from the airport is much more leisurely - they spend only a small proportion of their time actually queueing or being processed. The rest of their time is spent in a relaxed manner, making use of the ancillary facilities of the air terminal building.

THE SURVEY OF PASSENGER EXPECTATION

The survey to assess air passenger expectations took place at Heathrow at about the same time as the survey to monitor their behaviour. The survey sought to find out what air passengers thought of Heathrow, and what improvements to the airport they thought were necessary. The first step in the survey was to devise a questionnaire which could be handed out to passengers to fill in for themselves and then return to us by post. A considerable effort was expended in unstructured interviewing of passengers, analysis, and questionnaire testing, and this led finally to the questionnaire shown in Appendix 4.4. The questionnaire asked passengers to assess a list of possible improvements to the airport, and decide which improvements they thought were important and which were unimportant. They were then asked to rank in order of priority the items they had marked as important. The The replies obtained would therefore give us a measure of what passengers felt they should expect at an airport.

We obtained responses from some 2,000 arriving and departing passengers using Heathrow. The main conclusions of the survey were as follows:

- The four improvements which passengers thought most important were:

	% of passengers rating item important
"Get your bags to you more quickly when you land"	70%
"Make the walk to and from the plane shorter"	63%

	% of passengers rating item important
"Make check-in quicker"	53%
"Reduce the crowds in the waiting areas"	50%

The least important improvements were:

	% of passengers rating item important
"Provide a wider selection of shops"	20%
"Provide more porters"	13%

- Passengers flying on business tended to be more concerned with items relating to queueing and speed of processing, while leisure passengers tended to be more concerned with items relating to the ancillary facilities and services provided in the terminal building.

	% of passengers rating item important	
	Business	Leisure
"Get your bags to you more quickly when you land"	79%	59%
"Make it quicker to get through Immigration"	42%	34%
"Reduce the price of goods in the shops"	34%	42%
"Provide more baggage trolleys"	41%	47%

- Passengers who had used Heathrow at least once in the previous year generally considered most improvements more important than did the passengers who had not used Heathrow in the previous year.

- Older passengers were much more concerned with walking distance and help with their baggage, and less concerned with processing speed, than were younger passengers.

	% of passengers rating item important	
	(Aged 26-40)	(Aged 60+)
"Make the walk to and from the plane shorter"	63%	71%
"Provide more baggage trolleys"	42%	61%
"Provide more porters"	17%	25%
"Get your bags to you more quickly when you land"	73%	59%

	% of passengers rating item important	
	(Aged 26-40)	(Aged 60+)
"Make check-in quicker"	58%	42%

(Detailed results of the survey are shown in Appendix 4.3.)

The results of the survey can therefore be summarised as follows. Passengers are not only concerned with speed of service - they also have some interest in the quality of the service they are offered at the airport. Furthermore, different groups of passengers have different views and priorities - business passengers are mainly concerned with speed, leisure passengers have more interest in improvements to other aspects of the terminal, and older passengers are much more concerned about walking distances and baggage assistance.

IMPLICATIONS FOR AIRPORT PLANNING AND MANAGEMENT

What general conclusions affecting airport planning and management can be drawn from the two surveys?

- Air passengers are very concerned about the length of time they are forced to spend either queueing for, or being processed through, the various activities associated with getting on or off an aeroplane. This concern is very strong even when, in the case of departing passengers, relatively little time has to be spent in being processed. Time spent queueing is resented by passengers much more than time spent, as it were voluntarily, by the passenger in other ancillary activities.

- Although passengers are primarily concerned with speed of processing, there is also a need for the airport to provide an adequate service in respect of the other ancillary facilities - assistance with baggage, shops, catering facilities, and so on. Adequate provision of these services will make a significant contribution to passenger satisfaction.

- Compared with the time they spend airborne, both arriving and departing air passengers spend considerable lengths of time in the airport. In this respect the function and design of an airport is significantly different from that of other transport interfaces (such as railway stations) which are not normally designed to cater for passengers dwelling within them for any length of time. The long dwell time of passengers within the airport is one reason for air passengers demanding a much higher standard of comfort and provision of facilities at the airport than is normally provided at other types of transport interface.

- Finally, passengers do not behave in a uniform manner, nor do they have stereotyped requirements. Business passengers are different from leisure passengers, old passengers have different priorities from younger passengers, and so on. The design and operation of an airport must be flexible enough to cater satisfactorily for the needs of all the various different types of passengers who make use of it.

APPENDIX 4.1.

Arriving Passengers - Airside Activities			Arriving Passengers - Landside Activities (after leaving Customs)		
Activity	% of passengers undertaking activity	Time (in minutes) spent by passengers undertaking the activity	Activity	% of passengers undertaking activity	Time (in minutes) spent by passengers undertaking the activity
Walk from disembarkation gate to Immigration	100	4.0	Greet friends/escorts in concourse	42	3.7
Queue at Immigration	81	3.7	Visit enquiry desks	11	1.7
Process at Immigration	100	1.6	Visit bank	16	4.1
Visit toilets	21	2.4	Visit other shops	7	2.0
Use telephone (airside)	3	6.9	Visit car hire or hotel reservation desks	6	7.4
Wait for baggage at Baggage reclaim	82	8.3	Use telephone	10	5.3
Reclaim Baggage	89	1.5	Visit toilets	8	3.0
Find porter or trolley	28	0.9	Movement around concourse	100	1.1
Pass through Customs - Green Channel	88	0.4	Sitting down	7	12.2
Pass through Customs - Red Channel	13	3.7	Visit catering facilities	2	7.0
			Wait for surface transport to depart	79	2.8
			Boarding surface transport	100	0.4

APPENDIX 4.2.

Departing Passengers – Airside Activities			Departing Passengers – Landside Activity		
Activity	% of passengers undertaking activity	Time (in minutes) spent by passengers undertaking the activity	Activity	% of passengers undertaking activity	Time (in minutes) spent by passengers undertaking the activity
Queue for Passport Control	12	1.2	Find porter or trolley	16	1.1
Process at Passport Control	100	2.1	Queue at check-in	17	4.8
Visit enquiry desks (airside)	8	1.1	Process at check-in	97	4.8
Visit duty free shop	49	7.1	Visit enquiry desks	14	3.4
Visit bookstall (airside)	15	3.3	Visit bank	19	5.5
Visit other shops (airside)	3	4.7	Visit bookstall	28	4.8
Visit toilets (airside)	16	3.6	Visit other shops	21	5.2
Movement around departure lounge	100	2.5	Visit toilets	19	3.6
Standing still	36	3.8	Movement	100	2.0
Sitting down in departure lounge	66	15.1	Standing still	47	4.8
Use telephone (airside)	7	5.2	Sitting down	39	11.0
Visit catering facilities (airside)	27	17.0	Use telephone	10	5.4
Watch the aeroplanes	3	5.8	Visit catering facilities	17	22.5
Walk to boarding gate	100	2.5	Watch the aeroplanes	3	7.7
Queue for security check	39	5.4	Say goodbye to friends/escorts in concourse	22	3.1
Process through security check	100	1.7			
Wait in gateroom prior to boarding aeroplane or coach	100	4.2			

APPENDIX 4.3.

PASSENGER RATINGS OF VARIOUS POSSIBLE IMPROVEMENTS TO THE AIRPORT

1. The views of the passenger population as a whole

Items in overall rank order of importance	% of passengers rating item important
1. Get your bags to you more quickly when you land	70%
2. Make the walk to/from the plane shorter	63%
3. Make check-in quicker	53%
4. Reduce the crowds in the waiting area	50%
5. Provide walkways so you can always walk to/from your plane and don't have to go by bus	47%
6. Improve the transport services to and from town	47%
7. Provide more baggage trolleys	44%
8. Reduce traffic congestion in front of the terminal building	41%
9. Make it quicker to get through immigration	38%
10. Give better security against terrorists	38%
11. Improve the quality of airport food	38%
12. Reduce the price of food	38%
13. Keep the building cleaner	34%
14. Reduce the price of goods in the shops	32%
15. Provide better information signs	32%
16. Improve the service in the buffets	31%
17. Train the staff to be more helpful	31%
18. Improve the car parking facilities	31%
19. Make the seats in the waiting area more comfortable	30%
20. Always take you to/from your plane by bus so you don't have to walk	21%
21. Provide a wider selection of shops	20%
22. Provide more porters	13%

2. The views of different passenger groups

(a) Percentage of passengers in specified rating item important
(b) Rank order of importance of item to passengers in specified group

Item	Passenger's reason for travel		Passenger age group (years)					Use of LHR in previous 12 months	
	Business	Leisure	16	16-25	26-40	41-60	60+	Yes	No
1	79% / 1	59% / 2	78% / 2	63% / 1	73% / 1	72% / 1	59% / 2	76% / 1	53% / 2
2	64% / 2	60% / 1	56% / 9	48% / 6	63% / 2	64% / 2	71% / 1	64% / 2	58% / 1
3	59% / 3	46% / 5	79% / 1	50% / 3	58% / 3	51% / 3	42% / 4	58% / 3	39% / 4
4	53% / 5	46% / 6	56% / 8	49% / 5	53% / 4	49% / 5	41% / 5	53% / 4	42% / 3
5	55% / 4	39% / 10	28% / 19	35% / 14	49% / 6	52% / 3	39% / 6	52% / 5	34% / 11
6	50% / 6	42% / 7	51% / 10	50% / 4	50% / 5	44% / 7	39% / 7	49% / 6	39% / 5
7	41% / 9	47% / 3	42% / 16	42% / 9	42% / 8	44% / 6	61% / 3	46% / 7	38% / 7
8	43% / 7	40% / 8	49% / 12	45% / 8	40% / 10	42% / 8	37% / 8	43% / 8	36% / 10
9	42% / 8	34% / 14	60% / 7	37% / 13	44% / 7	35% / 10	24% / 18	42% / 10	27% / 15
10	36% / 12	39% / 9	78% / 4	47% / 7	40% / 11	34% / 11	31% / 11	38% / 11	38% / 6
11	39% / 10	37% / 11	64% / 5	40% / 11	42% / 9	37% / 9	25% / 17	42% / 9	27% / 14
12	34% / 13	42% / 6	76% / 3	55% / 2	38% / 12	34% / 14	35% / 9	38% / 12	37% / 9
13	37% / 11	29% / 17	49% / 11	31% / 17	36% / 13	34% / 12	23% / 19	36% / 13	27% / 16
14	34% / 13	42% / 6	76% / 3	55% / 2	38% / 12	34% / 14	35% / 9	33% / 16	30% / 13
15	29% / 18	35% / 13	25% / 21	42% / 10	32% / 17	30% / 18	30% / 12	30% / 19	37% / 8
16	32% / 15	30% / 15	43% / 15	33% / 15	33% / 15	31% / 16	19% / 21	34% / 14	22% / 20
17	31% / 16	30% / 16	35% / 18	18% / 18	33% / 14	31% / 15	26% / 15	33% / 15	27% / 17
18	34% / 14	27% / 20	27% / 20	27% / 19	31% / 19	34% / 13	22% / 20	33% / 17	23% / 18
19	29% / 19	29% / 18	44% / 14	31% / 16	31% / 18	29% / 19	26% / 14	31% / 18	26% / 19
20	14% / 21	28% / 19	37% / 17	21% / 21	18% / 20	19% / 20	33% / 10	18% / 21	30% / 12
21	20% / 19	19% / 21	45% / 13	27% / 20	21% / 20	18% / 21	22% / 22	20% / 20	18% / 21
22	8% / 22	18% / 22	17% / 22	17% / 22	17% / 22	13% / 22	25% / 16	12% / 22	16% / 22

APPENDIX 4.4.

A TYPICAL PASSENGER OPINION SURVEY QUESTIONNAIRE

A. First some facts about you.

Please tick one box and one box only in each section below.

S.N. (1)—(4)

(1) How will you leave London Heathrow airport today? *(If you use more than one form of transport tick the one you will use first).*

1. Plane (5)
2. Car *(including self drive hire car)*
3. Airline Bus
4. Other Bus
5. Taxi or Minicab
6. Other Means

(2) How old are you?

1. Under 16 (6)
2. 16—25
3. 26—40
4. 41—60
5. Over 60

(3) What sex are you?

1. Male (7)
2. Female

(4) What is (or was) the purpose of your trip?

1. Business (8)
2. Pleasure
3. Other reason

(5) How many times have you flown in the past 12 months? (There and back counts twice)

1. 0 times (9)
2. 1 to 4 times
3. 5 or more times

(6) Have you flown out of London Heathrow airport in the past 12 months?

1. Yes (10)
2. No

(7) How much have you paid for your airline ticket?

1. The scheduled first class fare (11)
2. The scheduled economy fare
3. It is part of a package holiday
4. A reduced fare
5. Don't Know

(8) Where do you live? *(If you live in more than one place tick the one in which you spend most time)*

1. United Kingdom (12)
2. Elsewhere in Europe *(Including Eire)*
3. USA or Canada
4. Elsewhere

(9) Is English your first language?

1. Yes (13)
2. No

Now we would like to know where you think we should spend our money at London-Heathrow Airport.

B. Below you will see a list of ways we could improve the airport. You will probably consider some of these improvements important and others unimportant. Simply go through the list and for each item mark whichever of the two boxes on the left you think appropriate. Of course if you feel an item is already very good and does not need improving mark the 'not important' box; mark as important those items where you feel improvements are necessary.

C. Now please put those items you marked as important in an order of priority. Go through the list again. Look at all the items you marked as important and pick the one you think most important. Write a '1' alongside it in the 'Order of Priority Box' at the right hand side of the page. Write a '2' in the box by the second most important item and so on. Continue until you have given a number to every item you have marked as important.

Please ignore the Order of Priority Box for the moment

Not Important	Important (for Heathrow)		Order of Priority Box
		Improve the car parking facilities	(14)—(15)
		Keep the building cleaner	(16)—(17)
		Provide more baggage trolleys	(18)—(19)
		Make the seats in the waiting areas more comfortable	(20)—(21)
		Provide a wider selection of shops	(22)—(23)
		Make check-in quicker	(24)—(25)
		Improve the transport services to and from town	(26)—(27)
		Provide better information signs	(28)—(29)
		Reduce the crowds in the waiting area	(30)—(31)
		Make it quicker to get through immigration	(32)—(33)
		Reduce the price of food	(34)—(35)
		Get your bags to you more quickly when you land	(36)—(37)
		Improve the quality of airport food	(38)—(39)
		Reduce the price of goods in the shops	(40)—(41)
		Provide more porters	(42)—(43)
		Reduce traffic congestion in front of the terminal building	(44)—(45)
		Make the walk to/from the plane shorter	(46)—(47)
		Train the staff to be more helpful	(48)—(49)
		Improve the service in the buffets	(50)—(51)
		Always take you to/from your plane by bus so you don't have to walk	(52)—(53)
		Give better security against terrorists	(54)—(55)
		Provide walkways so you can always walk to/from your plane and don't have to go by bus	(56)—(57)

D. Please now describe how much you like/dislike Heathrow Airport's facilities in general:

			Neither or				
Extremely	Quite	Slightly	both equally	Slightly	Quite	Extremely	
Like						Dislike	

(58)

Space to (77)

Job No. (77)—(80)

Chapter 5:

TWA Corporate Identity

Jules Rondepierre

This chapter is a study of the new Corporate identity adopted by TWA, ranging from aircraft livery and interiors to uniforms, facilities and print graphics. The reasons for adopting the new policy are rooted in the airline's history and the evolution of TWA's Corporate identity over the fifty years of its history is briefly summarised. An explanation of both functional and economic aspects and a review of the design methodology in formulating the new policy are covered.

The TWA identity, (Figure 5.1.), as it exists today, was adopted in 1975 as an update of previous graphics, resulting primarily from a change in aircraft livery.

We, in the transportation industry, and perhaps particularly in the airlines, are recognised as much by the paint schemes on our equipment as by our graphic symbols appearing on printed materials, on signs and in our advertising. In the early days of commercial aviation, the Corporate identity was frequently taken from the symbol which appeared on the side or tail of the aircraft. This type of marking was already a tradition of pilots and squadron leaders of the great world war, where in fact most of the early commercial pilots had learned to fly. And now, 50 years later, the situation is not too different: what works well on the side or tail of the aeroplane often sets the pace for other graphic applications and thus the Corporate identity.

In order to understand how TWA's identity got to be what it now is, it is necessary to briefly review its history (Figure 5.2.).

Western Air Express, a TWA predecessor company, was organised during 1925 and obtained a Los Angeles – Salt Lake City mail and passenger route. It began operations on the 17th April 1926, thereby becoming the first scheduled commercial route flown in the United States. In 1928, Western Air Express began service from San Diego to Los Angeles and San Francisco.

The year before this, three young flying instructors organised Standard Air Lines which began commercial operations from Los Angeles to Tucson, later extending the route to

El Paso. Also in 1927, the year aviation gained tremendous impetus from the transatlantic flight of Col. Charles A. Lindbergh, a line from Los Angeles to San Diego and Agua Caliente, Mexico, was established by Jack Maddux. Service was later extended from Los Angeles to San Francisco.

In 1929, Western Air Express inaugurated daily flights between Los Angeles and Kansas City. This same year Western Air Express and Standard Air Lines were consolidated into Aero Corporation of California, which continued to operate Western and Standard as mail and freight carriers with a three times a week passenger service.

At that time, not much existed in the way of aircraft paint schemes other than the placement of the Company logo whereever there was a large enough section of fuselage to accommodate it. You should note, however, that in addition to the Western Air Express logo, consisting of an Indian head and arrow, their first paint scheme on the Douglas M-2 included two parallel white stripes on a red background.

During this period of almost constant route expansion and mergers, the conception of a great transcontinental system of transportation emerged. The system would combine air and rail service to reduce coast-to-coast travel time and the Curtiss-Keys aviation group was formed to operate the model airline. The Pennsylvania Railroad was chosen in the east and the Atchison, Topeka and Santa Fe was invited into the group to form the western rail link, and a new company known as Transcontinental Air Transport was organised.

The obtaining of airport sites, the selection and testing of equipment, the formation of flying and ground personnel, the co-ordinating of rail and air schedules, and building of air stations, depots, terminals and weather stations – all of this was a mammoth undertaking which fell to Col. Charles Lindbergh, who served the line as Chairman of the technical committee. Passengers travelled by air during the day in ten passenger Ford Tri-motors and by rail at night from coast to coast, over 3,500 miles, in just 48 hours. The Tri-motors bore the new TAT logo which notably carried an arrow, as did the logo of Western Air Express.

In late 1929, TAT merged with Maddux Airlines, thereby extending its routes to those cities served by Maddux. Western Air Express had also continued to expand, but in 1930 the United States Government announced that it would award an air-mail contract to only one company for the entire cross country air route. Since no airline could make it on passenger revenue alone, this decision forced yet another merger, that of TAT/Maddux and Western Air. Thus, on the 1st October 1930, Transcontinental and Western Air, Inc. was born and the initials TWA appeared in unembellished block letterform on aircraft for the first time.

Figure 5.1. The red TWA logo and double line motif adopted in 1975.

Figure 5.2. The evolution of the TWA corporate identity — from its predecessors in 1928 to the current logo and motif.

As terminal facilities and ground support equipment became a part of the growing air travel industry, airline identification was extended to signs and courtesy vehicles and with service becoming almost predictable, timetables were introduced. They carried the airline logo and were great souvenirs treasured by those daring enough to fly. In time, the inevitable happened, hostesses came on the scene and while they were required to be registered nurses, the Company provided their uniforms which became another extension of the Corporate identity.

The plain TWA logotype appeared with relative consistency on the variety of aircraft types used for both mail and passenger operations. The experimental DC-1 sported the standard letterform enclosed in a graphic device, very much resembling the world globe and it's polar axis. The DC-2 retained these, and coincidentally, added two parallel stripes first seen on the Western Air Douglas M-2. The Lindbergh Line was also added with the reappearance of an arrow of sorts. All of this continued through the DC-3 days where the globe logo was used on blankets and headrest covers in TWA's skysleeper service. Later, Boeing Stratoliners were added to the fleet with virtually the same livery except the Lindbergh Line was changed to the Transcontinental Line, but retained the same arrow. The war years produced some patriotic efforts and in this case for some unexplained reason, the arrow has reverted to the Indian style of the early Western Air Express logo, perhaps recalling the American war with the Indians. The war years also saw TWA's aircraft and technicians diverted to military service with the Boeing Stratoliners airlifting men and equipment across the Atlantic to Europe and Africa. This ability led the airline to urge the Government to allow extension of its domestic routes in post war years beyond the continental limits of the United States and, in June 1944, TWA applied for authority to fly around the world. The first Lockheed Constellation in TWA markings was rolled out of the hangar in April of that same year.

The now familiar livery was standard on all TWA aircraft. At the close of the war, the Stratoliners were returned by the Army Air Corps and underwent substantial modification before resuming scheduled airline service. These modifications included a new paint design, adopted for all TWA planes that same year. This scheme seemed to combine the best of everything in its past. The parallel stripes of the tail were extended to the length of the fuselage and the block TWA letters had been italicized giving them a more contemporary look and our old friend the arrow was again pressed into service. With routes spanning most of the world, the airline appropriately changed its Corporate name from Transcontinental and Western Air, to Trans World Airlines. This change was made in 1950 and was added to the aircraft exterior.

The next nine years saw almost no change in markings with the Constellations forming the backbone of the fleet. In all, TWA received 147 Connies from Lockheed in eight different models. The most significant technological advancement was, of course, the introduction of the jet aeroplane into commercial passenger service. TWA heralded the new era with a change in paint design, first seen on its inaugural jet flight from San Francisco to New York in March 1959. The red dart, as it became known, was developed as a symbol of speed, with its rocket shaped nose, widening to a swallow tail shape somewhat reminiscent of the automotive styling of the time - fins on many American cars, for example.

Hostess uniforms continued to change with the styles of public dress and became more important to the overall Corporate look. Gone were the nursing qualifications, replaced by such chauvinistic requirements as good looks, poise, outgoing personality, youth and above all, single status. Airline executives recognised their market to be the businessman and reinforced the glamour of flying by providing glamorous employees to perform the expanding on-board service. The in-flight uniform had already become a marketing tool, unifying the appearance and giving pride to those who had met the qualifications to wear it.

Aircraft interiors were still quite utilitarian in the waning days of the propeller. Unable, because of tubular shapes, weight and size restrictions, to build in the opulence of the fine rail cars, airlines had settled for fabrics and carpets which at least covered the bare metal and absorbed some of the droning noise. Not exactly by coincidence were the colours frequently chosen to absorb coffee stains which were unavoidable in the bumpy altitudes to which these aeroplanes were restricted.

Ground facilities were becoming identifiable with the individual airline. As each attempted to out-do the other with comfortable departure lounges, credit was sought for their efforts and the Corporate symbol was prominently displayed. Competition for passengers also dictated the need to identify each airline's ticket counter at the airport and the Corporate logo began to dominate these sales areas. Ground employees were also uniformed, giving the airline yet another method of identifying itself to its passengers.

The aircraft paint scheme was now more correctly named with the surface coating of most of the fuselage to reduce corrosion and the maintenance cost of polishing bare metal. For many obvious good reasons, white was chosen as the background colour providing good contrast to TWA's long-used red markings.

Changes in aerodynamic design had produced the large futuristic looking empenage, particularly suited to the application of identity graphics. The TWA letterform, by now a well recognised type style, was positioned on this prominent flying billboard. Recognised as it was, it was not in keeping with the designers' state of the art. It was not a symbol which portrayed in graphic form what its letters represented. The jet age seemed to require a more sophisticated logo and the well established, prestigious design firm of Raymond Loewy Associates was retained to analyse TWA's graphic needs. Numerous graphic devices were developed, some including previously used elements and some totally unrelated to TWA's past. Selected symbols were submitted to consumer groups for reaction and after considerable market research, the overlapping globe symbol, surrounding the already established letterform was adopted. Affectionately referred to as the bird cage, this Trans World symbol was added to every element of TWA identification. The new logo first appeared in 1960.

Calling attention to the new symbol seemed appropriate and it was a TWA mechanic who developed the first logo light, intended purely as a promotional gimmick. The brightly lit tail had the unexpected benefit of easing night taxiway identification for both pilots and controllers.

The Jet Age, with safer, higher speed, higher altitude aircraft and increased payloads also seemed to require a more sophisticated aircraft interior. The psychology of colour became recognised as an important element in passenger appeal. It was at about this time in our history that the design discipline was recognised as an important marketing science. The economic planners were identifying the potential growth market segments and recognising the value of visual appeal to the consumer. There began an organised effort to unify the appearance of the airline in all of its graphic applications. Capitalising on TWA's round the world routes, serving the major cities on four continents, including principal leisure destinations in the US, the target market became the vacation traveller. "Great Cities" was selected as the marketing theme and was reflected in the design elements with bright, festive colours. The airport and city ticket office identity walls featured brightly coloured square tiles, each colour representing a continent served with appropriate "great city" names on the various titles. The same bright colours were repeated in the gate hold area vinyl seat covers, and again in the aircraft interiors in high quality woven fabrics of orange, gold, hot pink and blue, and even in the wide body movie screen murals done by the well known illustrator, Bob Peak. The murals also represented the four continents in overall colour tones, e.g., Africa - hot pink, Asia - gold, North America - blue. The same bright colours were repeated in the flight attendant and agent uniforms: orange, yellow, blue.

The same approach was carried through in print graphics: ticket envelopes and menu covers by Bob Peak, destination orientated in bright colours. Other colour co-ordinated items included tray liners, paper napkins, drink stir rods, and boarding passes. The exterior appearance of the airline continued in the familiar red and white, centred around the aircraft exterior and globe logo.

These design decisions of the 1960's proved their worth in improved market share and aircraft load factors. Data from routine surveys indicated a strong passenger acceptance of TWA's appearance, and senior management and the Board of Directors recognised that the influence of co-ordinated design in all areas of public contact is what creates the public's image of the corporation, not just the logo alone. The success of these programmes evidenced by continued acceptance over several years has given credibility to the designer's role in influencing public opinion, even in the

green shaded eyes of our Corporate accountants and comptrollers.

The early 1970's saw some major changes in world economics with significantly increased labour and material costs and, of course, the fuel crisis. Our market research and economic analysts were predicting a change in the market. Spiraling inflation was having a serious impact on the individual consumer. The once famous bargains of Europe were no more and the holiday traveller was simply staying at home. The target market had become, once again, the business traveller and our design approach would have to be different. Inflation had caught the airline in more ways than one; not only were our passenger loads and revenue down, but our labour and material costs were up. Our competitors had updated their image more recently than we and our survey data were now indicating a serious decline in preference ratings. The 1974 design assignment was not simply to create a new identity for TWA, it included some difficult budget restrictions. Begin with the aircraft exterior, our most visible identity.

Because familiarity has a significant influence on favour as well as recognition, our design approach would be an updating rather than a radical departure from our established identity. By taking the major existing element and re-positioning it on the aeroplane, and combining it with the double stripe scheme of earlier TWA aeroplanes we could create a contemporary livery which would preserve its historical lineage. The bird cage, despite its high recall value, had become dated by current graphic standards and would have to go the way of the arrow, still a sore subject with some of our more senior employees. The tapering stripes, which create an "in motion" illusion would be overpowered by a heavy letterform and so, outline Helvetica was selected for the Corporate signature. While it disappears

Figure 5.3. TWA Lockheed L1011 Tri Star showing new livery (1975) with tapered version of double line motif.

at a distance, longrange identity is assured by the dominant tail marking.

A number of alternate designs were required for the senior management presentation, but they were so cleverly radical that rejection by conservative executives would be assured in favour of the designer's preference. With approval of the new scheme came the green light to proceed with new designs for other image components.

The tapered dual stripes of the aircraft would be simplified to two parallel lines for ease of adaptation to a variety of complex shapes. Having only two colours to work with makes it possible to reverse the scheme wherever desired. Ground equipment, for example, has a red background, the darker colour to reduce maintenance costs and white markings in reflective material for night safety. Airport and city ticket office and gate room identity walls feature white markings on red backgrounds. The letterforms duplicate those of the aircraft. Wall carpeting was chosen because it absorbs noise and hides minor defects in wall surfaces. Some areas display a 4' x 8' mural – flags of countries served by TWA, made up of various types of carpeting in appropriate colours. This theme suggests our internationality and is repeated on our ticket envelopes. Ticket counters and other cabinetry are standardised in appearance with dark brown plastic laminate fronts accented by natural teak wood grain.

To differentiate directional and informational signage from identity graphics, white Helvetica lettering is used on dark brown backgrounds. Gate area seating colours have been reduced to brown and beige. Carpeting throughout all TWA public facilities is standardised red with an accent carpet of red, brown and beige stripes used in high traffic areas to hide soilage and wear, significantly reducing maintenance costs.

All of the above, together with the advertising, is what the customer sees before the ticket sale is made, or at least, before he experiences the basic product – the aeroplane trip. It for the most part is bold, large scale (supergraphic), attention getting, identifiable TWA red and white. It is consistent, applied uniformally to the extent possible at all locations, giving TWA a unified, family resemblance from one facility to the next. Once the ticket sale is made, the environment in which the passenger will spend anywhere from 45 minutes to 9 hours must be treated with a subtlety and mood evoking feelings of security, warmth and comfort. The aircraft interior, like our personnel, must be hospitable, not abrasive. In the new TWA interior programme, presently being installed, first class fabrics are of a soft camel colour with slight blue and red accents in plaid and ribbed patterns. Three fabric patterns in blue and white were chosen for the coach cabins. Corporate identity, although subtle, is not totally ignored with a fourth coach fabric of TWA red used in row pairs to simulate our two-stripe motif. In narrow body aircraft, the red rows are transverse which serves to break the cabin visually, reducing the tunnel effect without the use of physical dividers. In wide body aircraft, the red stripes run fore and aft. Bulkheads and partitions seen upon entry and when facing aft are also TWA red in plush carpet material. When seated and facing forward, a more soothing dark blue carpet covers the vertical surfaces. The Corporate symbol is respresented here in two parallel polished chrome bars.

We have made major, and we feel organised changes to the airline's appearance in the last three years, updating first our aircraft and ground equipment liveries, then passenger facilities and graphics and now our aircraft interiors. Only one major element remains – our people. From mid 1978, all customer contact employees will be in new uniforms. Since a 1978 uniform is designed in 1976 and worn until 1982, award winning fashion designer Ralph Lauren was commissioned to create career apparel for TWA which responds to our

Figure 5.4. Interior of TWA wide-bodied jet showing double parallel line motif formed from two centre rows of red upholstered seats.

employees' needs and which will look as good five years from
now as they do today.   Like our aeroplanes, our ground
equipment and facilities, the design approach is simple,
direct and professional.   Rather than the mix and match,
multi-coloured uniforms our people are wearing today, the
new programme will provide a unified look with all people of
each work category (male and female in-flight , male and
female ground) in identically styled outfits.   To avoid the
boredom of a four-year programme for both our employees
and customers, each work group will be issued summer
ensembles in lightweight Air Force blue and winter weight
garments in Navy.   Corporate identity is achieved by
inclusion of the logo in wings and name badges and by application of the red stripe markings to all jacket sleeves.

Other areas of Corporate design influence, contributing to
our "look" or "image", include print graphics for standard
Corporate forms and service support materials; i.e., menu
covers and inserts; tray liners, napkins, and drink stir
rods; ticket covers, ticket envelopes and boarding passes;
food packaging graphics; Corporate and executive letterheads, envelopes and business cards; use of the logo and
logotype; graphic standards for a variety of Company forms;
bulletins, publications, promotional and collateral materials.
Because of the high attrition rate of many of these items, they
are continually being redesigned to assure their compatibility
with major design elements and used to support specific
marketing programmes where possible.

I have tried to cover half a century of design at TWA in
less than half an hour.   In the invitation to prepare this
contribution, it was suggested that the chapter could include
reasons for adopting the new TWA identity.   I hope the
history didn't bore you, but I feel, in fact, that the history is
the reason.   It seems that the more we change, the more we
stay the same and the designer's role is to ensure that the
relationship between the travelling public and the visual
presentation of the transporter, balances the need to be up-
to-date with the need to be familiar.

Part 2 Discussion:

Case Studies — Passenger Handling Design

Chairman: Dick Negus

P.J. BROWNING (National Bus Company, Peterborough)
Reassurance is one of the critical factors in providing information about bus travel. All passengers are at one time first-time passengers. I seem to remember a recent suggestion that in any stable traffic position the turnover of passengers on a particular bus route was about twenty-five per cent per annum. If this is so we have to give a great deal of thought and consideration to the provision of information, not because we think it is a good thing to do but because we have to ensure that a 25% loss is replaced by 25% new passengers and not by only 22% or 23%. Once a passenger has made his first journey (and by his first journey I do not just mean in another town, but on another route or at a different time of day) he has 50% of the problem solved; by the time he has made his second journey he has got about 95% of it solved. I remember standing on Stamford Bus Station, which is not a very big bus station, a few months ago waiting for a bus. I was trying to get a bus to Peterborough; there were several buses coming into this Bus Station and I was darting backwards and forwards with an interested set of people watching me. Suddenly another bus arrived, to me totally indistinguishable from the others, and they all hurried forward to it. It was then that I really began to think about the question of reassurance for when I arrived at this little bus station there was nothing to reassure me that I was eventually going to get to my destination. The only point I would like to add is that it is important to reassure people when they are on the vehicle that they will get to where they want to go.

C.J. HOLLAND (R. Travers Morgan and Partners) We have heard a lot about information and the need to provide it, but we have not heard much about budgets in the Design Process. I wonder if some of the contributors could indicate what proportion of their turnover they are spending on information, or whether indeed they have a specific budget for this area?

RICHARD DEIGHTON (British Airports Authority) The British Airports Authority is responsible for providing flight information services at its airports. We are just now entering an era of computerised information systems. Our rate of investment in these is of the order of £1 million per annum, about 1% of our total annual income. The systems which we are installing are mainly of the Solari Board type and the idea is to provide information of various types and in various parts of the terminal building, corresponding to the different needs that people have in different areas. Thus passengers in the check-in area are given a fairly comprehensive information board which gives details of flights, departure times, whether they have been delayed, which gate, and so on. As they move forward the information becomes more sparse because it is felt that once passengers are on their way through the building they know reasonably well what is happening. By the time they reach the gate the only information they need is that their flight is at that particular gate. So the information is purely and simply a display over the gate room saying which flight is at the gate room.

On arrivals, the information requirements are fairly straightforward. Firstly the passengers need to know which reclaim unit they should be collecting their baggage from, so we have a flight number repeater board over each of the reclaim units. Secondly, the people who come to the airport to meet passengers, the people whom we call escorts, need fairly comprehensive information; and the kind of information they are provided with is when various flights are due to arrive, whether they have been delayed, whether or not the baggage has been delayed in reaching the reclaim units, and so on. So I think we make a reasonable job of providing information. The main problem we face is not so much in the display of information as in collecting it from the airlines in time to display it to the passengers. I think we would be hard pressed to provide more than we already do.

JULES RONDEPIERRE (TWA) The budgeting process for TWA is perhaps different from nationalised airports. First of all we have thirty-six airport locations in the United States and twenty-two overseas. It is in fact the overseas locations which are more difficult to budget for. Once we can establish what the particular information system should cost in the U.S.A. it is usually prohibitive to have the international stations buy from the United States manufacturers because of the import duties; so we simply send them the specifications and ask them to solicit quotations from local manufacturers to duplicate that system and budget for it locally, so that it will be paid for in local currency.

P.R. EVANS (Greater Manchester Transport) In relation to our bus fare turnover, which is about £50 million a year, and in relation to our total revenue of about £80 million a year, we spend a pittance on the sort of thing we were looking at earlier: about £150,000 a year on printed publicity and promotional material, and about another £50,000 a year on the programme for signs. This is not a high percentage. It is much lower than what I understand to be the advertising figure for the entire manufacturing sector in Great Britain of some 1.1% of sales, although some industries spend far more than that – soaps and detergents, for example, are around 27% followed by toilet preparations at 26% and tobacco at about 17%.

RAYMOND PLUMMER (Design and Industries Association) In the photograph of the Altrincham Interchange there were two sign-posts, one considerably larger than the other. The larger one had the British Rail logo and the word Altrincham on it, and the other one had the separate sign and it had an arrow with it and said "Station". Do you think that both were necessary and if they were, could they not have been combined on one post?

P.R. EVANS (Greater Manchester Transport) On one side of the interchange where there is access to both buses and trains there was a joint logo, Greater Manchester Transport and British Rail. The other side had access only to the trains and therefore there was just the rail logo. Were it possible to gain access to the buses without buying a rail platform ticket, to have to do which I agree is nonsense, there would be the joint logo on this side as well.

RAYMOND PLUMMER (Design and Industries Association) One sign said Altrincham and it had a British Rail logo on it and as far as I was concerned it was recognisable as a Station. Quite close to it with an arrow accompanying it was a single sign on a separate post, occupying valuable pavement space, which said "Station". Were they both necessary?

DICK NEGUS (President, Society of Industrial Artists and Designers) Do I take as an implication then that there is a certain point when a corporate identification sign starts to actually spell out words so that the British Rail symbol now means station to people and you do not need to say station. In other words you can start to cut down on superfluous information some years after you have got a good identity scheme going.

B.D. ATKINSON (British Railways Board) I think the confusion arises due to the fact that the sign saying "Station" is provided by the Local Authority and is a Department of Transport sign. The Corporate Identity sign is provided by British Rail. Obviously there has been lack of co-ordination in this instance, but usually the two signs are not seen together. The Department of Transport sign provided by the Local Authority is usually some distance from the station, guiding pedestrians and vehicles to the station.

M.A. TAUNTON (British Aerospace) Mr. Deighton presented statistics which show the much longer time spent at airports by passengers who were departing than by those who were arriving for reasons which he explained and which are fairly obvious. On the face of it you would expect this situation to improve if more and more shuttle services were introduced where people are not so committed to catching one particular aircraft. Has he any comments on that and would it be to British Airports Authority's advantage or disadvantage to have less people hanging around the airport, in other words, would they then lose a lot of revenue?

RICHARD DEIGHTON (British Airports Authority) Mr. Taunton has raised a very interesting point. Yes, I think there are two trends, which are working in opposite directions. The first trend is that towards shuttle services and variations on the shuttle technique like gate check-in or late check-in, and these obviously allow the passenger the

option of spending much less time at the airport prior to departure than was previously the case, and I think that trend should be encouraged.

Running counter to this is the second trend, towards larger and larger aircraft sizes, and it does appear to be the case that the bigger the flight load, the longer the airline requires to collect all the baggage from passengers at check-in, and load it into the aircraft. This is reflected by airlines telling passengers to check-in earlier and earlier prior to the departure of the aircraft. And as Mr. Taunton says, this does have an influence on congestion in the airport and in the capacity of the airport. If, for example, all our passengers decided to spend twice as long at the airport as they did previously, we would have twice as many people in the terminal. This means that either we need an air terminal which is twice as big in floor area or else that an air terminal of a given size can only handle half of the previous passenger throughput.

Thus anything that takes place to induce passengers to arrive at the airport nearer their departure time than at present should be encouraged – it will give us an improvement in our airport capacity and, for the next few years, certainly in the London area, airport capacity is something we are going to be very much short of. As to whether this would have much influence on our income – it obviously would, but I feel it would be relatively slight. I just hope that people would turn up early enough to visit the Duty Free Shop and not time their arrival so fine that they have no time to go there at all.

P.R. EVANS (Greater Manchester Transport) First, the incremental revenue and incremental cost at Altrincham Interchange. This was measured by passenger sampling which gave us a pattern of all journeys made before the interchange was opened, and before the services were so revamped that the buses better met the trains and the trains better met the buses, and before the publicity campaign was launched. After the opening of the interchange and the pattern of services was changed, extra passenger trips amounted to something like 13% on the buses and 17% on the trains. Of the new bus trips, nearly 9% were journeys which would not have previously been made at all, 1% had transferred from other modes and 3% were extra journeys. The rail trips were 7% which would not have been made, 8% transfer and 2% extra journeys. The extra revenue to Greater Manchester Transport for the whole project exceeded the extra costs by some £33,000 per year and whilst this is not a vast amount in the context of £50 million in fare revenue, it is however most encouraging against the backcloth of usual industrial trends.

N. TOWNEND (Greater Glasgow Passenger Transport Executive) It is my personal experience that the shuttle service between Glasgow and London demands my arrival at the airport earlier than the previous straight booking system. This is simply because the business man in Glasgow aiming at a meeting in London knows that the 8.10 from Glasgow is ideal and he can plan a meeting in central London for 10.30, and British Airways will provide a back-up plane if you do not get on the first one. What they cannot guarantee of course is what time the back-up plane will arrive and therefore the business man with a tight schedule must make sure that he is at Glasgow Airport within the numbers of the first plane load. If you are going by another airline which has a fifteen minutes booking time with hand baggage you can get yourself there precisely fifteen minutes before takeoff, so for me personally Shuttle is not all that some people would have us believe.

Turning to the money spent on design and publicity, someone earlier seemed to make an almost disdainful reference to the fact that something might cost money. In operations we are fairly used to that sort of comment. Could I therefore ask Mr. Evans, whose publicity is some of the finest of a Passenger Transport Executive in England, how he arrived at his incremental revenue benefits for the Altrincham Interchange and could I also ask Mr. Rondepierre how he and his predecessors could identify those improvements to market share and load factors, which stemmed from 'design', rather than to any other features, such as new aircraft, new routes or other improvements?

P.R. EVANS (Greater Manchester Transport) The incremental revenue and cost of Altrincham Interchange was measured entirely by passenger sampling ending in a pattern of all journeys made before the interchange was built and before the services were revamped so that the buses connected better with the trains and vice versa. This was also before the publicity campaign was launched. After the opening of the interchange with the changed pattern of services, extra passenger trips amounted to something like 6%. These were trips made up of new journeys, which had not been made by people on public transport before the interchange was built and extra journeys made as it was that much more convenient. The extra revenue exceeded the extra costs of the extra buses which were needed in certain cases and the extra rail costs by something like £120,000 a year, which is not a lot in the context of £45 million total revenue, but we are talking of just incremental revenue and incremental costs.

JULES RONDEPIERRE (TWA) The question was how we could identify the increase in passenger load related to changes in graphics or changes in overall design. As a matter of fact TWA, like most major U.S.A. airlines, spends an awful lot of money on market research. In addition to measuring the size of the total market, we compare ourselves to our competition and there is also Federal agency data available on boarding figures for all the airlines. In fact, our share of the market, against our competition, improved considerably after major changes were made in the corporate appearance. I think it was generally accepted by our people that this was largely the result of the appearance changes.

T. GLASGOW I was wondering if it was possible to have guides on certain rail trips. In Scotland they used to have one from Queen Street Station, Glasgow to Mallaig, giving descriptive information on the trip and they also used to have

one for the trip down the Clyde; and I know the Swiss did one from Bern to Milan which is a fantastic route and I think it would make travel much more interesting if one could get such information when travelling.

P.R. EVANS (Greater Manchester Transport) Leaving our Travel and Touring Divisions aside, we have about half a dozen leaflets that describe excursion routes by bus, but Greater Manchester is perhaps not the country's most popular tourist resort – although I think it has much more to offer visitors than many people think. The scope is therefore somewhat limited but the idea basically is a good one.

D.R. VERNON (Greater Manchester Transport) Public patronage of the bus industry has just about halved in the past thirty years and I think all we have been saying to-day should be regarded in that context. I was most interested in Peter Evans' suggestion that the purchase of a bus ride might be considered a distress purchase whereas both Eirlys Roberts and Alfred Wood thought of travel as a joyful occasion. I wonder if we might not be in danger of overlooking a number of other related matters, which in my experience of the bus industry, and it may apply to other industries, have a direct or indirect impact on the corporate image and the identity of any organisation. Kenneth Robinson mentioned total design. I am not quite sure what he meant by that, but I think he did mean a little more than design and architecture. I feel a design policy is all very well as far as it goes, but it does need a great deal of backup by line and functional management determined, for instance, to keep garage floors, workshops, canteens and office premises clean and tidy; to keep the inside and outside of buses clean (they all too often seem dirty with oil spillages), to maintain a good standard of internal and external advertisement (not to use window stickers that become so messy), to insist on reasonable appearance and attitude of all staff who have contact with the public, to insist on the correct display of destinations which you have heard a great deal about already, and to constantly up-date maintenance facilities and so forth.

The image is affected very often by breakdown and delays on the road, which need to be monitored and resolved if possible, or by failure to operate scheduled trips, and in general to supervise the adequacy of the services. I think it is also appropriate to remark about vandal damage to our fleets. The cost to Greater Manchester Transport is thought to be in the region between £150,000 to £250,000 per annum and there is no doubt of the effect of that upon the transport environment; it is very depressing. I would also say that our corporate image takes a hard knock every time our service is affected by industrial action. It may be said that these are all operating matters but I do not think design policy can exclude these practical considerations in achieving the corporate image. I wonder, would Mr. Evans care to comment whether to achieve somewhat better total design, design ought to be an important function of operations or alternatively operations should be an important function or design?

P.R. EVANS (Greater Manchester Transport) I think it is no use having good design in the first place if, for example, your beautifully designed buses or your lovely bus stations are covered with dirt. Obviously the implementation and the maintenance of the design standards are more important. The evolution of the original design involves many considerations. It should involve firstly the passenger, as he is the one who pays for the whole thing; we must provide what he needs. Equally however, it has to be governed by operational constraints. It is no use designing a bus for the customer that will not run properly. The co-ordination of design must be by design experts, but no design will ever succeed if it ignores (a) the passenger and (b) the man who has to drive the bus, using the driver as an example of "Operations" as you, I think, are meaning it.

DR. R.W. CRESSWELL (University of Wales Institute of Science and Technology) I would like to refer to the question of route information leaflets provided within trains. When the then new Mk. 1 coaches were introduced in 1951 (Festival of Britain year) British Railways placed leaflets in certain named trains giving information on places of interest en route. Also, London Transport tour buses now have similar types of leaflets.

Regarding the effect of corporate identity policies, I would like to ask Peter Evans and Jules Rondepierre how far their respective schemes have given a boost of morale to their staffs. One gets the feeling that if a transport organisation, whether it be a bus, rail or air undertaking, adopts a positive corporate identity policy, it gives the impression, to both its customers and its staff, of caring. So often many of the organisations that feel that a good design and corporate identity policy does not matter give the impression that they "couldn't care less", which appears to permeate through all their activities.

P.R. EVANS (Greater Manchester Transport) The answer, both subjectively and objectively, is "Yes". Subjectively, from my own impressions and my own discussions with our staff. Objectively, from measurable research and statistics. Just to give one example: at Altrincham, where we did upgrade the design and decor standards, and the general image, of bus station, route furniture, publicity, signing, etc., the lost mileage from Altrincham garage (lost mileage being one of the industry's measures of the extent it lets the public down for mainly two reasons - mechanical failures of buses and staff absenteeism or illness) fell dramatically and is now running at about half the rate for the rest of the organisation. There are other reasons for this (the proportion of newer buses is slightly higher at Altrincham, for example) but those other reasons are not enough to explain the difference and the results are definitely better. The other two aspects are: we log all our complaints, and we do get fewer complaints, not markedly fewer, but fewer, from Altrincham than from elsewhere; and we also get, which is perhaps more significant, more suggestions (sensible suggestions) from our staff, on the Staff Suggestion Scheme. These are just some indications that it is working.

JULES RONDEPIERRE (TWA) We have an expression, or at least we have developed an expression in the last two years,

that the flight attendant is our most frequent traveller. That person is on the plane four or five days a week and his morale is very important. This comes through not only in the aircraft interior but in the uniforms for flight attendant people. It really is not necessary, as least from a wear point of view, to change the design of uniform every four years, but after a four-year cycle the garments are beginning to wear and the feeling is that there will be some cost associated with replacement even in the same design. There is an additional cost in making a change, but it is virtually offset by what would be required to replace the existing uniforms. It is more than offset by the morale booster it gives people. They just get tired of wearing the same thing day-in and day-out, and in fact it seems to go in cycles because we survey our people and give them the opportunity to provide information as to what they would like to wear. It is very difficult to get more than 50% of the people to agree on anything. We have 10,000 people in uniform. The last time we surveyed our people six years ago for the current uniform, they were in a fairly rigid form of dress at that time as the style of ordinary dress was changing, they indicated very strongly that they would prefer a more casual non-uniform uniform - something where there was an opportunity to look different from one another. The creation was a mix-and-match series of garments where the colours worked fairly well. The current survey which was taken about a year and a half ago gave just the opposite result as they wanted a more-uniform uniform, and I think that was pretty predictable.

With regard to the aircraft interiors, again it is a subjective thing and I think you would be fortunate in my job to find 50% who like a particular scheme. We are talking now specifically of the reaction of the flight crew, but it affects all the employees in general. I think they feel comfortable, if somebody up there is doing a reasonably good job regardless of the fact if the dress is not to their personal taste. If they think it is something of which they can be proud as an airline symbol, we are not going to get a lot of complaints from passengers. This does have a very definite morale impact and enables us to get some of those relatively expensive programmes through management. There is always the intangible thing - we go through the brief exercise where we write the cost of the programme and the benefits - there are some economic benefits, but always the last paragraph has a few intangibles. Fortunately in my case, senior management has accepted them as having some value even if we cannot define it specifically.

W.M. SHULTZ (Boeing Marine Systems) The U.S. Department of Transportation made a survey a number of years ago which turned up a very interesting fact. People travelling value their time five times higher when waiting than when moving. It is probably the reason that we humans, when we come on a traffic jam, will inevitably skirt around it, even if it means going way out of our way, just to keep moving. Therefore, it is little wonder that when people have to queue up at airports they get upset.

As a regular international traveller, I happen to have good service to the continent through London by a daily non-stop 747 flight from Seattle. However, those of us travelling on have a little problem. The minimum transfer time for baggage at Heathrow is one hour, so we are forced to have a connection of at least that long to have baggage make the next flight. Therefore, we are amongst those cluttering the Heathrow lounges because we are forced to do it. And if the inbound flight is late, you do not get your bags at the other end of the trip. For example, the last five times I did not have my bag in either the States or Europe. I must admit one does not play favourites, for it was four different airlines and four different cities. I am curious as to how much you are aware of this, how big a problem it is, and more importantly, are you doing anything to try and fix it?

RICHARD DEIGHTON (British Airports Authority) We are very much aware of the problems transfer passengers at Heathrow have to face. The underlying reason why there are so many delays is simply the layout. Somebody in their wisdom about twenty-five years ago decided that Heathrow would consist of three separate terminals, and they built those three terminals between two runways, and unfortunately they put the two runways so close together that there was not enough room for an adequate airside and landside road system in between the three passenger terminals. That really is the underlying reason why baggage takes much longer at Heathrow to transfer between terminals than it does at some other European airports.

   As to what we are trying to do about it, we are at present engaged in collaborative studies with the airlines at Heathrow to look at various ways and means of speeding up the transport of baggage between the three terminals. Potentially we think we could reduce the interconnect time from the existing figure of one hour to something like thirty or forty minutes, which would be comparable with most other European Airports.

   The only other comment I should like to make is that we have done studies to establish whether the fact that Heathrow has a long interconnect time actually diminishes its attractiveness to passengers who have a choice of interlining through Heathrow or some other European airport. It does appear in fact that reducing the interconnect time would not really increase the attractiveness of Heathrow as an interlining airport. But certainly I take your point that something needs to be done about it, and we are trying to do something about it.

K. WARD (Lanchester Polytechnic)   I would like to express some doubt about the benefits of corporate identity schemes. I feel they should not be completely dictated by the needs of an organisation for an identity, but should take into consideration the nature of the localities in which the organisation works and the nature of the passengers using its services.

   It may be appropriate for an international operator to have a corporate identity that is uniform throughout the world. It may be appropriate for an organisation serving Manchester to have an identity uniform throughout Manchester. However my main experience of transport operations was driving buses

for a small local concern. When it was taken over by the National Bus Company it received a corporate identity, which came from outside making our buses look like buses from the rest of the country for no reason that was related to the people who travelled and worked on them. Far from increasing staff morale, we felt the company we worked for to be removed one step away from us and the passengers. Buses in this context were a small local affair and needed a local identity. It seemed thoroughly inappropriate in the name of a corporate identity to impose the vast national scheme on local operators.

N. WILSON (Norman Wilson Associates) This question could take rather a long time. I think this could apply to all corporate identities and I do sympathise with our academic colleague from Lanchester Polytechnic. Perhaps the short answer is, if you were in the Ribble Area or the North Western Area they would have already previously taken over six private companies with various liveries underneath them. So I think this is a continuing problem on the national and multinational scale. Apart from the local stage carriage bus, we had not a marketable intercity bus like the Greyhound so we produced the National Coach livery, which has been quite successful. Perhaps when we have just got this organised, somebody will suggest we have a Eurobus with a new livery.

J.R. GRAY (British Railways Board) Speaking as a bus user, may I disagree with the idea of a local bus livery. It is all very well for the local yokel who knows what the bus looks like but to the new bus user or to anybody from outside the locality arriving by train, the local bus service becomes a total mystery. At least having it in a National or PTE livery is a reassurance that this really is the bus that has arrived.

F.R.F. EVANS (Midland Red Bus Company)   I was wondering if it would be a good thing for airlines to always run their own buses. Surely airlines would like to see their intending passengers arrive on time for departure and would find it in their own interests to provide transport from the central area bus station to the airport for their own air travellers?

RICHARD DEIGHTON (British Airports Authority) If you have a transport system which suffers from inadequate design you can overcome that deficiency with intelligent and forward looking management. The converse, I think, is that even if you have a system which is designed to a very high standard and has been provided with the best possible intentions it will not work unless it can be managed in a sensible fashion. I cannot stress too highly the importance of effective management in ultimately producing what the consumer really wants.

JULES RONDEPIERRE (TWA) I can offer a comment as somewhat an outside observer. I travel quite a lot around the world, frequently in England, and I am a user of the local buses, Underground and British Rail, as well as the airlines. Frankly, I would like to compliment you on just being here and having the interest. Frankly, I think you have taken an excellent approach and are much more aware of what improvements are needed locally. To an outsider you are in advance of much of what we are doing in the States at the local level. It is good to realise that there are people elsewhere in the world who have similar problems to us and are doing something about them.

P.R. EVANS (Greater Manchester Transport) Firstly, regarding the communication role of design, I think we must all assume that the passenger does not know. Just as the speed of the slowest is the speed that often has to be adopted, so is the comprehension of the slowest the one we must take as our yard stick. Secondly, in our experience nearly everyone respects good design. The better it is (and that is not necessarily the most expensive), the higher is the morale of the people who are working in the environment of that design and the less likely is it to be the subject of vandalism. Thirdly, as a passenger transport industry we must not assume we have always got it right, or that we are always right. Mr. Wood quoted Murphy's law earlier – or rather part of it – that the piece of bread always falls buttered side down. We must not forget that the full law says that the bread always falls buttered side down except when dropped expressly to illustrate the validity of the law.

Part 3

Vehicle Design

Chapter 6

Aircraft, Trains, Buses and People

Rachel Waterhouse

In 1977 'Which?' asked its members what they thought of British Rail. The results were not complimentary. Apart from complaints about cost and punctuality, there were comments on cleanliness: 'Why go if you have to add a dry cleaning bill on top of the fare?'; on comfort: 'have been frozen on some occasions – no heat at all – but sometimes roasted'; on information: 'when delays occur, passenger frustration is aggravated by lack of explanation or apology'; on food: 'subsistence-level food at Hilton prices'.

'Which?' accepted that 'at least some of the members' complaints we've quoted paint a less than fair picture of British Rail'. But they are certainly symptomatic of a certain dissatisfaction, which is not uncommon among travellers.

This dissatisfaction springs mainly from two sources. First, the fundamental design of train, bus or aircraft. Secondly, the standards of repair and maintenance. Most of the 'Which?' members' complaints fell into this second category of operational short-comings. This may well be because in the last decade considerable attention has been paid to designing for passenger comfort, much less to problems of cleanliness and easy maintenance. New techniques of designing for passengers are becoming standard practice; these include applied ergonomics, the study of passenger behaviour and the use of passenger surveys. Can these techniques now be used in the design of vehicles and carriages that are cheaper and simpler to maintain and which will encourage passengers to be cleaner and tidier?

THE AGE OF PUBLIC SERVICE VEHICLES

There is no one standard for vehicles; there is no average passenger. At any one time the types of vehicle being used by local and national bus companies, the rolling stock of British Rail or London Transport, and the planes being flown by private and national airlines cover a wide age-range, which parallels a considerable span of design sophistication. As a result, one passenger will be demanding the better quality seating, lighting and heating that another already takes for granted, while the traveller whose personal comfort has been increased by an improved environment will be demanding better amenities in terms of cleanliness, refreshments and perhaps entertainment.

Many London buses, still manned by a conductor as well as a driver, have draughty rear access platforms whereas in Birmingham one-man operated buses, with front access and closing doors, are now almost universal. Each system has quite different advantages and disadvantages which will be reflected in passenger reactions.

Similarly, Inter-City or the High Speed trains have improved carriages, with better heating, lighting and seating which give a smoother ride than older rolling stock relegated to long distance cross-country routes like the Newcastle to Plymouth run.

On London's underground the book-life of rolling stock is 40 years. So, even in 1977, pre-war rolling stock was providing all or part of the service on the Bakerloo, District, Northern and Piccadilly lines together with the East London and Highbury branch services, while the new Victoria line travellers enjoyed cleaner, brighter carriages and faster journey times.

Private airlines serving local needs often fly older turbo-prop aircraft providing standards of comfort and ride which are well below the characteristics of larger and heavier jet planes. Their marginal utility lies in the time saved on relatively short hauls or the convenience of flying direct from one's home town without having to go first to Heathrow or Gatwick.

In these terms, the problem of increasing comfort for many passengers is not primarily one of better design, rather of the economics of capital investment by British Rail, the bus companies or the airlines.

INNOVATION AND CHANGE

As in large families, improvements come in two ways: belongings can be "handed down" or new ones bought. The arrival of the Advanced Passenger Train may put, for example, the longer cross-country routes straight into the forefront of British Rail's technical development both in the engines and carriages. The decision of a local bus company to adopt one-man operated buses, involves the fairly rapid re-equipment of the whole fleet of vehicles. Automatic train operation, if adopted, would require a similar re-equipment programme. Such decisions often involve "handing down" the existing rolling stock or vehicles to less well-provided routes or to other companies. In such circumstances some upgrading overall is likely to take place, but the major benefits will go to those passengers who happen to be living on the right route or in the right place.

Major changes in vehicle design are not usually introduced by gradual modification of existing vehicles. Frequently they are part of a completely new system - electrification, jet engines, high speeds, automatic controls, or one-man operation. Passengers need to ensure therefore that the most advanced designs solve more problems than they create. User testing of all new types of vehicle during design development and the incorporation of the most advanced ergonomic knowledge should be normal practice for the benefit, not only of the immediate user, but also for possible secondary, or even tertiary, users.

LIMITATIONS ON THE POTENTIAL NUMBER OF PASSENGERS

Personal mobility is even more variable than vehicles and rolling stock and fundamentally affects the quality of people's

lives.   For the young and agile almost any form of transport
is practicable; for the handicapped, including age as a major
handicap, for mothers with young children, for housewives
burdened with shopping, the possibilities of using public
transport may be severely limited.   Easy access to vehicles,
adequate numbers of comfortable seats, easy disembarkation
would considerably extend the number of potential travellers.

The importance of this mobility to the housekeeping budget
of people without cars, living at a distance from the
competition of the high street shops, is well recognised.
Country dwellers have been particularly hit by the decline in
rural transport services; suburban mothers and old age
pensioners are equally disadvantaged unless they can readily
use public transport.   Vehicle design can therefore directly
affect not only the 'quality of people's lives' but also their
family budget.

Since the number of passenger miles achieved by a given
number of journeys is closely related to the profitability of
any transport enterprise, passengers must be attracted from
alternative forms of transport.   British Rail has been most
active in pursuing this policy.   If the suburban commuter is
regarded as almost a captive animal to be packed into heavily
overloaded, ancient rolling stock twice a day, the inter-city
businessman is in a different category.   The development of
the Inter-City, High Speed and Advanced Passenger Trains
alongside the extension of the national motorway system
brings trains into direct competition with cars on middle and
long distance journeys.   These potential business passengers
have to be wooed by speed, comfort and amenities, as well as
by frequency of service and punctuality.

In the air the overall consideration on the part of the
operator appears still to be maximisation of load.   The discomfort of the journey for the passenger is balanced by the
over-riding advantage of speed and mitigated by the assiduous
attentions of personable young ladies providing drinks and food
or, on longer journeys, by choice of film entertainment.
Only larger jets provide that easier space and movement,
reduction of noise and vibration and properly pressurised
cabins, which make longer flying times tolerable.

MAINTENANCE
   When 'Which?' discovered that its members' complaints about
rail travel were particularly concerned with cleanliness and
maintenance, it undertook a survey to find out how far the
criticisms were justified.

'Which?' looked at over 1,400 carriages about four-fifths of
which were second class.   Seats were less than satisfactory
in a quarter of second class carriages. First class did rather
better. On Southern Region suburban trains more than a
quarter of the seats were very dirty - often full of dirt and
grease. Very dirty seats were found on comparatively few
Inter-City trains, though quite a number were 'less than
clean'. Windows were especially dirty on Eastern and
Southern Region suburban trains. Floors were especially
dirty, as one might expect, in smoking carriages.   Over 700
carriages had toilets.   About a quarter of these weren't

clean - and a fifth of those in second class carriages were
very dirty.   Many lacked amenities too - in second class
a fifth had no paper, a fifth no soap, a quarter no towels,
and half had no hot water.   First class toilets were in general
better.   Litter was an increasing problem because of the
introduction of paper cups and plates in the buffet cars
without the provision of litter bins.   The development of a
proposed table clearing trolley has been very slow.

Heating and ventilation was also criticised but came only
ninth in the list of priorities for improvement - rated by
passengers below litter bins, improved toilets and cleaner
carriages.

In modern open carriages the lighting, heating and
ventilation work well unless standards of maintenance and
repair are allowed to fall.   The best designed system needs
proper care and attention, and quick replacement of broken
parts.   Essential to the heating system in air-conditioned
carriages, for example, are well fitting doors, so passenger
comfort requires quick repair of any door that refuses to
stay shut.

'Which?' found that the order of preferences for passengers
changed over the length of the journey: less vibration, less
noise, cleaner carriages, improved heating/ventilation and
better lighting all decreased in importance with the increased
length of time on the train.   In contrast, the importance of a
public address system, extra entertainments, and a newspaper
stall increased with the length of time already spent on the
train.   The authors suggested that this indicated a progress-
ion from concern about physical comfort, through boredom and
a need for things to do, to a need for information as the
journey neared its end.

A public address system is a matter of great importance to
passengers.   Even more important is its use, especially
when there is a break-down or an unscheduled stop.   To sit
for an hour and a half in a stationary train which has a
totally silent public address system is one of the most
frustrating experiences a passenger can be asked to endure.

The 'Which?' findings suggest that many of the earlier
demands of rail passengers for comfort have been at least to
some extent met, and that current demands are for designs
that can be cheaply cleaned and maintained.

MINIMUM STANDARDS FOR PASSENGERS
   During the past two decades considerable advances have
been made in defining minimum standards of safety and comfort
for passengers.   Individual passengers seem to take safety
somewhat for granted, believing, perhaps , that the liability
of the operator and national licensing requirements ensure
adequate standards.   Only the occasional major accident -
the DC10 crash over Paris, the Moorgate tube disaster, or
a series of brake failures on coaches - undermines public
confidence.   The accidents themselves tend to stimulate
safety research and development, though the results are not
always accepted.   The deformable coach seat, for example,
recommended by a committee of the Society of Motor

Manufacturers and Traders is opposed by the operators because it is also less vandal-proof. The Committee was set up, however, after a particularly unpleasant motorway coach crash which left passengers impaled on the backs of broken plywood seats.

Comfort, on the other hand, is a matter of daily experience, but an experience in the past difficult to quantify. The development of human factor studies and the extension of ergonomics from the work-place to people's everyday lives have widened our understanding of, and helped us to define, a comfortable environment whether in the home, the motorcar or public transport.

The first task of the early sixties was to begin to build up an anthropometric picture of the ordinary population. As late as 1973 Hoag and Adams (1) stated that 'existing literature on anthropometry represents an almost exclusive sampling of military personnel', which, as they pointed out, was likely to cover active individuals between the ages of 18 and 40, the majority between 18 and 25. This ignored the British Standards Institution's 'Anthropometric and Ergonomic Recommendations for Dimensions in Designing for the Elderly' published in 1969. Public transport, in particular, needs to be designed for the widest spread of the population.

The second task was to observe how people behave in relation to their surroundings. Only by watching actual behaviour patterns, can the physical and psychological tensions of any situation be evaluated and used to explain people's feelings or reactions.

THE PASSENGER SEAT

An early candidate for ergonomic evaluation was the passenger seat. The high incidence of back pain among populations who spend more and more of their time sitting down is due in great measure to the inadequacy of seats themselves. In 1973, H.W. Oxford (2) pointed out that too little research had been carried out into human posture and that too few seats in buses, trains and aircraft gave adequate support. His criteria for an adequate seat included proper support for the hollow of the back, the right height from the ground, ample space behind the calf to allow movement of the lower leg, no undue pressure on the thigh behind the knee and freedom from strain in the neck and shoulders. A seat which is too high causes most discomfort. Even at 425 mm, unless the depth of the seat is only 375 mm, or a footrail is provided, a seat is too high for almost 50 per cent of women, for men of short stature and for young teenagers. Oxford suggested that the depth of seat should not exceed 425 mm (450 mm if a footrail is provided), but some of the aircraft seats he measured were 500 mm in depth, which exceeds the thigh measurement of 90 per cent of men and women. British Rail have chosen a height of 400 mm for first and second class seats in the new High Speed Train. It is worth noting that the seat heights preferred by the elderly and disabled for buses were, however, 425mm and 450 mm.

Height and depth are not the only important factors. One of the major fatiguing discomforts of every traveller is the constant automatic physical adjustments he has to make to keep himself in balance every time the vehicle sways, rounds a curve, goes over a bump, accelerates or slows. During the whole journey he is moving his trunk, head and arms, weighing perhaps 36.25 Kg, through a succession of small distances. Perhaps it is this tiring process, together with the visual disturbance, which so readily induces sleep in train passengers at certain high speeds. Branton and Grayson (3) considered this movement factor helped to explain passenger behaviour in their evaluation of two seats for the British Rail experimental train XP64. Type I was the traditional softer seat, Type II a reinforced plaster shell with urethane foam cushions, giving a firmer feel. Male passengers were observed. In Type I, more men slumped into the softer seat, used the back support, and crossed their legs (shorter men crossed them less often), while in Type II they more frequently used the arm-rests, sat with uncrossed legs and neglected to use the back-rest, suggesting a less relaxed position. The firmer seat appeared not to hold the passenger in place as adequately as the softer one and therefore required its occupant to brace himself against the continual movements that the ride produced.

Studies like these have produced specifications for seats suitable for a wide spectrum of the population, which can perfectly well be incorporated within the economic constraints of the need to maximise the load. When it comes to width of seat it is a different matter. In the 'Which?' survey, travellers in both older and newer second class open carriages put more space as their top priority, whereas travellers in both the older and newer first class compartments thought them comfortable and spacious, so they primarily wanted less vibration and less noise. Despite improvements in design, therefore, the top priorities of both first and second class passengers remained the same whether they were travelling in older or newer carriages.

BAGGAGE

Problems of luggage and baggage are common to passengers on all public transport. Whatever the accommodation provided, passengers want to keep an eye on their personal baggage, so passengers and luggage begin to compete for space. If suitable luggage storage space in trains is inadequate, passengers will pile the table in front of them and fill the gangway beside them. They will also want to keep heavier items at floor level. The spaces between the bodies of seats now provided in open carriages makes this possible, though the width of the space available and the width of the gangway limits the size of storable luggage. Passengers apparently do not favour stowing larger luggage overhead because they fear the items might fall on people beneath. There is a short panic period on first joining the train when passengers mark out their territory. This panic is greater for occasional passengers than for regular travellers, and includes not only finding a seat, but also arranging their belongings. They tend to resent attacks on their territory by passengers joining the train at later stages of the journey.

The problem of keeping one's possessions nearby occurs

also in buses, where passengers are increasingly reluctant to leave cases or other parcels where they cannot observe them all the time. Considerable amounts of shopping and small bags are therefore taken to seats where there is scarcely room to accommodate them. The changeover to one-man operated two-door buses with a central luggage storage area has made boarding a bus with large cases or rucksacks a difficult exercise. For mothers with a baby, a folding push-chair, a handbag, shopping and other children, it is almost impossible. Even on aircraft, where each passenger is strictly limited to one piece of hand luggage for under-seat storage, that, together with a handbag and a couple of duty-free bottles, severely limits the amount of leg-room available in an already much restricted space.

GETTING ON AND OFF

In talking about seats, two assumptions have been made. First, that the prospective travellers can actually get aboard the vehicle; second, that there are enough seats for those travelling.

The Department of the Environment Circular of 1973, 'The Disabled Traveller on Public Transport', by suggesting improvements which would help disabled passengers, attempted to extend to moving vehicles the provisions of the Chronically Sick and Disabled Persons Act of 1970.

For the severely disabled both airlines and British Rail make considerable provision. Wheelchairs, and their occupants can be transported by air and British Rail have a folding wheelchair for transporting passengers from their car all the way to a seat. If you have to travel in your own wheel-chair, new British Rail Mark III Inter-City first class coaches are planned to have a removable seat at the end bay. Until now, subject to prior permission, wheelchairs with occupants have had to travel in the guard's van.

Although most people seem to know about the provision made for air passengers, they are largely unaware of the services offered by British Rail. In an investigation into the problems of travel and the handicapped carried out at Loughborough Institute for Consumer Ergonomics on behalf of the Transport and Road Research Laboratory, it was found that very few of the physically handicapped people interviewed had used trains or knew of the existence of British Rail's special facilities.

The same investigation showed that even where the physically handicapped can walk as far as the nearest bus stop, in itself a severely limiting factor, problems with steps make the use of buses very difficult. The distance from the curb to the bus step can be daunting, much worse if the bus parks away from the curb and the distance is increased from the road to the bus step. Hand holds are vital in order to pull oneself up. The process is reversed in getting off the bus. Again steps and unsuitable or non-existent hand holds cause the greatest problems.

The anxieties of the elderly are much increased if there are not enough seats. The custom of the able-bodied offering seats to the old appears to be demoded. London Underground

trains now carry little messages over four seats near the doors asking occupants to give up the seats if needed by the elderly or the heavy laden. Perhaps buses will have to use the same method to try to jog other travellers into some form of courtesy.

Do the able-bodied not rise to their feet because the difficulties of standing passengers have not been adequately catered for? The importance of being near a vertical pole is well illustrated every rush hour by the crowding of passengers near the carriage entrances of underground trains to the point where they are jammed tighter than sardines. Yet by moving down the centre of the carriage to one of the overhead swinging hand-holds, more space would be available for everybody. It is not only, I believe, that these hanging straps are less rigid; it is also that having even one hand above one's head produces a feeling of vulnerability and exposure, especially with seated passengers below. Shorter passengers cannot reach these straps without discomfort.

In London, 'Red Arrow' buses have been introduced to provide a basic transport system between commuter stations. With very few seats, and space for a majority of standing passengers, hand-holds are essential. Even with a large number of rails provided, the journey is not a particularly easy one.

Not only do buses frequently have insufficient stanchions or other hand-holds, modern traffic conditions in towns cause frequent stopping, starting, acceleration and deceleration, all of which put a strain on the standing passenger. Even when seats are available, the old and frail are afraid of falling. If the bus starts before they are seated or if they have to get to the exit before the bus stops there is a period when they are at risk. Sometimes a driver with a fierce foot on the brake can make all movement within the bus hazardous at all stages of the journey.

What has been called the 'Jerk and Ride' may be partly due to the driver - acceleration and braking in particular - but it may also be due to the suspension and gear systems. Improved suspension, automatic transmission and a well-designed braking system can make it easier for the driver to operate the bus smoothly.

News of the new British Leyland B15 bus, therefore, is particularly welcome and demonstrates what can now be done by careful research, identification of the problems and determination to solve them. The co-operation of the Transport Road Research Laboratory, British Leyland and applied ergonomists from Loughborough in an investigation of factors affecting the use of buses by both elderly and ambulant disabled persons began in 1972. The scope of the investigation specifically stated that the factors to be considered would include 'safety and comfort as well as speed and convenience and may relate to entry and extra steps, door configuration, ramping of floor, fare collection, seat and footstool dimensions, hand-holds, passenger surveillance by the drivers and the operation of stop signals'.

The B15 design has incorporated many of the findings of this investigation: air suspension fitted to reduce roll on corners, steps which are much lower than normal, stanchions placed where they are shown to be of most use to elderly people and seat pitch which reflects the need for adequate leg room. Air suspension and levelling maintains the entrance step at approximately 150 mm above the pavement. Further improvements may come. A Telford firm have now developed special valves to operate on single-decker air suspension type buses, which produce a patented 'kneeling' bus system. This enables a stationary bus to drop down 100 mm at the front so reducing the step height even further.

Developments such as these designed primarily to meet the needs of the infirm, by making travel easier and cutting down minor accidents benefit all bus users.

ONE-MAN OPERATED BUSES

Seasoned travellers have the advantage of knowing how to work the system, but the regular traveller probably has a greater advantage over the occasional bus user on one-man operated vehicles than on any other. For this reason he becomes easily irritated by delays caused by those who don't know what to do.

Consumers generally have not welcomed the introduction of one-man operation seeing it as bringing a reduction in personal service - no one to help children or the old - an increase in journey time, and an increase in traffic congestion. But Canterbury consumers (4) as early as 1970 were not prepared to pay higher fares for the re-introduction of conductors.

Various ways have been devised to speed up the procedure. Season tickets, PTE Inter-travel cards and free passes for the elderly, all of which offer financial incentives, have been very successful. Flat rate fares also save time. In Birmingham no change is given, so that after one or two embarrassing episodes involving attempts to obtain change from fellow travellers, passengers are drilled into knowing the right fare and having the right change. This doesn't help the once-only stranger or the first-time traveller, but it ensures that the non-conformist is made to feel guilty of anti-social behaviour. Traffic congestion, caused by long waits at stops, has been reduced by parking bays for buses at busy loading points.

LOOKING INTO THE FUTURE

The general trend in all travel is towards more semi-automatic or automatic systems. Investigations into what this entails for the passenger have been widely undertaken. The more automatic, the more foolproof must the system be.

The new Helsinki underground system planned for 1978/79 will be automatically run without any operators in the train. This presents problems of interchange, stopping times and safety margins. In 1972 a short line was built with six coaches for experiments. The Ergonomics Section of the Department of Psychology of the Institute of Occupational Health carried out a study into passengers' opinion of the coach, traffic flow inside the coach, comparison of two

prototypes of seat design and travelling possibilities for, and problems of, special passengers (invalids, old people, children). A travelling mock-up train was organised, test subjects' behaviour and reactions noted, and recommendations made for improvement of seating, the number of handles and support pillars, and seat design.

A similar ergonomics evaluation has been carried out at Loughborough Institute for Consumer Ergonomics into a mini-tram system consisting of small cabs holding 10 - 20 people, travelling on guide lines at speeds of up to 60 m.p.h. between stations spaced approximately a quarter of a mile apart. The system, which will be computer controlled, will programme cabs to arrive every 20 seconds at peak hours. A station complex and a mock-up train vehicle were built on the campus. Experiments went on for nearly a year with passengers drawn from the general public travelling on the vehicle going in and out of the 'station'.

The passengers were divided into a commuter group and a non-commuter group. The first consisted of the young to middle-aged, active section of the population, carrying no more than a briefcase; the second was a more varied group of 'shoppers' carrying baggage, mothers with children, elderly persons, handicapped persons, including wheelchair users, and people temporarily incapacitated as a result of injury.

Selected mixes of passengers were used, taking imaginary journeys according to a programme shown on their ticket. Thus a passenger may find that he has to get on the tram at Station 1, alight at Station 4, get on again at Station 6, get off at Station 7 and so on. In actual practice each 'station' is the beginning and end of a tram journey out of the 'station' along a path for 100 metres and then return to the next station. In this way the experimenters were able to control the number of people on the platform, the number of people in the tram, and the number of people getting on and off, and type of people involved. Thus experiments can be carried out with different sized trams, with different seating arrangements and with different platform configurations in realistic conditions involving a tram moving in and out of a busy station.

The results so far have indicated a preferred cab configuration of three seats placed at each end of the vehicle with comfortable standing room for six people in the centre. Such a layout gives space for wide opening doors without interferring with the legroom of the seated passengers. Wide doors not only allow rapid movements by passengers in and out of the vehicle but also enable mothers with pushchairs and wheelchair users to gain easy access.

This work at Loughborough is part of the world-wide interest in human factor evaluation and applied ergonomics which will forestall consumer discomfort and complaint by providing future transport systems tailor-made for the maximum number of potential passengers. From the consumer's point of view, it is vital that, in the design of any novel form of public transport, human factor guidelines and advice are available to the designers during all, and particularly the early, stages of system development.

Soon the business man may expect, on his way to the office, working facilities like those provided in Leyland's experimental Super-Commuter Bus (5) including tape recorder/dictaphone, radio telephone, writing desk, radio and television.   Perhaps he will want to join a series of extra-mural classes, such as those launched by Michael Young in 1977 on the Cambridge Commuter Train.

In the meantime, however, for today's ordinary passengers could we have less noise, please, as much space as possible, warm and well-lit carriages, easy entrances and exits, comfortable seats, but, especially, cleaner vehicles and regular, efficient maintenance?

REFERENCES

1. LAVERNE HOAG , S. KEITH ADAMS: Human Factors in Urban Transportation Systems, Proc 17th AGM Human Factors Society 1973

2. OXFORD, H.W., Factors in the Design of Seats used in Public Transport, Proc 10th Ann.Conf.Ergonomics Soc. Australia and New Zealand, 1973

3. BRANTON, P., and GRAYSON, G.: The Evaluation of Train Seats by Observation of Sitting Behaviour

4. Better by Bus? , The Canterbury Consumer, November 1970

5. SPEED, JOHN: The Super Commuter and other Public Transport Developments, Coaching Journal, 1973 Vol.41 May

6. SAARI, J.T.: Coach Design for the Helsinki Underground, Applied Ergonomics 1974 5.3. 147-152

7. TAINSH, M.A.: The symptons reported by long-distance travellers, Applied Ergonomics 1975 6.4. 209-12

8. 'Which?' Puts Trains to the Test: 'Which?' November 1977 634-638

9. WILLIAMS, J.C.: Passenger Accompanied Luggage, Applied Ergonomics 1977 8.3. 151-157

Chapter 7:

Vehicle Suspension Systems and Passenger Comfort

Dr. M. G. Pollard

INTRODUCTION

In the context of this chapter two questions require answers at a very early stage in the design of a vehicle. Firstly, one must question how comfortable the vehicle should be for its intended application and secondly, ask how a reliable and cost effective suspension can be designed that will meet this requirement. Of course, there are many other factors which will impinge upon the design but this chapter is addressed to these two problems.

Comfort in a vehicle can be defined as a general feeling of well-being and it is affected by a large number of factors which are both physical and psychological, for example, noise, visual environment, temperature and vibration. For the purpose of this chapter it is vibration that will be considered. In terms of frequency the range will be restricted to 0.5 – 30 Hz. Railway vehicles have little energy content below this range and at higher frequencies the perception of motion diminishes and the problem gradually becomes one of noise. The quasi-static lateral acceleration experienced when negotiating a curve, where the track is insufficiently inclined to balance the effects of the centrifugal acceleration, will be discussed separately.

A railway vehicle running along a nominally straight track experiences irregularities at the wheelset. The function of the suspension is to attenuate the effects of these irregularities so that the vibration level in the passenger compartment is at a level which can be classed as comfortable. It is not cost effective to incorporate a de-luxe suspension into every vehicle; for example, one would expect a different standard of ride in a vehicle where the average journey was twenty minutes, to one where the average journey was three hours. Consequently techniques have been developed whereby the design of a suspension can be quantitatively assessed at an early stage. In this way the most satisfactory and cost effective solution can be found without proceeding to the expensive hardware stage. It is not only in the vertical sense that a satisfactory vibration level must be achieved. In the lateral plane also, the suspension must filter the effects of irregularities in alignment of the track. This is more difficult than the vertical problem since there are

Figure 7.1. End-of-rake bogie for the Advanced Passenger Train (British Rail).

forces between the wheel and rail which can cause instability of the wheelset, or bogie, or vehicle body. So the lateral suspension must give a good ride in response to track irregularities whilst adequately controlling the potential instabilities.

The chapter will discuss the definition of comfort levels and the techniques that are in use to enable suspensions to be designed to meet the stringent demands made of them. By way of example the APT suspension will be described to illustrate the various facets discussed.

SPECIFICATION OF STEADY STATE COMFORT LEVELS

The human body responds to vibration at different frequencies in various ways. Since passengers in moving vehicles experience a wide spectrum of acceleration frequencies, the effect of the different components must be assessed. In Figure 7.2. is shown a typical acceleration spectrum taken from a high speed vehicle. The measurement was made on the floor of the vehicle and one can identify various modes of vibration. For example, the rigid body

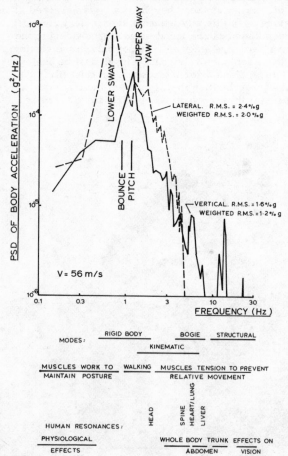

Figure 7.2. Vehicle accelerations and the effects on humans.

modes, such as body bounce, can be clearly seen, the effects of bogie pitch and bounce in this instance are clear and the broadness of the peak shows that the modes are well damped by the suspension. The bogie modes do not intrude into the body of the vehicle with this suspension, as great care has been taken to arrange the geometry and stiffness of the various connections so that they do not influence the acceleration in the body. Kinematic effects are generally only noticeable in the transverse plane but they do influence the roll of vehicles and hence the vertical acceleration off the vehicle centre-line. The sharp peaks of the structural modes are also clearly seen. The figure also tries to relate the various responses of the human body to frequency.

The use of power spectral density in assessing the ride of a vehicle is now a well defined technique which shows the vibrational energy distribution with frequency. It is not usual, however, to specify in advance of a design a target p.s.d. This is because it is not possible to compare two spectra in terms of relative comfort. For example, one cannot say whether a generally low spectrum with one large spike is better or worse than a spectrum at a generally higher level but with no dominant component.

For quantification of the ride quality given by a particular spectrum, one requires a number which takes into account the varying sensitivity of the human body to different frequencies of vibration. It is now necessary to introduce the concept of constant comfort curves. Much work has been done, particularly in the railway field, to relate the various sensations experienced by a human being undergoing whole-body vibration to the frequency and magnitude of that vibration.

One set of such curves much used by railway administrations is called the Ride Index Curves. These are based on early work by Reiher and Meister (1). In these tests subjects, both standing erect and recumbent but not seated, were vibrated both horizontally and vertically, not together, on a vibrating table. A verbal method of discomfort assessment was used and they produced equal comfort contours corresponding to six subjectively assessed levels from "not discernible" to "extremely annoying". The work was extended in 1935 and although it did not include seated subjects the importance of the work was in the establishment of the technique. In 1941 Helberg and Sperling (2) used the technique on seated persons to define seven discomfort levels. They found that the numerical value in the range 1 (barely perceptible) to 4 (unbearable) was given by a mathematical expression involving vibration frequency and magnitude. This was found to give too high a discomfort rating in the railway environment and a reducing factor was introduced. The British Railways' Ride Index is based on this work but the constant comfort contours were somewhat modified before inclusion and the origin of this modification, by Sperling, is obscure. The intention was, however, to "take human reactions more closely into account" and was based on some later German work in the early 1950's.

The Ride Index relies on curves determined using a verbal method of discomfort assessment, a method which has been shown to produce a large scatter of results. By contrast the more recent methods of determining equal comfort contours have been either a cross-matching technique against a standard vibration, or a magnitude estimation technique. Both techniques have been shown to produce less scatter than earlier methods. It is the results of these new methods that have been used to produce the International Standards Organization curves (3). These curves well represent the latest results available in the range 1 – 30 Hz. It is seen, Figure 7.3., from the equal comfort contours that for vertical vibration a broad region of maximum sensitivity exists in the frequency range 4 – 8 Hz. and this broadly agrees with the earlier results reflected in the Ride Index. Any benefit the seat might provide in attenuation, above about 4 Hz. typically, is beneficial and is not allowed for. The interior designers must ensure that the seat cushion itself has adequate damping since amplification of vibration at 4 Hz. is undesirable. For lateral vibrations, however, there is a marked difference. The ISO curves show maximum sensitivity in the range up to 2 Hz. and in this respect they differ markedly from the Ride Index curves. The difference in sensitivity may be due to the amount of restraint applied to the subject and whereas ISO is for seated persons the Ride Index was deduced from data on standing subjects. Work subsequent to the publication of the ISO curves has confirmed peak

sensitivity to lateral vibration to occur between 1 and 2 Hz. However, if one considers writing tests there is a suggestion that maximum impairment occurs in the range 4 – 5 Hz. This is of less importance in railway vehicles where usually there is little energy laterally at these frequencies.

There is one further major difference between the ISO and Ride Index curves. This is the relative sensitivity, at a given frequency, of the body to vertical and lateral vibration. According to Ride Index the body is almost equally sensitive to vibration in both vertical and horizontal directions, being slightly more sensitive in the latter. The ISO curves on the other hand show one to be three times more sensitive to vertical vibration than to horizontal at frequencies above 3 Hz. The latest experimental results demonstrate this relationship and one concludes that the ISO curves more accurately represent true constant comfort curves.

To extend the ISO curves below 1 Hz. is not easy, since the assessment is complicated by the phenomenon of motion sickness which occurs at frequencies below 0.6 Hz. and is most serious in the range 0.2 – 0.3 Hz. Railway vehicles rarely induce sickness presumably because they generally have little vibrational content below 0.5 Hz. and for this reason our assessments are usually truncated at 0.5 Hz. with little loss in accuracy. An assessment of the limited experimental data available, however, leads to the extension of the ISO curves which are shown dashed in Figure 7.3.

It has been shown that the ISO curves are the most reliable. The method of using them to produce a single figure assessment of ride quality is the ISO recommended "weighted sum" method. The acceleration spectrum to be assessed is modified throughout the frequency range using a weighting function (Figure 7.4.), the inverse of the constant

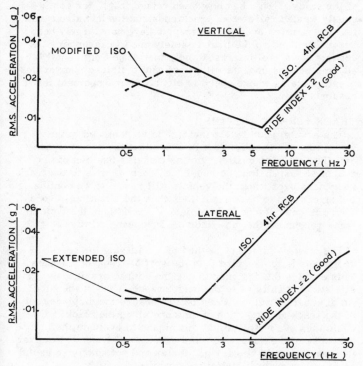

Figure 7.3. Comparison of Ride Index and ISO constant comfort curves.

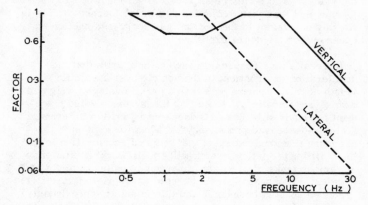

Figure 7.4. Weighting functions.

comfort curves. By integrating the spectrum the weighted mean square value of acceleration can be obtained. This is now related to the acceleration in the range 4 – 8 Hz. vertically (weighting =1), or 1 – 2 Hz. laterally, and the resulting figure can be used to compare the ride quality of two very different acceleration spectra. The method has the shortcoming that one is required to treat the vehicle ride as vertical and lateral vibration separately. There is no satisfactory information which assesses the sensitivity of the human body to vibration applied simultaneously in two planes. Furthermore the data which is used has been obtained from the application of discrete frequencies. There is no data available which describes the response of the human to a spectrum of vibration although there is some evidence that human sensitivity increases in the presence of broad band vibration. The experimental evidence is very confusing and the suggested increase in sensitivity ranges from zero to 100%. These are two areas where further work is required. It must be said that the data that is available is generally poor quality due to deficient experimental techniques and the data is rather inconsistent, but the ISO curves do represent a good mean drawn through the mass of experimental evidence available.

In an attempt to confirm the low frequency situation a writing test experiment was carried out by the Research and Development Division to determine the effect of vibration on writing ability. The time taken for a subject to trace a saw tooth maze was measured and at the same time the vibration was measured in terms of amplitude and frequency content. The experiment was designed to avoid long term and short term learning effects. The effects of vertical vibration had been previously shown to be small, when compared with the effect of lateral vibration, and so the maze completion times were compared only with the lateral acceleration levels treated with various weighting functions. Since the dominant motions of the coach were below 2 Hz. the raw acceleration and the ISO and Ride Index weighting functions gave very similar results and the task impairment was well correlated with, for example, the ISO function. The experiment did enable the target levels of lateral acceleration to be set and the value was to be less than 2.6%g for at least 50% of the journey and less than 3.2%g for 80% of the journey. This is roughly equivalent to the ISO fatigue decreased proficiency boundary for a 6 hours exposure.

In specifying a suspension one can now write that the acceleration environment in the vehicle over a specific length of track must be less than a certain value of weighted r.m.s. acceleration. In setting the number a value judgement is required. The ISO document is written in terms of "fatigue-decreased proficiency". Thus for a given exposure time one can specify a weighted acceleration level that will lead to fatigue which will impair working efficiency at various tasks. The data is based on studies of pilots and drivers. For passengers, the more appropriate figure is the "reduced comfort boundary" and this is set at approximately one third of the decreased proficiency level. This value is based on a number of studies carried out for various transport industries.

An examination of current Inter-City railway vehicles gives acceleration levels between 2 and 3%g vertically and 1 and 2%g laterally which are roughly equivalent to a two hour exposure to give reduced comfort, although the best Inter-City stock permits 3 - 4 hour exposure.

SPECIFICATION OF RESPONSE TO DISCRETE IRREGULARITIES

There is very little work available to describe peak values of acceleration that are tolerable to passengers. One type of discrete irregularity is that associated with switch and crossing work. Here high acceleration levels last for a very short length of time, the energy content is very small. If one examines the ISO curves these lead one to believe that very high levels would be acceptable. This is not the case, however, as the psychological effect of such large accelerations would be unacceptable. Typically railway passenger vehicles have resilient bump stops set near the limits of their suspension travel and one would expect to see no more than 7 - 8 times the r.m.s. value as a peak acceleration and this very rarely indeed. This seems to be acceptable.

Another type of discrete irregularity in the acceleration environment is the effect of a curve. Railway track is canted in order that trains negotiating the curve lean inwards so that the resultant force is normal to the line joining the tops of the rails. When the curve is traversed at a speed greater than the equilibrium speed there is a residual lateral component of the centrifugal force. The maximum size of this component can be related to the cant of the track and a series of subjective tests in 1949 led to a limit of $3\frac{1}{2}^{o}$ of cant deficiency being applied. The figure was based partly on passenger comfort grounds but also on the strength of the track. This has now been raised to $4\frac{1}{4}^{o}$ for continuously welded rail. New track construction has also meant that the worries over track strength have now largely been superseded and so the limit is solely one of passenger comfort. It is of interest to note that some Continental administrations operate with 7° of cant deficiency on various prestige trains where speed is clearly more important than comfort.

TRACK IRREGULARITIES

The acceleration levels that are to be achieved in the vehicle can be specified but in order that the designer can calculate the ride quality, via the transfer function of his proposed suspension, he requires information as to the track roughness over which the vehicle will run. If we confine the discussion to passenger lines then the situation is good. There is now a large body of data which defines the typical track roughness that one finds on European railways.

The most satisfactory method of quantifying the track roughness is to describe it in the spatial frequency domain. This enables the designer to use the data to provide statistical results as to the performance of the suspension. An alternative method would be to measure the displacement of the track as a function of distance along the track. One could then use mathematical techniques to evaluate the response of the suspension to that length of track. However, the results would be very particular and not nearly so useful as the more general statistical quantities.

A major survey was carried out over BR main-lines to determine the track roughness and this still provides the basic data (4). A special machine was developed to measure the vertical and lateral irregularities of the centre-line of the track and the cross-level variations. 25 main-line sites, each of 2 miles length, were then measured and statistically stationary lengths were analysed in terms of power spectral density over wavelengths between 50 m. and 1 m. The results are presented as Figure 7.5. where they are compared with European spectra (5).

Consider firstly the vertical irregularities. At long wave-lengths the spectral density falls with the square of the frequency. There are peaks associated with rail lengths and the effects of joints. At shorter wavelengths the spectrum falls more sharply. The two lines shown for each Administration define the envelope within which all the measurements fell. There is generally an order of magnitude difference between the upper and lower boundaries equivalent to a factor of 3 on the r.m.s. displacement. This represents the range of main-line track at any frequency; it is extremely unlikely that any single track length would lie on the boundary throughout the frequency range. Also shown is the interesting comparison made with measurements made by other European railways. It is shown that there is little difference across Europe.

The lateral irregularity has a slightly different pattern and generally the spectra fall with the third power of the frequency. At the long wavelength end the spectrum of both the vertical and lateral irregularities is rising and it can be shown that this rise continues to very long wavelengths as the track responds to geographical effects. Conversely the cross-level is tending towards a constant value at long wave-lengths. This is because the cross-level can be set to a directly measurable datum.

The results described can be used to predict the behaviour of vehicles under steady conditions. As suggested in the previous section there are also discrete irregularities which need to be treated on a different basis. The principal discrete irregularity has been in the past, and still is for freight vehicles, the dipped rail joint where the rails dip over a span of 3 m. or so to give a drop of perhaps 15 mm. at the joints between rails. This is less of a problem today where continuously welded rail is predominantly used for passenger network track. There is still a small problem, however, in that something very similar to a dipped joint occurs at each weld and the effect of a dipped joint is met at switch and crossing work. The major effect, however, is on the structural integrity of the vehicle and generally speaking the magnitude of such irregularities is maintained at a low value, such that large forces are not experienced by the vehicle structure and the accelerations felt by the passengers are not large.

In the lateral sense there is a similar effect at switch and crossing work where there is often a step change in the rolling line the wheelset is attempting to follow. This, of course, produces a perturbation in the riding of the vehicle which is generally attenuated to acceptable levels by the relatively soft lateral suspensions employed in passenger vehicles and which are discussed below.

VERTICAL SUSPENSION DESIGN

Consider in the first instance the movements of the vehicle in the longitudinal/vertical plane on the vehicle centre-line. Motions in this plane are only excited by the vertical irregularity of the track and there is negligible cross-coupling from the lateral inputs. The problem in design is to satisfy the comfort requirements whilst riding over track which has a known roughness. The background work done on vehicle suspension analysis has recently been discribed by Wickens and Gilchrist (6) who have also given a comprehensive bibliography.

The technique used is to mathematically model the suspension. The vertical suspension is relatively simple and can be easily represented by a spring, mass and damper system. The modelling is helped by the fact that modern suspensions use components with generally linear characteristics. For example, frictional devices are used very little nowadays, on passenger vehicles. The establishment of a mathematical model enables one to obtain the transfer function of the suspension. In this case, for instance, it could be the

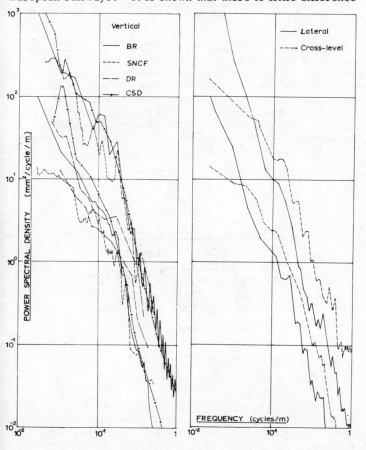

Figure 7.5. Comparison of track roughness spectra.

function describing the body acceleration for a unit displacement of the wheelset.   A knowledge of this function and the spectrum of track irregularity, enables one to define the acceleration spectrum in the body since there is a known relationship between the input, the transfer function and the output of a system.   Much work has been done in the past on the verification of this technique and it has been demonstrated on a number of occasions that the vehicle ride can be well predicted.   This is very important in that the mathematical technique can be used to define and refine the suspension at an early stage before expensive hardware has been bought or manufactured.   Furthermore many different suspension schemes can be examined and the most cost-effective solution chosen.

Acceleration of the vehicle body is only one aspect that must be considered in the design of the vertical suspension. Among others one must consider the ability of the vehicle to negotiate twisted track and the prevention of wheel hop and unacceptable displacements of the body.   For the passenger vehicle these requirements are generally easier to satisfy than for freight vehicles since the laden/tare ratio is smaller.

The simplest suspension one can imagine is a spring and damper mono-cycle at each end of the vehicle (Figure 7.6.a.). This suspension has all the necessary ingredients and one can write the equations of motion very easily;   the forcing terms appear on one side of the equations and the suspension terms on the other.   In the calculation of the vehicle response, of course, there is a fixed relationship between the values of z_t at each wheelset that is dependent upon the wheelbase and forward speed.

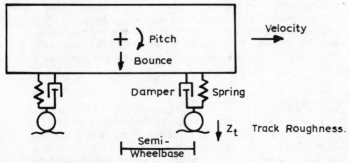

Figure 7.6a. Basic suspension.

The evaluation of this suspension shows it to be inadequate in providing the necessary level of comfort and it is necessary to introduce firstly a flexible end to the damper (Figure 7.6.b.) so that the high frequency content of the track roughness is not transmitted to the body.   This suspension is typical of those used in freight vehicles;   although usually the springs and dampers are designed to increase in rate as they are deflected, so that the natural frequency of the body on the suspension remains within acceptable limits, with an appropriate level of damping, and the suspension travels are not

excessive.   For passenger vehicles at high speed, however, this suspension is inadequate.   The arrangement is unable to attenuate the inputs sufficiently and reference to Figure 7.5. shows that the input power at any given frequency increases with speed.   The substitution of an air-spring, where one can have a very low frequency suspension because the self-levelling ability eliminates problems of tare-laden travel, may allow this single stage suspension to be used for some passenger applications but generally for high speed the mono-cycle is inadequate.

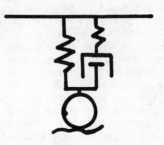

Figure 7.6b. Damper-end stiffness.

Consequently two steps are generally taken.   Firstly the concept of the bogie is introduced (Figure 7.6.c.).   By mounting the secondary suspension midway between two wheelsets the inputs to it are minimised.   Secondly, the bogie frame is attached to the wheelsets at each end by further suspension elements.   Then the high frequency inputs from the track are attenuated both geometrically and by two suspensions, and this is sufficient to reduce the acceleration in the body to acceptable levels.

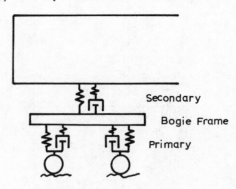

Figure 7.6c. Bogie suspension.

The primary suspension is required to be much stiffer than the secondary suspension for reason of wheelset control and also so that the isolation effects offered by the two-stage suspension can be properly utilised.   Typically the bogie frame bounce and pitch frequencies are in the range 4 - 8 Hz. where they do not interact with the secondary suspension which has frequencies between 0.5 - 1.5 Hz.

Figure 7.2. shows a typical response of a vehicle running on a bogie designed on the analytical basis described. The bogie is shown in Figure 7.8. where the major suspension components are identified. The response data was measured on a vehicle running on continuously welded rail. The dominant effect of the rigid body can be seen in the 1 Hz. region. The efficiency of the suspension in suppressing the bogie modes can be seen. The primary coil spring and hydraulic damper suspension gives bogie frequencies of about 6 Hz. with 30 to 40% damping. These values also control the wheelsets which see the bogie frame as a large inertia against which to act through the primary suspension to minimise normal force variations. The vehicle structural modes appear at 12 Hz. which is adequately high. If these modes occurred at lower frequencies they would be excited in sympathy with the bogie modes and being lightly damped the effect would be very serious. The r.m.s. acceleration, the square root of the area under the curve, increases approximately as the square root of the forward velocity, (Figure 7.7.). There are, of course, other effects such as frequency coincidences of railwelds with bogie or body frequencies which cause local perturbations in the variation of the acceleration with speed. Coil springs are not the only method of providing a primary suspension and rubber units are also popular.

Around resonance the airflow through the pipe is sufficiently throttled to provide effective damping. At high frequencies the pipe is to all intents closed and the spring volume alone acts as the spring. Represented as a spring, mass and damper system the air-spring is as shown in Figure 7.6.d. The mass m. on the lever, ratio n., is the effect of the air mass contained in the pipe connecting the spring to the reservoir and the designer is required to minimise pipe length and maximise diameter to keep these terms small.

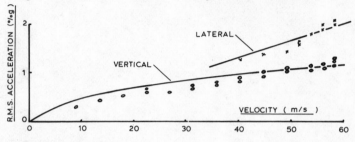

Figure 7.7. Accelerations in the body over an end-of-rake APT bogie.

k   Surge Stiffness

rk   Pedestal Stiffness

pk   Change of Area Stiffness

c   Damping

mn   Surge-pipe Effective Air Mass

Figure 7.6d. Air-spring model.

The secondary suspension in this case is an air-spring of such a rate that the body has a natural frequency upon it of 0.8 Hz. Experiments are in hand to reduce this to 0.5 Hz. to evaluate the improvement so obtained. The damping of the body in the vertical sense is about 15% of critical and is obtained pneumatically by connecting the spring to an auxiliary reservoir mounted in the body. The connecting pipe has an orifice in it. At low frequencies the arrangement acts as a spring with the whole air volume being compressed.

There are, of course, other ways of providing the secondary suspension. The air spring is popular, however, in that one can have very low natural frequencies, and hence good comfort, without the penalties incurred by large suspension travels. Furthermore, the latest designs of spring also incorporate the lateral suspension which is discussed in the next section. There are penalties, however, such as the high initial cost and the necessity of including an anti-roll bar to prevent the vehicle having too soft a roll suspension.

Typical results over a range of speeds obtained in the vehicle body over the APT end of rake bogie – one example was given as Figure 7.2. – are shown in Figure 7.8. This shows that at 125 mile/h (56 m/s) – the design speed – the acceleration level in the vehicle body was around 1.2%g. These results were obtained on the Research Department Test Track, CWR and jointed tracks, and on the WCML North of Lockerbie. The figures show that vertically a very acceptable ride standard is achieved.

LATERAL SUSPENSION DESIGN

The design of the lateral suspension of a railway vehicle is more complicated that that of the vertical suspension. Not only are there more degrees of freedom in the spring, mass and damper system but non-conservative forces are generated at the wheel/rail contact patch and the suspension must properly control the wheelset in the presence of these forces. The analytical approach to suspension design allows one to choose the most cost effective combination of suspension components and one can readily examine variations in the components and design the vehicle to ensure that bad riding will not be encountered in any foreseeable circumstances during the life of the vehicle.

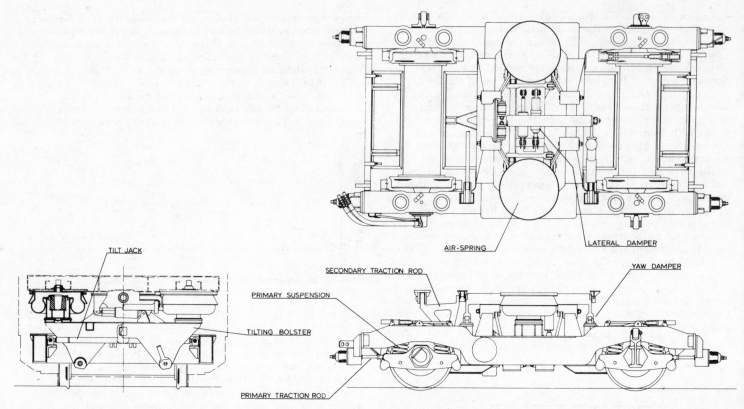

Figure 7.8. Layout of the Advanced Passenger Train end-of rake experimental bogie.

On the conventional railway wheelset two wheels are rigidly mounted on an axle.   The wheel has a coned, or otherwise profiled, tread, in the transverse direction, and a flange on the inside edge.   The gap between the flange and the rail on each side is typically 7 mm.   The origin of the coning seems to have been solely to prevent the flange rubbing continuously but quite early on the guiding ability of the arrangement was recognised (George Stephenson 1821) whereby a wheelset moving to one side of the track will yaw to steer itself back towards the centre.   In reality the wheelset does not proceed by pure rolling since this is modified by the action of forces in the wheel/rail contact plane which cause creepage.   As an example the longitudinal creepage can be defined as the change in the distance rolled by a wheel when transmitting a longitud-inal force relative to the distance rolled without it.   In practical terms it is more convenient to measure creepage in terms of velocity but the principle is the same.   The vari-ation in distance can be achieved without gross slip and is provided by the elastic distortion of the bodies in the contact region with a small amount of slipping at the trailing edge of the contact patch.   The relationship between creepage and tangential force is now well documented, for the longitudinal and lateral cases and the spin condition.   These results can be used in the analysis of wheelset behaviour by calculating the creepage and thus estimating the forces that are acting. The ideal value of force can be calculated but it is unusual for this condition to to be found in practice.   To overcome this problem the calculated forces are factored down by amounts based upon empirical knowledge.   A recently developed force measuring wheelset is at present being used to improve our knowledge of this area.   These forces, at the wheel/rail contact patch appear as terms in the equations of motion of the wheelset in addition to the inertia terms and the terms representing the spring and damper connections to the bogie frame or body.

There are also other terms in the equations of motion which depend upon the mutual geometry, in the transverse sense, of the wheelset and the track.   For purely coned wheels the contact angles between the wheel and rail are substantially constant and the rolling radius difference between the wheels changes linearly with lateral displacement.   However, the coned wheel does not remain perfectly coned and it becomes hollow and current practice is to design the suspension from the outset to cope with the hollowed wheel.   Furthermore so called "worn wheel profiles" have been developed which do not alter in essential geometry over long periods of running. For these profiles computer methods have been developed to survey very many wheel and rail profiles and their mutual geometric properties.   These results have shown that for a realistic range of conditions the rolling radius difference between the wheels will still vary linearly with respect to

the lateral displacement but that the constant of proportion-
ality, the "equivalent conicity" will vary, typically between
0.05 and 0.4. Additionally, the profiled wheel introduces
contact angle changes with lateral displacement which were
absent with coned wheels.

For the purposes of this chapter the full equations of motion
will not be described. The equations of motion of a wheelset
have asymmetric off-diagonal terms on the left hand side, due
to creep forces, conicity and contact stiffness, coupling the
lateral and yaw degrees of freedom, which indicate the non-
conservative nature of this system and result from the combination of creep and wheel/rail geometry. It is these terms
which give the wheelset its guidance and also its propensity
to instability. For the complete vehicle these expressions
are added to the straightforward Newtonian expressions
relating to the mass, spring and damper system by which the
vehicle and its suspension can be represented.

In the design of a suspension these equations are treated
in two principal ways. Firstly, the left hand side only is
examined, that is with no forcing terms. This enables the
characteristic determinant of the equations to be solved for
the eigen-values (frequency and damping) as a function of
speed. The eigen-vectors (mode shapes) can also be
evaluated. These results indicate stability margins and
some aspects of dynamic response. If the damping in any
mode is too low the vehicle will have an unsatisfactory
response. On the other hand if it is too high this will also
result in high acceleration levels in the body. For normal
railway vehicles the stability margin at low speed is high and
it reduces as speed increases. Figure 7.9. shows typical
results of the solution to the equations at different forward
speeds. The wheelset mode damping can be seen to be
falling rapidly leading to instability at 93 m/s with a very
high frequency; in the structural range. The most difficult
situation for this arrangement is that caused by the frequency
coincidence of the bogie modes (X) and the other kinematic
modes (C). In the middle of the speed range these modes
interact and the damping in each is perturbed leading to a
lightly damped mode throughout. At higher speeds the mode
X has become almost a pure kinematic mode which becomes
unstable at about 80 m/s. Up to the design speed of 56 m/s
there is adequate damping. The frequency, and indeed the
damping, of the modes can be drastically altered by alterations in effective conicity and creep coefficient. A reduction of conicity, for example, would reduce the rate of
increase of frequency with speed of modes C and A. The
coincidence effect between C and X would then be postponed
to higher forward speeds. On the other hand coincidence at
low speed between C and the rigid body modes Y and B might
be problematical.

In the design exercise the stability margins under all
conceivable conditions must be calculated and assessed.
Many factors must be recognised such as the condition of the
wheel/rail interface, variability in the parameter specification, mass and inertia changes in the body etc. Frequently
a compromise has to be made. One of the most significant
compromises is that between stability and curving ability.

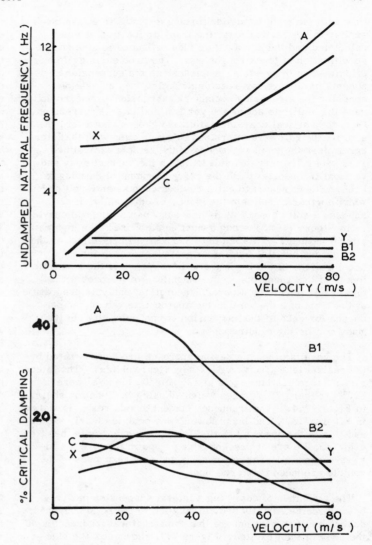

Figure 7.9. Simplified Eigen-value presentation for a vehicle on APT end-of-rake
bogies.

The former requires tightly constrained wheelsets whilst
good curving is only achieved with very flexible connections
to the wheels. The designer thus has to minimise the plan-
view wheelset suspension stiffness, whilst still achieving
an adequate stability margin at the operating speed by introducing dampers to the bogie frame, or in difficult cases
cross-bracing between the wheelsets.

Once the stability of the vehicle has been established and
the contribution of each suspension component examined the
designer can concentrate upon the lateral ride. The starting
point is again the equations of motion for the vehicle, this

time with the right hand side forcing terms. In a fashion similar to the vertical case the transfer function can be calculated and the steady state ride estimated for the chosen specification of track roughness. The problem is again more difficult than the vertical problem since the suspension components have more far-reaching effects. As an example consider the air-spring secondary suspension. Modern units have the ability to act as the vertical and lateral suspension. Once the vertical characteristics are chosen, however, these also fix the roll parameters and in conjunction with the lateral parameters the two sway modes of the vehicle are defined. It is generally very difficult to obtain the correct sway and vertical frequencies, and the correct amount of damping in each, without resort to extra devices such as anti-roll bars which further complicate the issue. Additionally, if one chooses a soft primary plan-view suspension for good curving, as in Figure 7.9., the bogie must be stabilised by a high rate lateral damper. This not only has a significant effect on the sway modes but also acts as a transmission path for the accelerations of the bogie frame in response to the kinematic inputs of the wheelsets. The magnitude of the problem is clear. It is only by a careful theoretical analysis programme at the start of a design that the appropriate values can be chosen for each of the suspension components, to meet the many conflicting requirements.

The results of such a design approach are demonstrated by the results taken from an APT bogie test vehicle. The lateral r.m.s. acceleration levels at 125 mile/h. (56 m/s) were 2.0%g, Figure 7.7., when weighted using the function shown in Figure 7.4. The frequency content of this result is shown in Figure 7.2. The large lower sway peak is clearly shown and this is the dominant motion felt by a passenger in the vehicle. We are at present taking steps to improve the lower sway response. The upper sway and yaw responses of the vehicle are much less prominent.

The technique of designing a lateral suspension has only been described briefly and, in addition to the rigid body modes described, one must ensure that the structural frequencies of the body are not excited. Figure 7.9. shows how the kinematic frequency of the wheelset can be sufficiently high to excite these modes. One major aspect of suspension design which has not been considered here is that of track flexibility and track forces. These are major items and play an important part in the definition of suspension parameters. In curves in particular it is very important that the suspension is such that lateral wheel/rail forces are minimised.

APT TILT SYSTEM

Major reductions in journey times can be achieved by running through curves at higher speeds than present day trains. At present trains run with $4\frac{1}{4}^{\circ}$ of cant deficiency and this is all felt by the passenger in his seat. By tilting the vehicle body with respect to the bogies the APT will proceed around curves with 9° of cant deficiency with the passenger unaware of the fact since the tilt system works to null the lateral acceleration in the vehicle body. This is a significant contribution to passenger comfort.

The tilt system design has to take account of the space envelope provided by the structural loading gauge, the length of the transition curve between straight and uniformly curved track, the minimisation of transient accelerations imposed on passengers and interaction with the roll and lateral dynamics of the vehicle. These considerations have led to a train in which each vehicle is tilted independently by an active electro-hydraulic closed-loop servo-system which responds to sensors measuring the lateral accelerations imposed on passengers. The electrical output of the sensor is converted by the control system into a movement of the hydraulic actuators which move the swinging bolster. Since the bolster is suspended on inclined links an outward lateral motion also inclines the bolster inwards. This has the effect of tilting the vehicle mounted on it, to null the lateral acceleration whilst minimising the movement of the centre of gravity. This technique means that the passenger senses little transient lateral acceleration but is subjected to movements that are essentially vertical. In the context of dynamics a major problem has been the resolution of conflicts between response rates, stability, ride quality and system power consumption.

This has been achieved by developing a control strategy which has two major features. The first controls the low frequency behaviour of the vehicle, say below 1 Hz. The sensors measure the lateral acceleration in the vehicle and this signal passes through a low pass filter to which the hydraulic system responds to null the acceleration. It is not desirable to respond to the high frequency content such as might be present due to kinematic motions of the bogie or the cross-level roughness of the track. If the control were simply this the stability of the system would be rather poor with serious conflicts between response rate and stability. However, by adding a second control loop which takes a signal proportional to the jack displacement through a high pass filter, exactly complementary to the low pass filter, the stability margin can be widened considerably and the response rate can be increased to a satisfactory value. At high frequencies the hydraulic actuators then appear very stiff to null movement between the swinging bolster and the bogie frame. To improve the response of the system a further feedback loop is added directly around the servo-valve and hydraulics. This suppresses various difficulties due to non-linearity.

Much theoretical and experimental development work has taken place both in the laboratory and on the track to determine the most satisfactory range of parameters. The situation at present is that the tilt system improves the ride of the vehicle running on straight track by about 20%. On curves the system follows the ideal line very well as is shown in Figure 7.10. where the ideal displacement line is calculated from a heavily filtered bogie lateral acceleration signal. It can be seen that there is some error in the transition, where the jack responds rapidly, due to lags introduced into the control system. However, the largest error is 1.6° and when compared with the 4.3° that passengers experience at present this is very small.

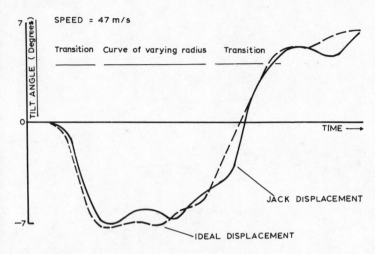

Figure 7.10. Tilt system response through curves.

CONCLUSIONS

The chapter has touched on a few of the many aspects of suspension design that must be considered in ensuring passenger comfort. Using the techniques that have been developed over the past decade, suspension design has ceased to be the empirical process that it once was and it is now possible to specify the necessary suspension parameters to ensure a satisfactory performance in the widest sense. The criteria that a design must meet are now reasonably established although more, careful experiments are required to improve the accuracy of the available data. It is still necessary to build prototype vehicles since it is not practical for the mathematical model to represent completely the intricacies of the suspension. Similarly, there are always differences in the parameters that are achieved in the engineering design as opposed to the theoretical specification and these must be measured.

Modern railway vehicle suspensions meet the stringent demands made of them and current work is aimed at maintaining comfort levels at higher speeds, improving reliability and reducing costs.

REFERENCES

1. REIHER H. AND MEISTER F.J. Die Empfindlich keit des Menschen gegen Erschutterungen. Forsch. Ing-Wes. 1931.

2. HELBERG W. AND SPERLING E. Critical Appraisal of the Riding Properties of Railway Vehicles. O.f.d.Fort. d.Eisebahn.V.96,No.12, 1941.

3. Draft International Standard ISO/DIS 2631. Guide for the Evaluation of Human Exposure to Whole-Body Vibration. 1972.

4. POLLARD M.G. Power Spectra of Track Roughness Obtained from the "APT Survey". BR Research Department. TN DT 2. 1969.

5. ORE Report. Question C116. Report No.1. Power Spectral Density of Track Irregularities. Definitions, Conventions and Available Data. 1971.

6. WICKENS A.H. AND GILCHRIST A.O. Railway Vehicle Dynamics – The Emergence of a Practical Theory. CEI·MacRobert Award Lecture 1977.

ACKNOWLEDGEMENT

The author thanks the British Railways Board for permission to publish this material.

Chapter 8:

Boeing Jet Foil

William M. Shultz

INTRODUCTION

Every metropolitan area is seeking ways to improve anti-quated traffic systems. Their plans seek to solve these problems by improving, and adding to, ground-based transit systems, such as better buses, subways, moving sidewalks, and suspended public transports, emphasising increased frequency, punctuality, and flexibility of service, and stressing circulation and distribution. Most of these solutions have the common feature of being capital-intensive, largely automated, based on dedicated guideways, and propelled by clean (often electric) power. They are all expensive.

But above all, they are, almost without exception, ground-based. Few plans consider water transportation.

The introduction of a fast ferry service between coastal points at something like normal (or better) road speeds gives an opportunity, not only to save time in water journeys, but to influence the travelling habits of the people. If the fast ferries can be operated at accepted fare levels and be linked with good public land transport, it is possible that commuters, shoppers, and people making short business trips would be willing, even pleased, to leave their automobiles at home. The greater speed of fast ferries makes it possible to use longer routes than present ferries and land-bridge crossings.

If the primary objective of a system is to move people, to be successful the system must:

Move them rapidly, with safety;
Move them without congestion, and with flexibility;
Move them at a reasonable cost.

Reliability is a key factor. The equipment must provide dependable, consistent operations under all conditions of weather, day and night, every day of the year.

Comfort and convenience are essential or people will not use the system, no matter how well it meets any other require-ment. Passenger acceptance is the most critical factor for any transportation system. Without it everything else is purely academic. This is of special concern for marine systems. The sea has always provided cargo routes between and within most of the world's major trade centres. Water routes are inexpensive to establish and to maintain, they don't disrupt, condemn or destroy areas of the community, and they are flexible as no land-locked transit system can be. Unfortunately for passenger transport the situation has not worked out nearly as well, although the benefits remain the same. If the wind never blew and the water surface always remained fairly calm, it would be a relatively easy matter to develop high-speed marine craft acceptable to people. The ride of most marine vehicles is passable enough at slow speeds or when the water is calm. But the pitching, rolling and heaving motions and accelerations encountered when speed is increased or when the seas get moderately rough can cause considerable discomfort and seasickness.

For conventional ships, improvement in speed has usually been obtained by improvements in propulsion (higher power, lighter weight engines, improved propellers, etc.). In some cases the hull shape has been modified to decrease water resistance and provide dynamic lift in addition to buoyant lift (planing craft, catamarans, ski type vehicles, etc.). This works as long as the water remains fairly calm, but when it gets rough, speed must again be reduced and ride quality deteriorates very rapidly. The motivation associated with developing surface-effect vehicles (SEVs) and hydrofoils was being able to increase speed substantially for small increases in power, by elevating the hull above the surface of the water to obtain substantial reductions in resistance. Amphibious hovercraft and surface-piercing hydrofoils were the vehicles on which most emphasis was placed. Again this has worked out quite acceptably as long as the water remains fairly calm, but almost all of the present SEVs and hydrofoils still exper-ience significant degradations in ride quality and speed when they attempt to operate in rougher water conditions. All of these craft are surface followers, in which pitching, rolling and heaving motions tend to follow the surface contours of the water (the waves).

One type of advanced marine vehicle that can effectively de-couple itself from the water surface is the fully-submerged foil hydrofoil employing synthetic stabilisation. This type craft, when properly configured and controlled, will display little tendency toward motion magnification at any frequency, and in addition, has very low values of accelerations at all encounter frequencies.

On the 29th September 1972, The Boeing Company initiated production of the Model 929-100 JETFOIL, a fully submerged foil hydrofoil developed specifically for the transportation of people. That decision was made only after careful examin-ation of a large number of facts and factors, - technical, economic and social. No single consideration was sufficient-ly persuasive to determine the outcome of the deliberations, but the firm belief by the Company that the JETFOIL would be an outstanding product and that there was a growing world-wide need for such a product exerted considerable influence. The JETFOIL design was based on more than twelve years of advanced hydrofoil research and development experience and seven years of market research.

SIZE, ARRANGEMENT AND OTHER ISSUES

One of the main issues that had to be settled early on was, what was the best configuration for the marketplace? In other words, how many people should it carry, what other loads should be accommodated and how fast should it go, what kind of propulsion should it have, and what kind of control? To resolve this issue was no simple task and the actual assessment covered a four year period.

Figure 8.1. Eighteen years of Boeing Jetfoil development.

Little Squirt.

High Point PCH.1.

Fresh. 1.

Tucumcari. P.G.H.2.

We were not interested in having a group of engineers design something and then see if it could be sold. What we wanted was to determine what was needed and then see if our technical know-how was capable of coming up with a good design that could meet that need.

In the Fall of 1968, as a result of a decade of hydrofoil experience on LITTLE SQUIRT, FRESH, HIGH POINT and TUCUMCARI, (Figure 8.1) and nearly four years of earlier market analyses, some technical issues could be settled quite quickly.

For a small high-speed hydrofoil, waterjet propulsion seemed to offer a more reliable and lower maintenance cost system than a water propeller with its associated gears, shafts, drive trains, etc. (Table 1). The technical information available indicated that the overall vehicle efficiency for either approach was about equal — with the lower waterjet propulsive efficiency offset by other considerations so that the required total power was the same for either system. The benefits of the higher reliability and lower maintenance costs resulted in waterjet propulsion selection.

A detailed comparison of the advantages and disadvantages of gas turbine versus diesel engine power had also been carried out. It was recognised that very few commercial marine operators had any experience with gas turbines and that, as a result, any craft that employed marine turbines would have to have significant benefits to overcome a normal operator reluctance to become involved with equipment with which they had little experience.

TABLE 1

HYDROFOIL PROPULSION SYSTEM COMPARISON

	Waterjet	Propeller
Propulsive Efficiency	1.00	1.10
Boat L/D	1.00	0.90
Required Horsepower	1.00	1.00
Propulsion System Weight	1.00	1.10
Propulsion System Cost	1.00	2.00
Boat Cost	1.00	1.20
Propulsion System Maintenance	1.00	2.00
Propulsion System Reliability	4.00	1.00

Our studies showed that by using turbines it was possible to carry about 1.16 additional passengers for each 1,000 HP of installed cruise power for every hour of endurance less than about 41 hours. For a vehicle with 5,000 cruise HP and four hours operating duration, 217 more passengers could be carried if turbines were used rather than diesels. Another way of looking at it was that if diesels had been installed in the Model 929-100 just about all of the available passenger payload weight would be taken up by the higher propulsion weight, or else the craft would have had to be substantially larger. This however, was not a sufficient reason to decide in favour of the gas turbine. Economic analyses for turbine versus diesel powered high speed hydro-

TABLE 2

MODEL 929 COMMERCIAL HYDROFOILS

45 KNOT SEASPEED, RETRACTABLE FOIL, OCEAN SERVICE, PASSENGER CARRIERS

Dash No.		-40	-60	-70	-100	-120	-150
Total Continuous Power	h.p.	1900	3000	3600	5000	6200	7500
Dynamic Lift	tons	38	60	72	100	122	148
Lightship Weight	tons	29.0	44.2	51.9	70.6	84.3	100.0
Crew Weight	tons	0.2	0.3	0.4	0.5	0.6	0.7
Fuel Weight (4 hours)	tons	2.2	3.7	4.2	6.0	7.5	8.7
Payload Weight	tons	6.6	11.8	15.5	22.9	29.6	38.9
No. of tourist passengers		55	99	129	190	246	324
No. of commuter passengers		68	124	161	250	308	405

foils showed that the lowest operating cost per seat mile could be obtained with a turbine powered design and that the economics were less sensitive to annual utilisation for the turbine configuration. (Figure 8.2.). When it was also established that marine turbines were available in the right power range, and that the manufacturers were willing to back them with fixed price spares' contracts, it was concluded that the operator benefits were substantial enough and the decision was made.

The economic studies also indicated that the optimum design cruise speed was approximately 50 knots in calm water for the turbine configured craft. This equates to a rough water cruise speed of about 45 knots with a corresponding block speed of about 40 knots for most operational routes.

Figure 8.2. Breakeven fares. Block speed = (Vo-lo) knots. Load Factor = 50%.

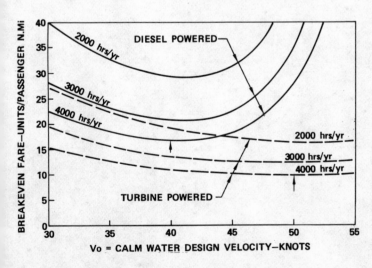

From the materials aspect, because of the weight sensitivity, the decision to use aluminium for the hull and passenger compartment structures was easily made. Once made, numerous other problems had to be handled in the design, including the type of aluminium, method of construction and method of fire insulation to meet existing regulatory standards for ships. For the speed range of interest, 40 to 50 knots, it was essential that the foil/strut material be of high strength to withstand the loads associated with high speed, rough water operations, and be able to resist corrosion without the need for protective coatings.

As indicated previously, the primary use for the JETFOIL was considered to be short-range passenger transport in both coastal and ocean waters. A world-wide route analysis was conducted at the University of Washington to determine the number and location of routes to which such vehicles could be applied effectively with reasonable expectation of profitable service. Extensive data was collected relating to population distribution, tourism, economic activity, quality and quantity of existing transportation, special legal restrictions, and water and weather conditions. A total of 335 routes were analysed of which 133 were established as good hydrofoil routes.

Six point designs were configured for the Model 929 series based on available marine gas turbines, (Table 2). Because of the large number of variables involved, a computer simulation was developed to make the comparative assessments. Inputs to the computer were vehicle performance and cost information, numbers and distributions of passengers, fares and block speed. Outputs were percent of market carried, load factor, utilisation hours, required fleet size, profit and return on investment. The programme was designed so that any type of vehicle could be analysed and therefore, compared with the hydrofoil designs. All designs were evaluated against the market demands updated from the previous studies; the conclusion reached was that the -100 was the configuration best suited to the worldwide market need.

Figure 8.3. The Boeing Jetfoil 'Spirit of 76'.

MODEL 929-100 GENERAL DESCRIPTION (Figure 8.3.)
BASIC SHIP STRUCTURE The JETFOIL is designed to
spend most of its operating time foilborne.   Hullborne speed
and range are secondary considerations and performance on
the hull becomes important only as it affects the ability of the
ship to return safely to port in the event of a malfunction.
The hull must be seaworthy in any sea conditions expected to
be encountered and considerations of hullborne safety, takeoff
drag, and the hull loads and accelerations encountered during
high-speed rough water operations are primary design factors
in determining the best hull shape.

    With a beam of 30 feet and a length of only 90 feet the
JETFOIL is much beamier than one is normally used to seeing.
While this may disturb the designer with traditional views
about naval architecture and how a ship ought to look, the
shape of the JETFOIL was very carefully developed from the

most advanced data and established design principles to
achieve a hull that was best suited for this application.
Additional benefits derived from the beamy configuration
include a much better volume within the length for passenger
accommodations and a more compact craft for operations into
smaller harbours, marinas and docks.

    Because the JETFOIL is an aluminium ship, considerable
insulation is provided so that the structure will meet existing
fire safety requirements of the regulating agencies.   It was
recognised at the outset that this would not be easy but we
never seriously considered requesting special rules for
JETFOIL operations since that could have defeated our
objective to develop a vehicle that could operate anywhere,
anytime and under almost any weather conditions safely and
with minimum restriction.   We also placed very rigid environmental criteria on the design to ensure that the JETFOIL
would be a good neighbour in the community.   Among other
things this meant achieving low noise emissions and therefore
appropriate acoustical insulation.   Unfortunately, materials
that are often excellent for fire insulation are very poor
acoustic insulators, and vice versa.   We also wanted

Figure 8.4. Jetfoil propulsion and foil systems.

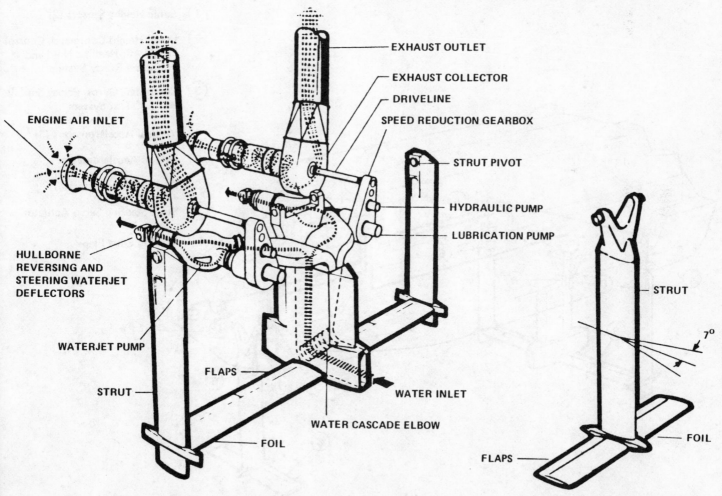

materials that were non—corrosive to the aluminium, low in moisture absorbtion, resistive to vermin, and simple to install and maintain. A feel for the magnitude of the insulation requirements can be gained by considering that the combined weight of the fire/acoustic insulation in the JETFOIL is greater than the normal fuel weight.

FOILS AND STRUTS The foil system is a fully submerged canard arrangement with a single tee—strut and foil forward, and a three strut full—span foil aft, (Figure 8.4. – see previous page). The canard arrangement provides positive directional stability and reduces vertical accelerations in rough water. A requirement imposed on the design from the outset was that the foils should not extend beyond the hull lines so that special docking camels would not be needed. The beamy hull and foil configuration permit this without penalising the performance advantages inherent in a fully-submerged foil system.

The foils and struts are retractable using slots in the bow and stern sections. When retracted, maximum draft is less than six feet. This provides unparalleled docking flexibility and route selection for a vessel of this size with no need for expensive and/or unacceptable dredging. Secondary benefits of retraction include easier inspection and maintenance.

PROPULSION SYSTEM The propulsion system consists of two parallel and independent gas—turbine waterjet plants, each located in its own compartment (Figure 8.4.).

The engine selected was the Detroit-Diesel-Allison 501-K20A, an aft—drive, free—turbine version of the T 56 aircraft engine. More than 10,000 of these engines had been built and they had accumulated more than 50 million operating hours. More than 250 million dollars had been spent to develop the 501 series into a mature industrial/marine engine. To maximise operational life for the JETFOIL, the turbine was conservatively rated at 3,780 HP.

Figure 8.5. Jetfoil Automatic Control System.

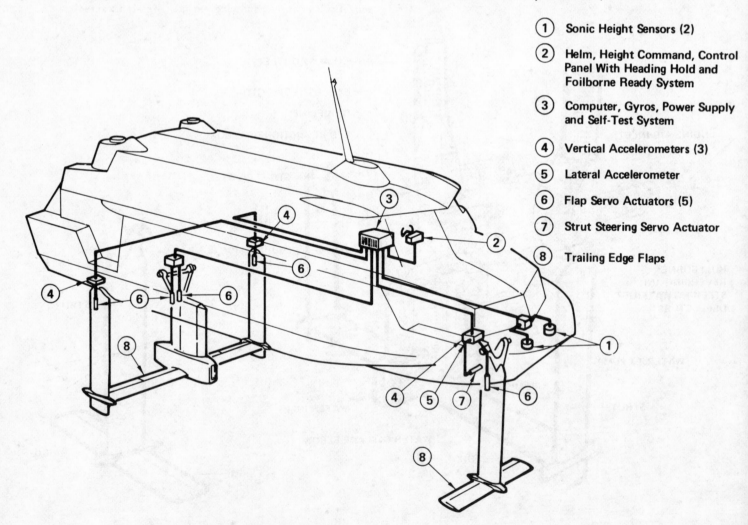

1. Sonic Height Sensors (2)
2. Helm, Height Command, Control Panel With Heading Hold and Foilborne Ready System
3. Computer, Gyros, Power Supply and Self-Test System
4. Vertical Accelerometers (3)
5. Lateral Accelerometer
6. Flap Servo Actuators (5)
7. Strut Steering Servo Actuator
8. Trailing Edge Flaps

Turbine combustion air enters through both port and starboard inlet grills and is passed through mesh-type filters to remove as much salt as possible before reaching the engine inlet. Vertical exhaust stacks duct the exhaust gases directly to atmosphere.

Considerable effort has been expended to make the JETFOIL extremely clean and quiet. External noise is less than 90 dbA at 100 feet. The JETFOIL exhuast emissions are extremely low. There is no visible smoke.

The pumps are self-priming axial-mixed flow type.

Hull mounted ducts connect the water passage in the aft centre strut and the central hull water opening at the keel to each pump intake. Each pump flow rate is 22,300 gallons of water per minute. The pumps discharge through nozzles on the underside of the hull. For ship control when operating hullborne, hydraulically operated vectoring and reversing buckets are installed downstream of the nozzles. The vectoring provides for 30 degrees deflection of the stream either side of the centre. The reversing provides for variable reverse thrust to approximately half of full forward thrust. The waterjets have no measurable effect on the water during passage through the system.

STABILITY AND CONTROL A fully submerged foil hydrofoil is inherently unstable in all axes and degrees of freedom when operating foilborne. If an external disturbance, such as a wave, imparts an upsetting force there are insufficient natural counteracting forces developed to restore the vehicle to its original equilibrium condition. Synthetic stabilisation must be provided and when properly done this is the technical feature which permits the de-coupling from the water surface and the resulting low accelerations and ship motions when operating in rough seas, even at very high speed.

In the JETFOIL the stabilisation is accomplished electronically by the Automatic Control System, (the ACS, Figure 8.5.). A solid state computer takes input signals from accelerometers, gyros, height sensors, control position transducers and manual input command signals, processes them and then issues commands to the control system to provide continuous dynamic control of the ship during takeoff, landing and all foilborne operations. In addition to providing ship stability, the ACS controls the hull height above the water surface, provides co-ordinated banking for all turns, and all but eliminates ship motions caused by the orbital particle motion of waves. The magnitude of rough water that can be handled depends on the strut length, or more precisely, the depth at which the foils can be flown without getting the hull too close to the water surface.

OUTFITTING AND FURNISHINGS
The outfitting is similar to that of any other boat of similar size. The general fittings for handling, mooring, etc. are essentially the same and other equipment also corresponds. Furnishing, however, is quite different and in many respects compares more closely to a jet airliner than to a ship, (Figure 8.6. - see next page). Interior finish is complete on all surfaces so that all walls and ceilings are covered and no

structure is visible. The partitions and cabinetry are made of honeycomb material covered with a wood-grained vinyl and the wall panels and trim are a plain coloured vinyl covering over sheet metal or honeycomb panel material. Decks are carpeted and the ceilings are an acoustical metal material with fluorescent lighting fixtures.

Versatility in the interiors is accomplished by mounting the seats on tracks. The seats, which are lightweight aircraft type, are supplied in modules of two, three and four abreast and are fitted with adjustable legs that can be adapted to the different seat tracks on the two decks. They can be located at different positions, fore and aft, on the tracks to provide varying seat spacing for a higher density or greater comfort as the customer requires. For longer trips the same seats can be replaced by galleys to provide food service or, if a large volume of baggage is expected, luggage racks can replace portions of the seating. The JETFOIL is outfitted with a complete intercom system which can also be used for entertainment by attaching a tape deck or other music system.

As a result of the flexibility described above, the interior arrangement is such that it can be modified to suit a wide variety of requirements of different customers. Many features such as coat racks, bars, tables, different seating arrangements, etc. have been developed. All these changes can be carried out quickly and with a minimum of revision to the boat, so that the operator can adjust the interior to changes in his type of service or in passenger demands.

CLASSIFICATION AND CERTIFICATION
The JETFOIL has been designed to meet the classification requirements of the American Bureau of Shipping (ABS) and the Regulatory Requirements of the United States Coast Guard and other regulating bodies wherever the JETFOIL operates. JETFOIL materials and machinery are individually inspected by the ABS as are the completed hulls and struts and foils, and are approved under an AMS classification. Unattended machinery spaces are classified ACCU.

To date, various JETFOILS have been certified for operation as follows:

By the US Coast Guard for domestic use in Hawaiian waters and international operation in the Straits of Juan de Fuca and the English Channel.

By the Hong Kong Marine Department for international operation between Hong Kong and Macao.

By the Minister of Transport, Japan for domestic use in the Sea of Japan between Niigata and Ryotsu on the Island of Sado.

By the Direccion de Navegacion, Venezuela for domestic use in the Caribbean between Puerta La Cruz and Porlamar on the Island of Margarita.

Certification is now in process by the Department of Trade in England for international usage over various routes in the Northern European area. The JETFOIL

Figure 8.6. Interior view of Boeing Jetfoil showing fittings and furnishings.

is also designed to comply with the IMCO (Inter-Governmental Maritime Consultative Organisation) rules, and equipment can be added to meet SOLAS (safety of life at sea) requirements.   Future JETFOILS will comply with the novel craft rules currently being developed by IMCO.

EXPERIENCE TO DATE
JETFOILS have been in service since 1975.   They have operated on four continents and six different services.   Route lengths varied from 34 to 136 nautical miles.   Passenger arrangements varied from 190 to 294 with one operator offering mixed classes of service.   Fares ranged from 17 to 40 cents per mile.

The JETFOILS have competed with conventional passenger ships, surface piercing hydrofoils and aircraft on these routes.   On one service more than 40% of all trips were run in Seastate 4 or higher seas with a weather reliability of 99.3%.

The JETFOILS have carried nearly 3 million people and their reactions to the vehicle have overwhelmingly confirmed the importance of comfort and speed.   Surveys taken on

three of the services showed that 84 to 93% of the passengers
carried were sufficiently impressed to say that they would use
the service again and between one-half to three-quarters of
them felt that comfort/speed was the most important feature
of the vehicle.   These results were for the service with the
two highest fare rates and for fares which were between two
and five times higher than the competing conventional ship
fares.

SUMMARY

We are convinced that the passenger transportation market
is energised on the criteria of speed and comfort.   These
criteria have been followed successfully in the past as demonstrated by the succession of jet aircraft which were able to
double the speed of piston aircraft and provide increased
comfort for the passenger.

During this century, there have been small incremental
improvements in speed for the sea passenger.   The load
factors that are being enjoyed by both hydrofoils and hovercraft today and the kind of passenger response that we have
seen to the JETFOIL demonstrates to us that high speed water
transport is highly appealing to the travelling public.

Figure 8.7. Boeing Jetfoil on P&O Ferries London-Zeebrugge service.

Part 3 Discussion:
Vehicle Design

Chairman: Thomas Beagley

D.S. BURNICLE (Leyland Vehicles Limited) In her present-ation Mrs. Waterhouse raised the subject of cigarette smoke extraction from buses. Recent innovations on buses such as the Leyland National give a complete change of air every three minutes, extracting cigarette smoke very well. Moreover, for overseas markets twin-fan installations are standard, giving a complete change every one and a half minutes. You can specify twin-fans in the United Kingdom, but I suggest that it would be rather draughty for our normal climate.

Our latest double-decker, the Titan, will have a very high rate of air change. However, I am afraid there are still very many long-lived buses running around without such efficient ventilation systems; it will obviously take a few years for sufficient Titans to come into service to solve these problems.

It is also very pleasing to hear a consumer arguing for planned obsolescence. Normally, I thought you argued for product longevity.

RACHEL WATERHOUSE (Loughborough University of Technology, Institute of Consumer Ergonomics) I accept, of course, the point about things lasting a long time. Indeed my argument was that if these vehicles are designed to last, then we should make sure that every conceivable ergonomic improvement is incorporated now.

Fortunately, we are much more aware of passenger comfort problems and their solution than were the designers of those long lasting buses. They were concerned more with engineering and longevity.

I hope that our vehicles will not have built-in obsolescence, but that they will be designed for the comfort of their passengers

H.R. ANDREW (University of Aston in Birmingham) I should like to ask Mr. Shultz two questions regarding the P. & O. operation of the Boeing JETFOIL from London to Europe. First: What has been the average load factor on this service? And second: What are the operating costs of this vessel compared with conventional hovercraft?

W.M. SHULTZ (Boeing Marine Systems) The service started in June 1977, and it was consequently difficult to capitalise, so late, on the peak summer market. By the end of summer the load factors had reached 60 - 65%, falling again in winter. Incidentally, before I left Seattle, P. & O. had already taken about 200 reservations for both next Saturday and Sunday crossings.

I do not know the hovercraft operating costs, but I suspect

that they are higher than JETFOIL mainly due to skirt and engine maintenance problems; engine problems have been caused primarily by salt ingestion. Our engines are located in a much more salt-free environment.

While on the subject of maintenance, I would like to take up Mrs. Waterhouse's point about the reliability of sophisticated systems. We offer the same support for our boats as we do for our aircraft; this has not been done by shipbuilders previously.

We realise that the JETFOIL is an expensive vessel – it costs £4 million – but it has been designed to run incessantly. If kept running it can make money.

JAMES COUSINS (British Railways Board) Could I ask Mr. Shultz what wave height can be accommodated, and also whether his company is working on a car carrying version.

W.M. SHULTZ (Boeing Marine Systems) I was responsible for testing the JETFOIL for the first 250 hours, when we performed rough-water trials, and have flown it in seas up to 24 feet high. In Hawaii they have exceeded 30 feet. For example, we are considering the application of our vessel to offshore oil support in the North Sea, and feel that it can operate there foilborne 90% of the time. Obviously there will be some very big seas which will preclude flying, because the struts are too short.

We have a car carrying version on the design boards, but I believe that it will be some time away; we find it difficult to justify the economics of carrying an automobile at high speed in comfort.

C.J. HOLLAND (R. Travers Morgan and Partners) I would like to address a further question on cost to Rachel Waterhouse. She has drawn our attention to many faults in, I feel, rather a negative manner, but has not mentioned constructively what the consumer might be willing to pay for improvements. The exception to this is her reference to a survey in Canterbury in 1970 which concluded that consumers were not prepared to pay for a change from one-man to two-man operation of buses.

What is being done by the consumer movement to try to establish how much people are prepared to pay for solutions to the problems which they are so good at spotting?

RACHEL WATERHOUSE (Loughborough University of Technology, Institute of Consumer Ergonomics) This is of course a very fair question and one that has been asked before. If there is to be a new vehicle, then there will be some expenditure. Given that fact, the design ought to contain all the latest features appropriate for the consumer. Clearly, there will be occasions when economic constraints will prevent complete freedom of choice, but the consumer will want the bus to be as good as possible within these constraints.

We must be perfectly clear that we are discussing two different aspects. One is the new design being planned now. The other is the criticism which consumers are voicing about those vehicles in which they are travelling today.   This is the only way in which the consumer can feed information back to the designer.

You ask whether consumers are willing to pay more.   Quite often consumers already pay more willy-nilly for a better service.   If you travel from London to Birmingham by rail you are obliged to pay the price for the new rolling stock.   You cannot choose to pay less and travel by older rolling stock.   So people do actually pay higher prices for more advanced forms of travel.

I do not think we are asking for the impossible.   All the criticisms we make can be met without enormous extra expenditure.

THOMAS BEAGLEY (President, Chartered Institute of Transport)   The balance between introduction of new features and costs does indeed present a difficult problem.   The more information that Mrs. Waterhouse and her colleagues can impart about the consumers' willingness to pay for additional features, the greater will be her contribution to the transport industry.

P. LEE (Martin and Voorhees Associates)   Dr. Pollard mentioned briefly the subject of "hunting" (the vertical movement of train on bogie and on track).   It was noticeable on the APT bogie shown that the wheels were very small.   Clearly the wheel and the tyre profile are significant in the hunting problem.   Could he give us some idea of the work carried out on this subject?

DR. M.G. POLLARD (British Railways Board)   Strictly, hunting is associated with a lateral movement, and it is generated because of the tyre profile.   Originally most vehicles start with a purely coned profile, but this wears to a hollow shape, and the effect is that, as a wheel set moves across the track, the rolling radius of the wheel on one side increases rapidly and on the other it decreases.   The wheel set then goes down the track rolling in a snake like movement. This is usually controlled by the springs to the bogie frame, but if the designer has not specified the parameters correctly there are some conditions under which this sort of movement will become unstable.   Now we have worked on developing profiles which do not change shape as they wear - that is, the wheel merely gets smaller while the profile remains the same. Once you can do this you can then design the suspension to accommodate all the foreseeable conditions between wheel and rail, and you should not have this phenomenon of hunting occurring in modern vehicles.

H.G. CONWAY (Deputy Chairman, Engineering Design Advisory Committee, Design Council)   A very distinguished French engineer from Citroen said some years ago that the real cause of discomfort in vehicles is not acceleration, but the rate of change of acceleration.   This seems logical enough because the muscles in your viscera have to change their tension in order to deal with acceleration.   In the case of aircraft ejector seats, for example, it is the rate of change of acceleration which allows you to be ejected.   This is a

subject not often discussed by those concerned with suspensions.   I would ask Dr. Pollard to comment on this point.

Recently I had the pleasure of viewing the Advanced Passenger Train (APT), and although I thought it was an impressive engineering design, the prospect of it ever working seemed to me to be in doubt.   To achieve reliability I believe that the tilting mechanism had duplicated or triplicated hydraulic systems.   It contained many control valves, and the idea of normal British Rail maintenance taking care of this highly sophisticated system seems doubtful. I would appreciate Dr. Pollard's comments.

DR. M.G. POLLARD (British Railways Board)   Rate of change of acceleration is termed "jerk".   There is very little information on human response to different levels of jerk.

The acceleration experiments which have been carried out, except those very recently, have been badly planned, yielding dubious results.

The only information about jerk comes from American experiments on their people-mover systems.   Apparently, if the jerk was associated with a loud noise or with an obvious track feature, nobody seemed to mind that it was at a very high level.

With regard to the reliability of the APT tilt system, I share your concern.   The built-in hydraulic system is very sensitive, and we have accordingly designed it with as few moving parts as possible, and also as a single replaceable unit.   Maintenance sheds are being designed for complete unit removal and replacement and its subsequent rectification away from the train.

The system is indeed duplicated to give train safety in a failure condition.   Each end of the vehicle is controlled independently, but each can take over whole vehicle control in the event of failure.   In such an event, the vehicle will ride upright, the passengers being then subjected to some cant deficiency.   This is not much worse than current French practice which runs at around 7 degrees of cant deficiency, and the vehicle is perfectly safe.   In tests we have run around a curve with the vehicle leaning over the wrong way to 12 degrees, while we ran demanding 12 degrees the other way, giving 24 degrees of tilt error.   It was uncomfortable but not unsafe.

THOMAS BEAGLEY (President, Chartered Institute of Transport)   Mr. Conway's question is indeed pertinent, and I share Dr. Pollard's views on it.   British Rail are sensible enough to realise that the new APT development will need a trial period, and are accordingly constructing prototypes, soon to be in operation.   British Rail will clearly wish to see how these operate in practice before making major investments.

P.A. HAMILTON (Bicknell and Hamilton)   It appears that

when the APT comes into service, most of the existing stock is to remain. I believe that the riding quality of some of this needs improvement. In view of the impressive progress of APT and HST I wonder to what extent the new techniques are being planned for use on improving existing stock.

DR. M.G. POLLARD (British Railways Board) The Board's long term plan is to cascade new stock down through the system. For example, the APT will come on to the West Coast mainline, the electrified line. Then the new rolling stock, which is currently being hauled by locomotives on that line, will be used on other routes. I agree that there are some vehicles which do not approach the standard of our newer inter-city stock, but I can assure you that work is progressing to improve that situation. Perhaps it is not fast enough for some, but we are working towards higher overall standards. For example, new stock currently running from London into Hertfordshire is designed on the sort of principles outlined. I understand that it is very comfortable and reliable.

K. GRANGE (Pentagram Design) I understand that an essential difference between APT and the well-known successful Japanese train is the necessity for large scale Japanese investment in new track.

Twenty years ahead, does Dr. Pollard believe that a new track design will become an inevitable part of an assumedly higher speed rail system?

DR. M.G. POLLARD (British Railways Board) I will give you my own view. You are quite right; since there was no track suitable for upgrading, a very expensive new track was necessary for the Japanese high speed train.

HST and APT optimise the existing infrastructure by running at 125 m.p.h., the present signalling system remaining suitable and track maintenance not being worsened. For the future, while speed may extend to 150 m.p.h., I do not think that any greater speed is justifiable economically. Typical reductions in journey time by an increase to 200 m.p.h. are quite small, while the costs of the inevitable new track – and the additional power to haul at this speed – would be phenomenal. For track, once you have the right of way, it costs 3 or 4 million pounds per mile, and the power requirement increases as the cube of the speed. So I believe that about 125 - 150 m.p.h. is the likely future top speed in Britain.

THOMAS BEAGLEY (President, Chartered Institute of Transport) Is it not true that track construction depends upon geography and that building new track in the United Kingdom is generally more expensive than in the flat plain of Japan?

JAMES COUSINS (British Railways Board) I think this discussion has rather missed the point. I understand that the APT's vehicle dynamics are designed to corner at speeds 50% higher than conventional suspension systems. British Rail's main investment is in the High Speed Train which is operating on welded track, being generally straight, where there would be no great advantage in operating the APT.

On the West Coast route, however, there are curves on which the APT can take full advantage of its design specification.

Mr. Grange referred to the Tokaido line in Japan where they had the most appalling kind of old railway system. The Japanese simply built a straight elevated track.

In France, they have built high speed prototype trains, and are now building the TGV001 as a production train operating very smoothly at speeds up to 200 m.p.h. Again, this is on a straight track; the design solution really depends upon the type of train to be operated and its location.

The fundamental advantage of the APT is its ability to use curved track at higher speeds.

M.W. ANDERSON (British Airways) As an extension to an earlier question, would Mr. Shultz quote some comparative operating costs for the JETFOIL.

He also commented that, if the utilisation is kept high, the profits can be large. I understood the P. & O. Ferries utilisation to be about 6½ hours in every 24 hours, and would judge this to be relatively low. Are they making profits at this rate, or is the operation regarded as a promotional exercise initially?

W.M. SHULTZ (Boeing Marine Systems) Costs obviously vary with specific routes. On average, we calculate that, at 45 - 50% load factor and a fare of 19 - 21 cents per mile, you could make a 10% profit on investment after interest is paid. I believe that this is acceptable for these types of operations.

I should just mention the experience of Sado Kisen, who have operated conventional ferries for years between Niigata and Sado Island. The success of the JETFOIL has enabled them to operate profitably for the first time in three years. As a result, they have decided to purchase another JETFOIL.

Our design objective was to achieve a utilisation of 4,000 hours per year for a mature service. The aircraft fleet achieves this, and we felt that it could be reached eventually by the boats. Initially you are lucky to reach more than 2,000 hours per annum, because everyone is learning. Over three years the average underway time per boat has increased from 5½ hours to 6½ hours, and will continue to increase as more vessels come into service.

Part 4
Case Studies — Vehicle Design

Chapter 9

The Interior Design of Wide Bodied Aircraft

Gerry Molony

INTRODUCTION

Large high capacity aircraft are produced in order to keep down cost and fares by improved productivity.

This chapter discusses the basic constraints to be met in designing successful aircraft interiors and equipment.

1. Aircraft Interior Design

2. Constraints:

    (a) Weight – The Hidden Constraint
    (b) Cost
    (c) Time

3. Seat Basic Dimensions

4. Interior Materials Safety Regulations

5. Decor

6. Food Service

7. Toilets

8. Baggage Handling

9. The Future Task

1. AIRCRAFT INTERIOR DESIGN

The starting point of a good interior aircraft layout is the basic dimensions of the fuselage. The most important of these dimensions is the cross-section of the fuselage structure, which will never be altered and sets the family type from a particular manufacturer.

The length of the fuselage may be altered during the long development of an aircraft type, spread over the years as the markets develop and technology improves to match.

New aircraft models are introduced with the same fuselage cross-section but with other major changes, which usually consist of alterations to wing configurations and propulsion, and a longer fuselage to allow more revenue payload in the form of passengers and freight to be carried.

The important fundamental dimension in fuselage width is the effective distance between the walls at 25 inches armrest height and 38 inches shoulder height from the floor of the interior, after allowing for structural frames and furnishing thickness.

After a long period of carrying up to 14 million highly articulate passengers a year, who all possess the full

Figure 9.1. British Airways Lockheed L.1011 TriStar.

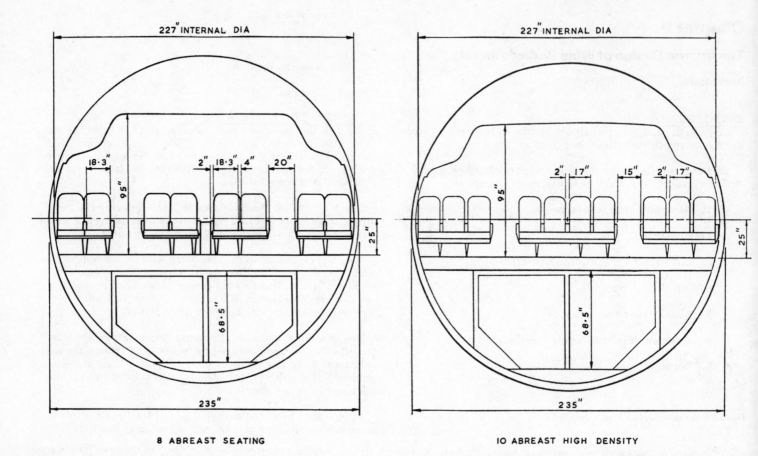

8 ABREAST SEATING   IO ABREAST HIGH DENSITY

Figure 9.2. TriStar seating densities.

equipment of eyes and posterior to test our results, we have now established that the minimum distance between armrests is 17 inches with 2 inch armrests.

The mandatory minimum width for a gangway is 15 inches. With a practical clearance from the wall of ½ inch minimum, it is possible to devise an aircraft which will be acceptable from the minimum comfort standard. This would be, plus or minus, steps of 19 inches in the width. Thus, an aircraft design for 10 abreast seating, using these figures, can provide 9 abreast luxury seating with wider gangways and wider seats, or, very luxurious 8 abreast tourist seating for longhaul routes (Figure 9.2.).

The mistakes we made in the past were in trying to design a fuselage cross-section for luxury travel.

There is no such measurement as a maximum width, and, following that line creates absurdities where you may be, for

example, aiming for a luxurious 5 abreast situation, only to find that you can get another seat in the width, making it 6 abreast with a 16 inch seat. This is workable, but extremely uncomfortable for the majority of passengers and would be unacceptable today compared with the comfort provided by our competitors' aircraft. Thus, the aircraft width should be designed around the maximum number of the minimum size comfortable seats.

The important length measurement is between fixed dimensions which will not alter in the particular aircraft as built. The main limitation is between the holes in the fuselage for doors, which are strictly controlled by legal requirements for emergency evacuation. For instance, the TriStar has four doors per side, each measuring 42 inches x 72/76 inches. The second limitation in length is the position of fixed toilet installations. These distances should be made allowing for a certain number of seats at the practical minimum dimension, which is currently 30 inch pitch. Our minimum, at present operated, is 30 inches. (Figure 9.3.).

The point here is that if you get this basic dimension right you can accommodate the maximum number of seats at 30 inch pitch, and yet if you were short of 4 or 5 inches in that

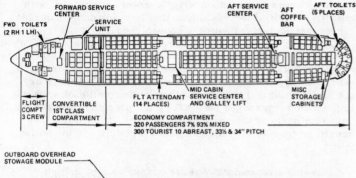

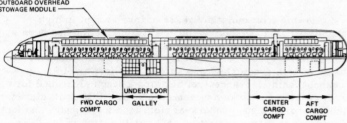

Figure 9.3. TriStar seating layout.

dimension you might well lose a row of seats, say, 10 seats out of an aircraft.

The loss of revenue if one passenger seat is removed from an aircraft type is roughly £40,000 per aircraft per annum. For a fleet of 20 aircraft this will be some £800,000 in loss of revenue.

The most important requirement for all the internal equipment, such as pantries, seats, bulkheads, partitions, and overhead passenger amenities is that they must be capable of installation anywhere in the aircraft to provide commercial flexibility of operation.

2. CONSTRAINTS
(a) WEIGHT – THE HIDDEN CONSTRAINT The success of the aircraft depends on its ability to lift the maximum payload over the required range. Any item carried which does not produce revenue is to be considered a constraint. The cost of weight to be permanently carried on a Tristar over all our routes is calculated at £52 per 1 lb. weight, per aircraft, per year. Thus, for 20 350-seater aircraft the increase of 1 lb. weight per seat results in a £364,000 loss of revenue a year for the airline, which is a considerable constraint resulting in a very delicate, easily damaged, interior structure and equipment with which we have to contend and maintain.

What we try to do is to strengthen by careful design the detailed parts which are subject to the most wear and damage. We have thin stainless steel caps on the ends of seat arms and stiffened metal hatrack edges and rails. The pantires and trolleys are locally stiffened to take the extraordinary battering they receive with the continual loading and unloading

of equipment year in and year out all over the worldwide network.

The art of the design is to strike a compromise, and, we find, in fact, that every detailed part of the aircraft has an entirely different requirement of weight and strength from the floor to the walls and hatracks. The lightweight and soundproofing requirements needed for a ceiling panel have led to the design of hollow, plastic, foam-filled laminates with tiny perforations over the surface area to produce the sound-deadening effect required. The plastic surface of this has to be treated with an impervious coating to reduce the onset of brown stains due to nicotine and dirt accumulation – all this within a very lightweight limitation because of the enormous area to be considered.

(b) COST When controlling the design of an aircraft interior, cost is the outstanding factor. The problem is the enormous amount of labour, toil and skill that has to be applied to design and produce production drawings; to develop the components to make them work satisfactorily; and then carry out the enormously complex task of equipping this vast interior with the detail built to the highest possible standards of function and furnishings which are required on a modern aircraft today.

The reliability achieved by aircraft nowadays has meant that times between major checks are being stretched up to a period of 3 – 4 years between the possibility of major refurbishing. During this period, the fleet is required to carry 14 million passengers a year, and the turnround of passengers leads to very heavy work loads on all component parts. Therefore, the original cost may be high, provided a trouble-free life can be obtained, because the cost of removal and replacement is overwhelming. For example, a downtime on a large shorthaul aircraft of one day may cost the Corporation £25,000 loss of revenue which can never be recovered. At the present time, the control of our costs is fairly effective considering the ever-increasing cost of furnishing equipment for commercial application.

(c) TIME It could be assumed that the purchase of a 30 million dollar aircraft would include all the interior equipment that you see when flying on one of our aircraft. The truth is, that owing to the complexity of route structures and the requirements of the airline, the manufacturers and the airlines long ago concluded that the equipment of interiors which are particular to that airline should be provided by the airline itself. This is reflected in the contract price, in that we are able to obtain this equipment far more cheaply than the manufacturers could produce it for us with their high aircraft manufacturing overhead costs.

During the TriStars' final acceptance at Lockheed California, I found it very exciting to sit in their production building with a large blackboard detailing the progress of our aircraft under construction. The blackboard showed that certain items of equipment, which we were providing and sending to Lockheed for fitment, were missing because they were still in the process of design and production in England.

A delay in the production of any of these items, leading to a contractual break, could not only cost the Corporation in downtime of an aircraft, £25,000 a day per aircraft, but a very heavy penalty in public goodwill.

It may seem that a year is a long time to produce some equipment for an aircraft, but a production time on a seat or a pantry, for example, is 18 months for initial design and commencement of production before the programme of agreed delivery to match the aircraft production dates can be met. The whole production of the aircraft type can be done within 4 years, so, the design, development, and production to the aircraft schedule leaves surprisingly little time for changes, mistakes, and trying out the new ideas we would wish to incorporate.

It follows then that the best line, as with the best human endeavour, is with the steady development of sound products based on hardwon experience.

3. SEAT BASIC DIMENSIONS
Apart from a few variations, there are three general types of seating, namely:-

1ST CLASS SEATING consisting of double units, wide and luxurious, at fore and aft pitch of between 36 - 42 inches.

EXECUTIVE TYPE SEATING which is usually triple seating at 34 inch pitch.

and

HIGH DENSITY SEATING from 34 inch pitch - the maximum agreed with the International Air Transport Association, down to 30 inch pitch, which is the minimum acceptable for a 2 - 3 hour flight with a full meal service. (See Figure 9.5.).

We have also invented a seat which is fully convertible, from a double first class seat to triple tourist class; retaining the different armrest and full reclining facilities with divided tables at the back. My section, in fact, originated the present back table concept which is unaffected by reclining backs, and also the folding break-back seat to improve the safety in close pitch seating.

The first class and executive seats are somewhat easier to design as they don't have the very rigid specification and weight constraint brought about by the large quantity of seats required to be installed in the aircraft's tourist section.

Consider the tourist seat and its minimum comfort. We have here a most interesting problem of giving the passenger the best possible comfort and safety within these tight constrictions, bearing in mind the variations between children and grown men. In this regard, most people consider the comfort from their own fixed standpoint of their personal point of view, no matter what their shape may be.

To meet the majority with the minimum of complaint, the compromise is struck to give the seat fairly firm support with gradual curves and as much wriggle-room as possible, with cushions provided for the longer flights which can be placed for the particular passenger's convenience.

We have several ingenious methods of providing inflatable adjusting backs for lumbar support, and sliding headrests which can be introduced on the longer flights, but these are not really practical on the short trips where a lot of emphasis is placed on turnrounds amd getting the passengers in and out. Different parts of the seats are, however, given a different density of foam to give the greatest adaptability to the human frame.

Following from our many years of involvement in high density seating, we believe our main contribution has been in the very special design of the lower seat frame which is shown in Figures 9.4. and 9.5. Thus, $1\frac{1}{4}$ inch diameter tubes of high grade steel are spaced well forward to give maximum shin clearance, yet allowing $2\frac{1}{2}$ inch clearance for seat cushion suspension movement above. The small diameter tubing provides good underseat clearance for baggage and foot space and is also a very important safety factor in the downward crash case to avoid trapping people's legs.

The seats are designed to meet British Civil Airworthiness Requirements of 9 'g' forward, 4 'g' downwards, $2\frac{1}{2}$ 'g' sideways, and $1\frac{1}{2}$ 'g' rearwards. In practice, this means a forward load of a 170 lb. passenger multiplied by 9, or, 1530 lb. to be applied to the seat per seat place.

Some years ago, we sponsored a dynamic test rig which was simple and cheap to operate on which we tested all our current seats at that time. What we were after was a seat that bent and deflected under load and did not tear away from the floor causing the passenger behind to swing over into a nest of broken tubes. These tests were satisfactory, and, in fact, showed that the ordinary mandatory static test, coupled with a photographic record of the mode of failure, is most effective. We did find, however, that some of our seat belts had a free end which flipped forward, and this led us to test our buckles separately. During the test we found that a flying free end could snap the buckle open. We discussed this matter fully with the Civil Aviation Authority and jointly re-wrote the CAA specification to prevent this happening on any of our current production seat belts.

4. INTERIOR MATERIALS SAFETY REGULATIONS
The present materials meet British Civil Airworthiness Regulations with regard to flameproofing. Regulations are now being proposed to step up this standard to include smoke promulgation amd toxicity, and a great deal of work is being done in this direction to test various materials. My own view is that we should eliminate entirely materials which propagate smoke and fire and not spend a great deal of time and money producing exotic materials to test on animals, but simply use metal wherever possible. The manufacturers are being encouraged to follow these lines. In fact, all the world's airlines and manufacturers are concerned with these problems and involved in producing new and improved regulations.

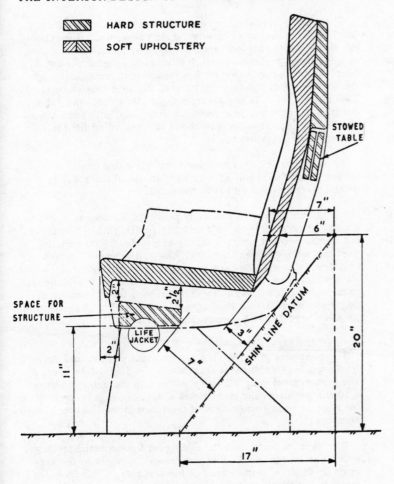

HARD STRUCTURE

SOFT UPHOLSTERY

STOWED TABLE

SPACE FOR STRUCTURE

LIFE JACKET

SHIN LINE DATUM

Figure 9.4. Seat basic envelope.

BASIC DIMENSIONS

OVERALL LENGTH, (BACK UPRIGHT)	25"
WIDTH OF EACH ARMREST	2"
SEAT WIDTH BETWEEN ARMRESTS	17"
WIDTH OF UPHOLSTERED BACK	17"
HEIGHT OF ARMREST ABOVE SEAT CUSHION	6"
HEIGHT OF FRONT OF CUSHION ABOVE FLOOR	18"
HEIGHT OF TOP OF BACK ABOVE FLOOR	43"
HEIGHT OF TABLE TOP ABOVE FLOOR	25·5"
RAKE OF SEAT CUSHION TO HORIZONTAL	7°- 8°
ANGLE OF LOWER BACK TO VERTICAL	
(UPRIGHT)	15°
(RECLINED)	30°

5. DECOR

The design of the interior of a large modern aircraft is a showpiece for the airline and is one of the main features of the product we offer for sale to the public of 14 million passengers a year, who have a good deal to say on the subject. It is, therefore, inevitable that there has to be a combination of the requirements of Engineering and Sales & Advertising in this area, with a free transfer of ideas between these branches.

The present TriStar interior design was arranged in the following way. We decided to produce three different schemes which could be considered as:

1. the soft Savile Row approach in muted colours.

2. the slick modern approach with many striped fabrics.

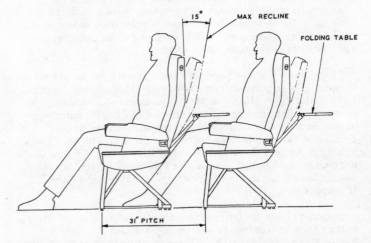

Figure 9.5. High density seating.

3. a decor split into four blocks of colours for the seating, using very decisive strong colours of red, yellow, blue and orange.   The carpets pick up these colours, but we keep the walls to a soft neutral colour with the minimum of pattern.

The impression created with the walls well lit is a startling effect of width, which is most impressive to anyone travelling on the aircraft for the first time.   The ceiling is sculptured and back lit.   This, associated with the colour blocks, which break up the length, can be very impressive indeed to those used to narrow-bodied aircraft, and completely overcomes the narrow tubular look.   It absolutely removes the fear of being crowded in with large numbers of people, and we never have any complaints in this direction.   The effect of this is most noticeable if you switch from an older narrow-bodied aircraft to the new wide look during the course of a transit flight, where you may spend some hours in one and then change to the other.   Indeed, a great deal of money is now being spent on trying to give the smaller aircraft more of a wide-bodied look.

We believe, after many years of discussion, that a new aircraft with a ten to twenty years life, must have a new interior to help sell this most expensive piece of capital equipment.   It is often said that these schemes and colours are a matter of opinion, but those of us who have spent a life-time attempting to please the public in these areas know that although the good interiors can be very different, a poor and dull interior is recognised immediately by the ordinary travelling public.

As an example of this, the method of approach on the last six aircraft we produced, including the TriStar, was to produce three schemes as mentioned earlier.   These schemes were in large card form with sample materials and three simple viewing models showing the amount and disposition of colours in 3-dimensional form.   This was produced very cheaply and no attempt was made to be accurate in detailed fittings.   These schemes and models were then shown to our Board of Management for policy guidance to be received. This was carried out and duly noted.

At the same time we produced ten different proposals for a theme.   These ranged from the use of Old Masters; Impressionist paintings; places of historical interest, such as castles; rocket and space travel; and children's paintings produced from the schools of Europe with prizes to be presented by the teachers and signed copies, with the labels of origin put into the aircraft.   Included amongst these was a cartoon by the English genius, Mr. Rowland Emett, who has succeeded in combining engineering, artistry, and humour. (Figure 9.6.).

In general our Management preferred, after a lot of study, colour scheme Number 3, and were intrigued by Emett's gentle humoured approach.   The executive then decided that this should be shown to a large number of staff, particularly junior staff.   We approach this with some trepidation, bearing in mind the well-worn cliché – "It is a matter of opinion".

However, a presentation was mounted and many staff were involved to view and write down their comments.   Everybody loved the Emett cartoon, and, out of many hundreds of people, their preference was for interior scheme Number 3, which coincided with that of the Management group, although the staff were completely unaware of any previous choice. There were only six people from the staff invited who did not like the scheme, and these six disagreed with each other. The verdict numerically was about 300 who voted for the scheme with 6 against.

We were particularly delighted that the cabin staff were pleased with the result as they have to spend their day in the interior and have to sell it to the public.

Since then, we have had many requests for copies of the Emett cartoons.   We have an exclusive aircraft use of these, but copies are, of course, freely available.   The amusing part that emerged was that Mrs. Emett, the sweet English lady from a Sussex cottage has contracts with General Motors, Nieman Marcus of Chicago, and Disney Productions, to name but a few.   And, by coincidence, the showpiece of the shopping centre in Nottingham is also an Emett production. We have here something endearingly British.

6. FOOD SERVICE

The problems of delivering drinks, tea, coffee, and duty free supplies to 350 passengers during a flight of 1½ hours, and then replenishing all these galleys on the ground during a 30 minute turnround many times a day, poses a large problem for a great many people around the international network and airports.

Our solution is to load the equipment into wheeled trolleys, which can be replenished on the ground, brought to the aircraft by vehicle, and located in the aircraft.   The food trolleys have ovens on the top which are plugged into the aircraft's electrical supply to keep the food heated during the whole of this process.   There is also a large capability for heating food on board for longer haul flights, if required. The TriStar food trolleys with ovens atop are loaded in the large underfloor galley area and elevated to the upper deck by two lifts, which can take trolleys or cabin staff.   We also have extra space above deck for trolley and pantry working areas.

The trolleys used are 12 inches wide, 36 inches high, 37/38 inches long and take up to 33 meals.   The principle of stowing the trays fore and aft in the trolley allows a large tray to be stowed in a narrow trolley, thus allowing these trolleys to be used in a 15 inch minimum gangway, therefore, a universal trolley standard is possible.   Advantages of the trolley principles are:–

1. Fast replenishment at the turnround by changing trolleys.

2. Easier cleaning and maintenance of the galley areas.

3. The flexibility of food standards by using different

The Retired Executive's car Powered by cast-off Vice Presidents and equipped with a continuous relayed board-room discussion of most acceptable character.

The 'Playboy' Special. Comes with twirled martini-glass steering, romance moonset with dimmerswitch, built-in bunny, and other pleasing features.

Figure 9.6. Cartoons by Rowland Emett used in aircraft interiors by British Airways.
© Emett

trolleys.

4.   The principle of satellite pantry working can be used.

This means that the trolleys have a special mushroom type locking capability at the floor which can be located in the door areas in flight, and in gangway positions while passengers are seated for the meal.   This gives more time for the cabin staff to serve the passengers without continually running back and forth to the pantry area and makes for a much more friendly and happier working atmosphere.

Coffee machines are provided on the aircraft to dispense good coffee quickly and effectively, thus obviating the need to carry large containers as we did in the past.   This is, in itself, a big improvement in the work load and service standard.

The trolleys themselves have required considerable design and development effort to bring them to their present standard of serviceability.   They are double ended, have six wheels, automatic hand brakes, and a foot pedal to release and engage the mushroom floor locking.

We make a feature of the colour and design of these trolleys which are on show continually to the passengers.   By using

Figure 9.7. TriStar aft lavatories.

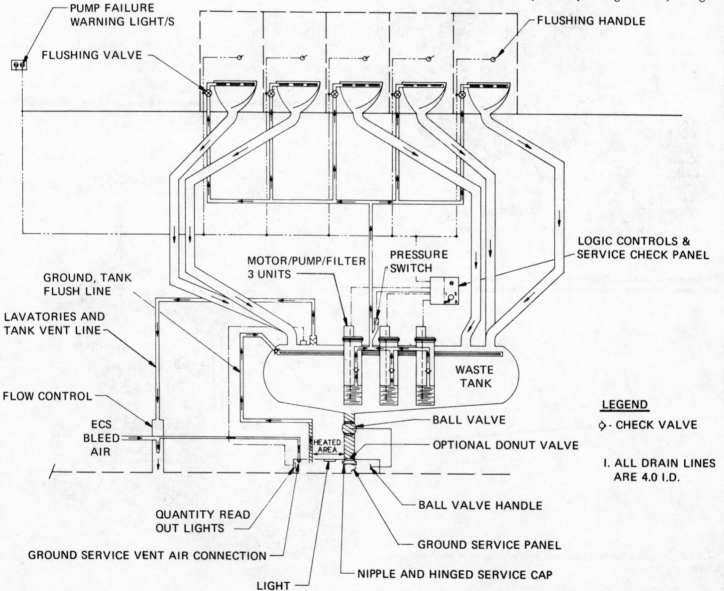

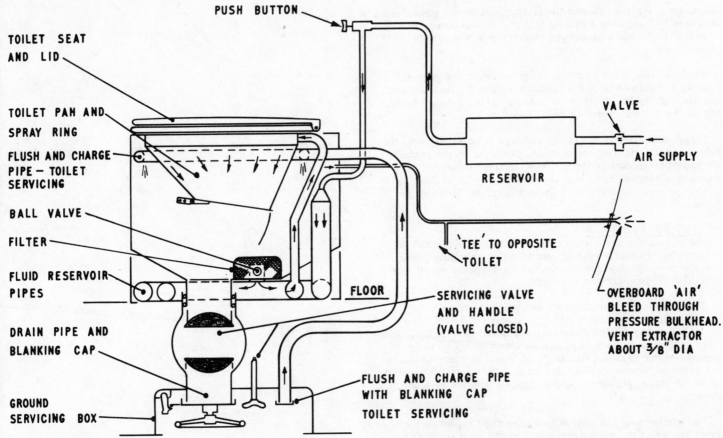

PUSH BUTTON

TOILET SEAT
AND LID

TOILET PAN AND
SPRAY RING

FLUSH AND CHARGE
PIPE — TOILET
SERVICING

BALL VALVE

FILTER

FLUID RESERVOIR
PIPES

DRAIN PIPE AND
BLANKING CAP

GROUND
SERVICING BOX

VALVE

AIR SUPPLY

RESERVOIR

FLOOR

'TEE' TO OPPOSITE
TOILET

SERVICING VALVE
AND HANDLE
(VALVE CLOSED)

OVERBOARD 'AIR'
BLEED THROUGH
PRESSURE BULKHEAD.
VENT EXTRACTOR
ABOUT 3/8" DIA

FLUSH AND CHARGE PIPE
WITH BLANKING CAP
TOILET SERVICING

Figure 9.8. Functional diagram — Toilet closet.

different colours to designate the type of trolley used for waste, the bar, or, for food etc. we find it a great help to the kitchen and cabin staff.

I believe that internationally there can be more rationalisation of catering equipment while still accepting progress. There is no point in competing in size of equipment, provided the passengers' requirements are met for the particular service.

7. TOILETS (See Figures 9.7. and 9.8.)
Some of the present fleet of aircraft have a toilet system of our own development which is shown on Figure 9.8.

Figure 9.7. shows the sophistication we are now involved in with the new large aircraft with triple electric pumps, revolving filters, and cross-feed to five toilets at the rear, with warning systems on the flight deck.

8. BAGGAGE HANDLING
Every air traveller now knows the old joke - "I left my heart in San Francisco, but my baggage is still in Instanbul".

Ground baggage handling, in fact, still remains a large problem with the airlines.

If you consider whether the aircraft should be tailored to suit the size of airport and local government requirements, or, whether you should allow aircraft to evolve freely, it must be agreed that standardisation would simply be stagnation and you have to go for progress.

Very few airports in the world would ever have accepted the Boeing 747 with its 500 passengers if they were in charge of the aircraft design; the aeroplane is the only form of transport which can transcend all land, sea, and national barriers. Thus, aircraft ground handling is being developed to a maximum degree to load and unload passengers and baggage as quickly as possible. Our TriStars are equipped with the capacity to carry a total of 16 containers; each container weighs 300 lb. and can take 3,200 lb. maximum of baggage. Eight are normally used for baggage and eight for cargo.

The in-plane loading system can unload the total baggage for 400 passengers to outside the aircraft in 4 minutes. A specially developed ground handling lifting device is attached to the aircraft and the containers are loaded onto a train of small, swivelling, bed trolleys, which takes them to the

buildings.   Having reached the buildings, the containers are
unloaded by hand onto a moving belt system and thence to a
carousel in the main passenger lounge for pick up by the
passengers.

There is still much room for improvement in the ground
loading and unloading of the containers, but it is evident that
the aircraft design itself is not being restricted by the building on the ground, which is as it should be.

Larger and more frequent aircraft are to be expected in the
future, which will require matching facilities on the ground.
To show how seriously the airlines consider the speed of
passenger baggage handling, the weight of in-plane loading
system is approximately 1600 lb. per aircraft for baggage
alone.

9. THE FUTURE TASK

The popularity of the twin aisle layout of the wide bodied
aircraft is now fairly established with the travelling public
and the lower seat kilometre cost of the larger aircraft has
established them with the operators.

Standards of comfort, decor, and galley service have
steadily risen whilst the costs to passengers in real money
terms (after off-setting financial escalation) have fallen.
This reduction in yield requires the interior design to be
capable of the maximum flexibility of layout in order to attain
the optimum results.   The interior facilities must be capable
of mixed class operation, long distance executive or high
density.

The airline that can best achieve the right layout on the
right routes at the right season will be the most profitable,
particularly if it can also be attractive and comfortable.
The aim of the aircraft interior designer is to keep one step
ahead, by being able to offer the commercial departments a
selection of viable and practical alternatives.

Figure 10.1. A production Leyland Titan bus in service with London Transport.

Chapter 10:

Bus Interiors — With Particular Reference to the Leyland Titan

David S. Burnicle and M. Heath

INTRODUCTION

This chapter covers the human and technical factors which have to be taken into account when designing the interior of a modern bus.

The point is made that no person is "average" so early decisions have to be made by the bus designer as to what percentage of the population he will design the bus to accommodate comfortably and safely.

Some factors which influence the passengers' comfort are connected with the mechanical specification of the vehicle such as ride comfort, noise level, floor heights, etc., other factors concern the interior layout of the body and some aspects border more on the psychological than on the physiological. For example, the selection of colour schemes where one is dealing with the less easily definable tastes of the travelling public.

The subject of vandalism is touched upon as it constitutes one of the most morale destroying aspects of the bus interior designer's work.

All the above aspects are covered against the background of the design philosophy for the new Leyland Titan double-decker which entered production in 1978. (See opposite).

THE "AVERAGE" PERSON

An omnibus is used by all types of people, it must accommodate and transport them with efficiency and comfort.

As very little of the interior of a bus can be designed to be adjustable the obvious approach would appear to be to design a bus to suit the "average" person.

But none of us is "average". We may regard ourselves as being average but a closer study will reveal considerable differences between individuals who all regard themselves as average.

A vehicle designed solely for the average person would satisfy no-one completely, indeed 50% of the population would find the vehicle virtually unusable.

We therefore have to take the ideal requirements and make compromises to achieve what is practicable and economic - a process common in engineering circles and one which ensures that engineering remains as much an art as a science.

EXTERIOR INFLUENCE

A bus interior is very much governed by its exterior. The "Dr. Who" model where the inside is larger than the outside

Figure 10.2. Population height percentiles — including shoes.

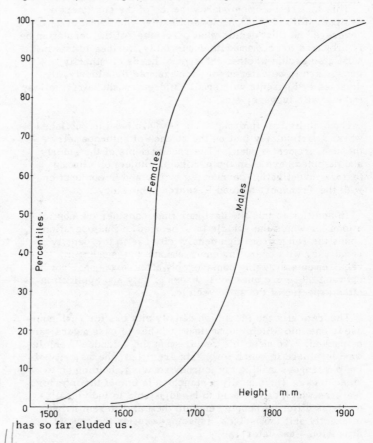

has so far eluded us.

The exterior is governed by its role as a vehicle competing for road space with the multitude of other road users. A spherically shaped bus would be ideal in that it would enclose the maximum cubic space for the minimum use of metal and glass, but unfortunately such a shape would not make best use of the limited road space available to it and would no doubt have problems of interior layout and access.

Years of evolution in matching vehicles to road space has led to the familiar cuboid shape with minor variations in proportions largely influenced by various generations of legislators.

We are therefore presented with this rectangular box to fill with people, together with a requirement to get them into it and out of it quickly and safely. It would be nice if in addition we could make their ride a pleasant one by accommodating them comfortably (and safely) and by providing them with a cheerful, relaxing environment.

All this would be relatively easy to achieve if the economics of the operating game did not demand that we have to cram into our rectangular box as many passenger spaces as possible.

INTERIOR DESIGN

This last requirement makes the job of the bus interior designer difficult.   Conscious of the fact that none of us is "average" he must decide what percentage of the population he is prepared to accommodate comfortably, further to this he must also decide whether the special needs of minority groups are to be catered for, for example the elderly, the disabled and parents with small children, pushchairs, holiday makers with luggage, etc.

Much statistical information is ready to hand in published works, particularly that on the science of anthropometry – the measurement of man.   The requirements of the elderly and disabled have been the particular subject of a human factors investigation carried out by Leyland in conjunction with the Transport & Road Research Laboratory.

In addition to this the designer must consider the applications for which the vehicle is to be used.   Bus operation spans the range from high density city use to low density rural use, with operating environments and passenger requirements differing considerably at the extremes, but in-between there are numerous shades of duty and application often expected of the same vehicle.

Theoretically the ideal high density city bus for rush hour use is one into which the maximum number of passengers can be packed.   To meet this requirement the "standee" vehicle was developed in which few seats are fitted, the majority of the passengers making the journey standing, holding on to stanchions.   Incidentally a stanchion is one of the interior features which can be said to be adjustable to individual's needs as different people can hold them at different heights to exactly suit themselves, (spacing becomes the crucial dimension – see later).

In a "standee" vehicle the only seats are situated over the wheelarches and to the rear of the vehicle.   An increase in passenger capacity of over 50% is achievable by this type of vehicle over a fully seated one, but the layout is only feasible on a single deck vehicle, and the "Cattle Truck" environment is only acceptable for very short journeys.   This class of vehicle although popular in certain continental cities has not generally met with much success in this country.

The most popular vehicle for high density city operation remains for the moment the fully seated double deck bus carrying in addition a number of standees in the lower deck gangways.

For rural low density bus service fully seated single deck buses are used.   Luggage space must be provided on these vehicles.   One day this may have to include bicycle racks also.

From this it can be seen that the maximum number of seated

passengers within the overall size is the target at which the designer must aim.   This is achieved by developing the seating plan – the layout of the seating arrangement.   This is one of the arts of the bus designer that we are endeavouring to make more scientific by the development of a computer programme which we call 'SEATSWAP'.   This programme is not yet versatile enough to warrant further mention here but it is already proving its use on some vehicle designs.

The development of the seating plan is subject to a number of influences; in addition to human factors, already mentioned, legislation and the layout of the running units have to be considered.

Legislation generally is concerned with setting minimum standards and ensuring that safety standards are met. Minimum seat sizes, spacing, gangway widths and heights, saloon heights, number and size of doors are its main concerns, suitability of details being left in the hands of the certifying officers.

The layout of the running units is dependent on the nature of the vehicle but with few exceptions the universal layout for modern double deck vehicles is to utilise a transverse vertical rear engine.

In the case of the Titan the aim was to produce a vehicle

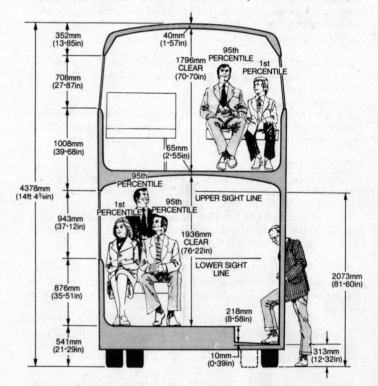

Figure 10.3. Saloon, window and step dimensions for the Titan.

which would offer the travelling public amenities well above the legal minima with consideration being given to:- step heights, floor profiles, gangway widths, general roominess, headroom, window area, ride comfort, noise level, lighting, handrail positions, driver comfort and decor.

Where possible these aspects were designed to accommodate a larger proportion of the populace than previous double deck designs.

The anthropometric sizes chosen to be covered ranged from 5th percentile giving overall heights for men of 1613 mm.(5ft. 3½ins.) and for women 1498 mm.(4ft.11ins.), to 95th percentile giving overall heights for men of 1854 mm.(6ft.2ins.) and for women 1701 mm.(5ft.7ins.). To simply accommodate only the largest people is not enough, smaller people must be considered where capacities such as reach are involved.

This design policy resulted for example in significant increases in headroom being provided and thanks chiefly to the integral construction of the vehicle these heights could still be accommodated within a normal "highbridge" overall height, giving Titan an overall height of 4378 mm.(14ft.3⅜ins.) without recourse to low profile tyres.

HEADROOMS

	Typical Previous Double Deckers	Titan
Lower Saloon		
Front	1848 mm.(6ft. 0¾ins.)	1936 mm.(6ft. 4¼ins.)
Rear	1790 mm.(5ft.10½ins.)	1902 mm.(6ft. 2⅞ins.)
Upper Saloon	1741 mm.(5ft.8 9/16ins)	1795 mm.(5ft.10 11/16 ins.)

The saloon windows were increased in height to 943 mm. in the lower saloon to enable a 95th percentile male passenger to see out without the need to stoop. The lower edge of the window was not moved as a higher waistrail would have given the passengers an "enclosed" feeling.

The statisticians tell us that in the rear of the lower saloon about 6 million people will be better off for headroom and in the upper saloon about 3.5 million people will benefit.

The large windows and the high ceiling lines contribute to providing a light and airy feeling within the saloons.

But is this enough? There is a danger that we may, with the best of intentions, be too short sighted. We can easily forget that not everyone is fit and agile and can jump on and off buses like the average commuter. We are all getting older and not all of us will be enjoying full health in our old age. The statisticians again tell us that this country has an increasing elderly population, and whilst they may still be a minority we are living in a socially conscious age and pressure groups do not allow us to forget the interests of such minorities. If we also consider that oil prices will inevitably have to increase, this elderly fixed income population will be increasingly dependent on buses. We therefore cannot and must not ignore the needs of this group - bearing in mind the lifespan of a new bus design.

At the request of the Department of the Environment an investigation of factors affecting the use of buses, by both elderly and ambulant disabled persons, was carried out by the Truck & Bus Division of British Leyland UK, who were acting as main contractors to the Transport and Road Research Laboratory. In this investigation the relevant anthropometric dimensions of one hundred elderly people, and one hundred patients with neurological and orthapaedic disabilities were recorded. The abilities of the same subjects to negotiate steps of various heights, to pull, twist and reach with their arms, were recorded together with their preferences for various seating arrangements, and hand holds.

The height of entry and exit steps seems to be the dimension that has the most daunting effect on the elderly and disabled. So particular attention has been paid to designing the entrance and exit areas to reduce boarding difficulty.

The effective use of hand holds to maintain balance is difficult for some subjects in a moving bus. The full results of the first stage of this investigation were published in June 1974 (1), the second stage has been completed and will be published shortly.

The various capacities of the subjects were compared with those of able adults to provide a realistic comparison, and some typical results are as follows:-
Almost 50% of the subjects used buses more than once a week, 19% never used buses; 86% had problems with the height of bus steps. The worst double arm span for a 5th percentile elderly female was 900 mm.(2ft.11½ins.) compared with 1114 mm.(3ft.7ins.) for an able adult.
Overhead reach for disabled, elderly or lame elderly is particularly limited.
The twist strength of one 10 year old boy exceeded that of half the female subjects.
Only 22% of the subjects could climb with ease the maximum permitted bus step height of 430 mm.(17ins.) using handrails. Without accessible handrails this was reduced to 9%.

This information was used in the interior layout of the Titan, the recommendation being followed as closely as possible.

Vertical handrails are used throughout the saloons positioned on alternate seats on each side of the gangway.

Step heights in the lower saloon have been reduced to 218 mm.(8⅝ins.) being the closest we could get to the 177 mm. (7ins.) recommended by the study. The external step height to ground is 313 mm.(12.32ins.).

Bell pushes are mounted on the stanchions so they can be operated from a sitting positon. The requirements of the other groups can be met but this is more dependent on the operator's requirements - children are generally very agile and adaptable – push chairs require a large luggage pen near the entrance door, which can be provided, if seating capacity can be sacrificed.

Given that most operators' economics will inevitably require the closest seat spacing, how else can the passenger be made to feel comfortable?

The Titan designers felt that a smooth ride was important. It may go unnoticed by the majority of passengers but in a way that was the idea – to let them relax and allow them to concentrate on their private thoughts, and not be jostled and jolted and have to concentrate on staying on the seat. The independently sprung front wheels and all round air suspension using widely spaced rolling lobe units assisted by torsion bars at

Figure 10.4. Titan independent front suspension.

the front give the bus the fine riding characteristics required.

Having given the Titan these excellent ride characteristics it had also to be made quiet on the inside to enhance the relaxing environment for which we were aiming. The target interior noise was set at 77 dB on the 'A' weighting scale but low frequency noises were not ignored and a parallel target of 85 dB on the 'C' scale is being aimed for.

We believe that low interior noise will be acclaimed by passengers, but knowing the perverseness and variety of human nature it is possible that the insulation from the hurly-burly of the outside world may accentutate the hurly-burly of their fellow passengers. This could cause more irritation than in a vehicle where the roaring of the engine and the whining of gears provides an all effacing background.

Familar sounds have a certain comfort about them and it could be that passengers in the Titan will request that some of the noise is put back in the form of piped music, or Radio 1!

One other basic aspect of passenger comfort is temperature. On a bus the doors are being opened very frequently and this places a heavy demand on the heating and ventilation system if a comfortable interior temperature is to be maintained in winter. Equally the heating system should be capable of supplying large quantities of unheated air in summer to provide adequate ventilation and prevent stuffiness.

The Titan heating system is rated at 30 Kw, which is powerful enough to achieve an interior temperature of $16^{o}C$ when the exterior ambient is $-5^{o}C$. It is a full fresh air system which provides regular air changes within the bus. The warm air is distributed through ducts at foot level in the upper and lower saloons from a central heater unit beneath the stairs. Temperature control is fully automatic, the heater units run continuously.

With all these features aimed at passenger comfort is there anything else we can do?

The large windows made the bus look different from the outside and this was further enhanced by employing a stylist to "clean up" the bus exterior by subtle alterations to curves and feature lines on the basic cuboid shape. This was considered successful as many people who were not involved with the project commented that the bus had a "new" and "different" external appearance compared with current vehicles. Excesses of fashion have to be avoided on a vehicle with a 15–plus years life expectancy. (See opposite).

The first complete prototype that was fully trimmed internally was criticised in that the interior appearance did not support the "new" look of the outside of the vehicle, or convey the impression that the passenger was aboard a vehicle which was technically advanced even though the features that gave the technical improvements were concealed "under the skin". (See opposite).

The main complaint was that once aboard the bus it looked

Figure 10.5. Titan exterior — Prototype No. 4.

Figure 10.6. First interior of a prototype Titan.

like any other bus, even though when on the move the differences became obvious.

In response to this, stylists were again called in and were briefed on the restrictions and requirements of the job. It was obvious from the start that the freedom available in the case of a car did not exist in this case, and that the styling exercise would have to be confined to a "cleaning up" of the interior, similar to that carried out on the exterior.

The first stage of the exercise was for the stylists to prepare their proposals - not all of which were practicable - in the form of art work. When this was approved the exercise moved to the next phase which included the preparation of a mock-up. (See overleaf).

The main aims of the stylists were to give the interior of the vehicle an "integrated" appearance and make features such as handrails on screens appear "built in" as opposed to "stuck on". Various colour schemes were proposed, three of which were adopted as standard options and the positioning of colour split lines was determined. Alternative seat fabrics - similar to those currently used in cars - were proposed, but

the wear and soiling characteristics of these in a bus environment were not sufficiently well known, so conventional moquettes were finally specified. (See overleaf).

One area which usually is very cluttered is the driving compartment and the header panel above the driver's windscreen. As the Titan driving compartment is based on the Leyland National very little alteration was required, but for the header panel the stylists proposed that all the "hardware" in this area - rear view mirrors, indicator winding handles, periscopes, etc. be recessed into a formed plastic panel giving a far neater appearance. (See overleaf).

All these were built into the mock-up and on receiving management approval the mock-up was exhibited to various operators for their comments.

Most of the features shown on the mock-up were then built into the 5th prototype vehicle with small modifications and will feature on production vehicles.

To recap, we have provided space, ride comfort, quietness, warmth and a clean, pleasant interior. It is said that

Figure 10.7. The interior of the mock-up built for styling development.

Figure 10.8. The interior of Prototype No. 5 incorporating revised styling features.

Figure 10.9. Final design of driver's header panel with recessed indicator handles.

good house interior decoration rapidly becomes part of the background and this has been the aim in the design of the Titan, that it too should recede into the background of the passengers' awareness.

Can more be done? How can we elevate a bus ride into more of a happening than just a mundane means of transport from A to B?

Well the scope is extremely limited when one is reminded that for urban bus travel in the UK, A and B are only 6 Km (3¾ miles) apart, (2). With this trip length of 6 Km the bus, on average, hosts a given passenger for a very short space of time; too short for television feature films, quadrophonic symphony concerts, taped language lessons, etc., etc. The designer is reduced to providing a few basic ingredients to assist the passenger to amuse himself.

On the Titan we have been careful to provide:-

- Good daytime amd night-time illumination for reading.
- Restful colour schemes.
- Large windows for looking out of, whether standing or sitting.
- High headroom to avoid discomfort to standing passengers.
- Sacrifice of some saloon spaciousness to provide advertising space on the lower saloon ceiling cove panels. This is a valuable source of revenue to the operator as well as providing something for the passengers to read (c.f. underground trains).

Unfortunately some passengers are not content to be amused by what the bus has to offer and so amuse themselves, at the operator's expense, in their own way. We are of course referring to vandalism.

Vandals may be roughly classified into two groups - the Enhancers and the Destroyers, although the latter category does seem to predominate.

Vandalism goes back I suppose to the Vandals, with a capital 'V', and archaeologists excavating Pompeii discovered graffiti scratched on the walls by the ancient Romans, so the problem is not a new one, just made a lot easier in recent times by the advent of the felt-tipped pen and the aerosol paint spray.

How can the problem be combated - at least by the bus designer? The use of modern self-coloured plastic laminates which are fairly scratch resistant is a help.

All fixing screws must be out of sight. The old adage "screw everything down" no longer applies here. A screw is a challenge to this first percentile of bus travellers.

Seats can be made vandal resistant by moulding them in glass fibre or by using moulded vulcanised fibre covers. Such seats are hard to sit on but need only be fitted in specific regions of the bus. The classic region is, of course, the rear of the upper deck of a one-man operated double decker.

We could go further by making the inside akin to a prison cell but in the end unless the vehicle is continuously "policed" by the driver or a conductor then the vandal will find a way to deface the vehicle.

One is tempted to argue for the provision of 1st and 2nd class accommodation in the vehicle but the society in which we live would perhaps rather live with the problem than have this as the cure.

So for the future the bus interior designer is faced with a dilemma. Whether to improve the quality and standard of the interior trim or instead to increase its damage resistance.

The availability of new materials will hopefully enable both to be achieved to a degree but we believe mink covered seats and velvet curtains will remain in the world of film star limousines'.

Would a bus so equipped attract any more passengers? We doubt it, but if any operator would like to try we are sure our bus interior design team would rise to the occasion.

REFERENCES
1. BROOKS, B.M., RUFFELL-SMITH, H.P., WARD, J.S. An Investigation of Factors Affecting the Use of Buses by Both Elderly and Ambulant Disabled Persons. Transport & Road Research Laboratory Contract Report; British Leyland UK Limited.

2. D.O.E. National Travel Survey 1972/3.

Chapter 11:

Inter-City Trains

James S. Cousins

INTRODUCTION

The greater part of the railway system in Great Britain was built in the forty years from 1830 to 1870 with steel rails replacing iron from 1870. The first railway telegraph system was installed on the Great Western between Paddington and Slough in 1842 – the first serious use of such a system.

The annual consumption of iron to provide the rails was soon in excess of the total national output before railways started. The effect on the national economy in building, engineering and in development of new technology, quite apart from the opening up of new sites for industry and housing, must have been relatively greater than the "spin-off" from the American Space Programme. Before the introduction of railways there was not even any accurate time-keeping between different parts of the country.

The grouping of the many railway companies of Great Britain under the provision of the Railway Act of 1921 took effect in January 1923. Of the four newly formed group companies, only one, the Great Western Railway maintained its original name. The route has retained its importance today in the introduction of British Rail's Inter-City 125 service, the world's fastest diesels, providing higher average speeds than any other railway in Europe between certain stations as part of a day to day timetable.

THE WORLD'S FIRST EXPRESS TRAINS

Five hours as a journey time from London to Exeter might still seem reasonable to a motorist with experience of being trapped in holiday traffic jams on the new motorway into Devon – and yet this is the time recorded for the distance by Daniel Gooch driving an Actaeon Engine with six carriages on the opening of the line between London and Exeter on the 1st May 1844. Daniel Gooch also records in his diary – "On the return journey we left Exeter at 5.20 p.m. and stopped at the Paddington platform at ten. Sir Thomas Acland, who was with us went at once to the House of Commons and by half past ten got up and told the House that he had been in Exeter at 5.20 p.m. .... the distance was 195 miles – a speed at 41.785 m.p.h."

In 1844 the impact of being able to achieve this journey time when compared with any other then available forms of transport, must have been even more dramatic than the reduction in space and time achieved by Concorde today. Indeed, Isambard Kingdom Brunel had the vision to conceive an Inter-City link between London and New York by the Great Western Railway, and built the SS Great Western to journey direct from London to New York by train and ship. Launched in July 1837, by 1839 it was the fastest ship in the Atlantic run, taking 16.12 days on the outward journey and 13.9 on the return.

Unfortunately this ship was out of service by the time the Great Western Railway was finally completed but the SS Great Britain launched at Bristol in July 1843 completed the link. Subsequently in 1909 the Cunard Liner "Mauretania" provided this link from the GWR port of Fishguard and the GWR ran special express trains to Dover for the Continental link.

It was also Daniel Gooch who took Prince Albert by train to the launching of the SS Great Britain at Bristol. In his diary, he describes her as a "Monster ship" and records the return train journey time from Bristol to London with the Prince on board as being two hours and four minutes, approaching a mile a minute, and remarked with some pride "Few runs have been made as quick as this ever since over so long a distance".

Such speeds by the 1850's must have been well established and alarmed Queen Victoria, who caused her Equerry, the Hon. Alexander Gordon, to write on the eve of a contemplated Royal Railway journey in August 1852 as follows.

> "I am desired to intimate Her Majesty's wish that the speed of the Royal Train on the 30th and 31st should on no account be increased at any one part of the line in order to make up for time lost by an unforeseen delay at another, so that if any unexpected delay does take place, no attempt is to be made to retain time by travelling faster than what has been agreed upon in the Time Bill you have sent me. This order has probably arisen from one of the Directors telling Her Majesty last year that they had been driving a train at the rate of 60 miles an hour, a gratuitous piece of information which very naturally alarmed Her Majesty although it was probably incorrect.
>
> I have to request that you will communicate Her Majesty's wishes to the Secretaries of the other Railways concerned."

Speed has been a cornerstone of Railway Marketing policy since their introduction and has reached present day fulfillment in the High Speed Train Inter-City 125, running over the Great Western Railway that Isambard Kingdom Brunel and Sir Daniel Gooch created. The Works at Swindon first came into operation on Monday the 2nd January 1843 and are still in use.

COMFORT AND CLASS

Conditions under which passengers were prepared to travel in the early days of railways are illustrated by an advertisement of the London and Birmingham Railway when it opened for business at Euston in 1837 – it read:

> "First class coaches (per compartment) carry six passengers inside and each seat is numbered. Second class coaches carry eight passengers inside and are covered but without lining

cushions or divisions and the seats are not numbered. Third class coaches carry four passengers on each seat and are without covering".

The prospect of third class travel at 40 m.p.h. in an open carriage on a wooden bench on a wet winter's day suggested considerable scope for improvement in passenger environment. Marketing policy on class still maintains certain differentials in comfort related to cost of travel on railways in the U.K. and it is perhaps encouraging to note that last year internal airlines in the Soviet Union are reported to have introduced first class seats and service - making some Soviet passengers more equal than others.

British Rail improvements in passenger environment in the latest Inter-City HST and Mk III Rolling Stock where coach construction, air conditioning, carpets etc. are standard in both classes, have reduced the difference in passenger comfort to elbow room in the seating arrangements and colour treatments in the interior.

For more than 100 years since their inception, railways held a monopoly in comfort, convenience, safety and speed. There is such romance and nostalgia for the long gone days of steam that an industry in catering for public interest in railway history exists. It is perhaps not generally realised that before World War II the railways pioneered U.K. Inter-City air routes with the Railway Air Services and more recently British Rail pioneered the large cross-channel Hovercraft the SRN4. The stretched version of these craft will carry 418 passengers and 60 vehicles.

THE RAILWAY BUSINESS - 1977 - 78

Every working day, British Rail provides 18,500 passenger trains, linking more than 2,300 stations. In 1976 these services catered for 708 million passenger journeys representing 17,800 million passenger miles. More than one third of this total mileage was accounted for by users of reduced fare tickets, apart from seasons, and about one third by season ticket holders leaving 5,800 million passenger miles at full ordinary fares. Of the 1976 total of just over £505 million paid in passenger fares, £52,590,000 came from first class ticket holders. (Figures published in May 1977 B.R. Annual Report).

Figures in 1977 suggest a 4% increase in passenger miles. Compared with motoring costs, the B.R. passenger can benefit from fares pitched at a very low average rate per mile.

Rail travel rate per mile	Jan. 1978 Average
Full fare	4.6p
Reduced fare	3.1p
Season ticket	3.0p
Average (all costs)	3.5p

The running cost per mile of the average family car (1,500 c.c.) covering 10,000 miles a year with petrol at 78p per gallon is currently 12.66p (AA Estimate). Even with the increase in fares from the 8th January 1978 - after a freeze

on fares for a full year - rail travel represents value for money.

INTER-CITY

Inter-City as a name and marketing concept was introduced by British Rail in 1951. At that time it was just one express train between London, Paddington and Wolverhampton known as "The Inter-City". The name is now applied to a national network linking more than 200 towns and cities with 1,800 trains each weekday. Although little more than one seventh of B.R. passenger journeys - 106 million - were attributable to Inter-City, in 1976 no less than 8,400 million passenger miles, almost half the B.R. total, were generated by Inter-City trains, representing fully half B.R. revenue from fares. Railways of other countries have copied British Rail in describing principal express trains as "Inter-City", including Germany and Holland.

Among the fastest trains in the world are those linking London Paddington, Bristol, Weston-super-Mare and South Wales. These Inter-City 125 trains are the world's fastest diesels and provide average speeds higher than any other railway in Europe between certain stations. More important than the high average speeds - around 98 to 100 m.p.h. in several cases - is the fact that these are the only trains in the world to provide such speeds as part of the normal day-to-day timetable at reduced fares for both second and first class ticket holders on a normal railway shared by local passenger trains and freight services. In Japan, top speeds of 125 m.p.h. or more are available only on the specialised "bullet" lines which have been newly built and carry no other trains (ordinary services remaining on their existing lines). In France these speeds are generally provided by first class supplementary fare trains and second class ticket holders who do not wish to pay an extra charge must travel on slower trains. On British Rail, first and second class carriages are provided with full air conditioning and comparable standards of environmental design, and Britain's concept of 125 m.p.h. comfort is to be extended to other routes, still with the principle that both classes should be available and cut price fares remain.

Passenger business on the London-Bristol/South Wales routes has risen by up to 20 per cent since the full Inter-City 125 timetable with more than 90 services a day has been in operation. Examples of journey time benefits are a cut in best times from London to Bristol from 1 hr 47 m to 1 hr 25 m and Cardiff from 2 hr 16 m to 1 hr 45 m. Trains timed at up to 125 m.p.h. leave Paddington station in London three times every hour - 15 minutes past to Swansea, 20 minutes past to Bristol, 45 minutes past each hour for intermediate halts from Slough outwards. Next 125 route is London Kings Cross - Newcastle - Edinburgh, with limited timings at this maximum from the 8th May 1978 and full timetable from May 1979. The preliminary 125 m.p.h. timings in May 1978 will cut the time of The Flying Scotsman from 5 hr 27 m to 4 hr 52 m for 393 miles between London Kings Cross and Edinburgh. This represents a steady improvement from the seven hours two minutes which applied in 1962. The full 1979 timings will trim London/Edinburgh still further to

Figure 11.1. Inter-City 125 High Speed Train (HST).

4 hr 30 m with other times such as London/Newcastle in 2 hr 55 m, London/Leeds 2 hr 13 m, and London/York in just over two hours.   Aberdeen at 7 hr 29 m will be as close to London as Edinburgh was twenty years ago.

In 1978 more Inter-City 125 trains are due to start between London Paddington and the West Country – Plymouth and Penzance.   Others are due to follow, mainly on the North East/ South West route linking such centres as Newcastle, Darlington, Leeds, Sheffield, Derby, Manchester and Birmingham with Cardiff, Britol, Exeter, Southampton, Bournemouth, Plymouth and Penzance.   On the London Euston/Glasgow line, where journey times came down from a best of about six hours to five hours in 1974 for 400 miles following electrification, the maximum speed will be stepped up in 1979 from 100 m.p.h. to 125 m.p.h. when the first passenger carrying Advanced Passenger

Trains start schedules of little more than four hours between cities.

The main APT advantage is in rounding curves at higher speeds than conventional trains.   At present speed is restricted for passenger comfort, not safety, on bends.   The APT tilt mechanism builds the banking into the train as well as the curve, thus allowing faster journeys without discomfort.

The London/Glasgow route has been chosen for the electric APTs because apart from the fact that the route is already electric, the cornering abilities of the new trains will have maximum advantage due to the curvaceous nature of the line. A conventional 125 m.p.h. train would save only ten minutes between London and Glasgow but an APT will save up to one hour at 125 m.p.h. maxima without any major track alterations. London/Bristol and South Wales and London/Edinburgh lines, on the other hand, have long fast stretches where the 125 m.p.h. capability of the more conventional Inter-City diesel sets can be exploited to the full with only a limited need to slow down on curves.

Years of research have gone into the development of both types of train. As part of testing programmes, the prototype Inter-City 125 or high speed diesel train as it was known at the time, achieved a world diesel record on rails of 143 m.p.h. on the 12th June 1973 between Darlington and York, and on the 10th Agust 1975 the experimental gas turbine version of the Advanced Passenger Train reached 152 m.p.h. near Didcot - a British record.

The foregoing is by way of introduction to the railway business and if we take as an example the Inter-City 125 service to Bristol, it is interesting to recall that the Great Western Railway officially began in August 1835 with a proposal to build one double line from Bristol to London for the benefit of the merchant community - it succeeded.

INDUSTRIAL DESIGN

The particular interest of the British Railways Board Design Panel and the Industrial Design Department is of more recent origin.

Competition from other forms of transport made it a commercial necessity that railways offer standards of comfort and design which at least equal those offered by air and road and also match in presentation the promotion of a modern image of Inter-City rail travel. It was an awareness of this need that led, in 1956, to the establishment by the British Transport Commission of the (now) British Railways Board Design Panel, whose remit is expressed as being "Concerned with the aesthetic and amenity design, both internal and external of such fixed and moveable equipment as is widely used by the Board's passengers, customers and staff, or is prominently visible to them or the general public".

Since its inception the Board's design panel has been able to contribute to improved design standards over a wide field which includes locomotives, the development of the Pullman trains, both diesel and electric, the Glasgow suburban electric stock, the XP64 train, the Mk III carriage, the HST and the Advanced Passenger Train. To this end the design

panel through the Industrial Design Department has retained the services of outside design consultants on specific projects and has established a small staff of industrial designers who work in close association with the Chief Mechanical and Electrical Engineer of the Board and the Research Department on new rolling stock.

BLUE PULLMAN AND NEW PULLMAN ELECTRIC STOCK

One major contribution to the modern design of rolling stock was the introduction of the new Blue Pullman vehicles in 1959. Much of the design character of these including the form of seating was assimilated into the present standard first-class open air-conditioned stock to the extent that the build of the MkIIC carriages is comparable with the Pullman vehicles in terms of passenger amenity. The Board's Design Panel retained the services of Jack Howe, RDI, FSIA, on the original Pullman car design; the Blue Pullman, now retired from service, was an example of a totally integrated design concept in which collaboration between the Board's engineers and consultant designers was fully realised.

In the major electrification programme on the London Midland Region, the appearance design of the AL6 electric locomotive benefited from the association of the design engineers with the late Professor Sir Misha Black of Design Research Unit - the design consultants originally retained by the design panel to advise on the proposals for a now corporate identity in livery application to rolling stock now applied throughout the system. A number of leading designers were involved in the appearance design of new locomotives and in the development of the XP64 train which introduced new standards of seating and interior environment into subsequent builds of Mk II carriages.

MK III CARRIAGES AND HST (HIGH SPEED TRAINS)

The greatest improvements in passenger comfort in Inter-City routes has resulted from the introduction of a new carriage, the Mk III. This is the current standard carriage on both locomotive routes and with the HST Inter-City 125 train routes. To facilitate standardisation and the resulting

Figure 11.2. Internal view of Mk IIIa first class coach as used in the High Speed Train.

Figure 11.3. Internal view of Mk IIIa second class coach as used in the High Speed Train.

economies in construction, the coach is of identical body structure relative to window sizes and door position for both first and second class.

The interior of the carriage is fitted out with modular components in the form of ceiling panels and lighting, luggage racks, window trim, bodyside panels etc. and with seating tracks to allow changes in seating configuration against a change in commercial requirements. A new seat design originally introduced into Mk II stock is also used in this carriage. Further economies were effected by an increase in coach length to 74 feet against the 66 feet of the Mk II carriage.

Coaches are fully air conditioned on first and second classes. While improvements in luggage space at the vestibule ends by replanning lavatory accommodation had been achieved in the Mk II E carriages, the Mk III also made use of automatically opening interior vestibule doors. High speed trains, which make use of the Mk III carriage also incorporate new design of catering vehicles based on the Mk III body design.

Proposals are also in hand for new air conditioned Mk III sleepers. The flexibility of the concept is illustrated by the adaptation of two existing standard Mk III carriages to provide the two new Saloons for the Royal Train which entered service in 1977.

The industrial design contribution to passenger environment in the new stock was realised through the development of sketches, models, and full-sized mock-ups on which the production details were based.

THE APT - ADVANCED PASSENGER TRAIN

A quite separate but parallel design exercise has been undertaken in the development over the past eleven years of the Advanced Passenger Train. The introduction of a 9° tilt to facilitate cornering at speed with the new suspension system and higher speeds produces a different cross-section to the HST. Reductions in weight have been achieved by the use of light-weight materials and the illustrations show the final mock-up proposals and exterior model that form the basis of the three prototype trains now completed for trials and introduction into service between London and Glasgow.

In this context the interior environment has been based on a similar component based interior configuration but weight, dimensions, vestibule arrangement etc. have necessitated a different design approach with new seats and interior finishes. The objective of the design of the APT is to provide fast operation around curves with the tilt mechanism compensating for the effect of centrifugal force. The train has been designed

Figure 11.4. Electric powered Advanced Passenger Train (APT) 1978.

for a maximum speed of 250 km. per hour. The energy consumption of the train should be two thirds that of a conventional train due to the aerodynamic efficiency of the train and lighter weight.

From the railway business point of view the Inter-City objectives of the APT in relation to existing trains are:

1. A 50% higher maximum speed.
2. Ability to operate at that speed over existing track with existing signalling.
3. High standards of passenger comfort.
4. Efficient energy consumption combined with low noise level.
5. An operating cost per seat similar to existing trains.

Detailed technical specifications of both trains are of course available, but from the passenger point of view, where journey time is of fundamental importance, the fully developed network of HST and APT trains show how competitive railways will be with the journey times offered by inter-city airlines, which require surface links to city centres from the airport.

CORPORATE IDENTITY FOR BRITISH RAIL

The appearance of trains has historically always been enhanced by the livery applied to locomotives and carriages. Railway companies had been identified by their distinctive liveries since the early 1840's. In 1922, immediately prior to the grouping into the four Main Line Companies, there existed 27 Main Companies with 94 subsidiary ones. All the larger Companies and many of the smaller ones, had their distinctive liveries and crests. These were, broadly speaking, absorbed into the four Main Line Companies' livery schemes which existed only for a period of 25 years until nationalisation in 1948. Subsequently, other variations appeared. In 1964, 16 years after nationalisation, the British Railways Board approved a plan for one corporate identity for the whole transport system.

Preliminary studies for this were commenced in 1963, and a Steering Committee appointed, whose job it was, through the Board's Design Panel, to make recommendations for an overall scheme, with proposals for its implementation. These proposals, which included versions of the symbol, namestyle and new alphabet, together with examples of the house style applied to stations, ships, rolling stock, etc., were agreed by the Board in November 1964, and priorities were laid down. First applications were to advertising and printed publicity material.

The scheme was launched in January 1965, to coincide with a public exhibition held at the Design Centre, London, announcing the new proposals against the background of overall modernisation of the Railways. Later that year the first part of the Corporate Identity Manual was issued. This defined the basic elements of symbol, logotype, lettering and colour, and gave directions for their use in applications to printed publicity, signposting and station fascias.

A second part of the Manual, issued in 1966, dealt with further applications of the elements to rolling stock, ships and small items such as a new house flag and letterheads. It contained further detailed information on signposting and notices, and publicity material. The Manual now runs into four volumes and all major areas of implementation have, as far as can be seen, now been touched on. Uniforms have been included and standards have been laid down for stationery, posters, timetables, linen, etc. Special services, such as Inter-City, Motorail, Accident Prevention, etc. are given individual identification within the corporate image, as are the 'Sealink' Shipping Services and the 'Seaspeed' Hovercraft. A separate house style for the rail catering services, now known as 'Travellers-Fare', compatible with British Rail's overall image, has been evolved.

The Corporate Identity Steering Committee meets regularly to advise on specific applications, to deal with any problems of implementation and to offer help wherever it is seen to be required.

British Rail is one of the largest undertakings in the world to have attempted a complete change of its public face, and a great deal has been achieved since the inception of the scheme; but an organisation like British Rail is always and inevitably moving with the times, changing and developing. New services are introduced which require to be fitted into the overall framework of the corporate identity so that all are clearly seen to belong to one establishment. The flexibility of the Board's corporate image is such that it can readily be adapted to changing circumstances and requirements.

Figure 11.5. Electric APT showing revised British Rail livery and special logo.

One example of this is the decision to change the now traditional grey/blue livery – well established on Inter-City routes, for the introduction of the APT.

British Rail's corporate design policy does, of course, extend to other forms of transport providing Inter-City links; Sealink, the cross-Channel ferry service and Seaspeed, the faster hovercraft link, both provide routes from London to the Continent.

While much of British Rail Rolling Stock will continue to operate to the end of the century and beyond, replacement locomotives, wagons and diesel multiple units will be required in the 1980's. The Railways Research and Development Division have a continuing interest in improvements in existing railway technology and in innovation. Magnetic levitation is under consideration and has potential for future development.

Improvements in performance and passenger environment in new rolling stock are self evident. Continuing research and development and innovation will ensure that the railways remain competitive with other forms of transport.

The High Speed Train takes BR to the limits of conventional technology, and it is therefore a logical development to introduce these train-sets on routes where the impact of new rolling stock, with accelerated schedules, will be greatest in terms of increased business. Part of the railway's philosophy is to introduce new stock on to the prime Inter-City routes every 5 – 10 years, and "cascade" the displaced stock on to other Inter-City routes, thereby achieving product improvement over the whole range of services.

1978 saw the introduction of HSTs on the East Coast Main Line, with a full service in 1979, and further trains are being built for London to West of England services in 1980.

Cross-country routes benefit next with High Speed Trains in 1981/82 on routes from the North East and North West to the South West, South Wales and the South coast.

The following table shows the improvement in journey time which the introduction of a full Inter-City 125 service brings:-

	Pre-HST	Post-HST	Improvement in journey time
London–Bristol	1hr 47	1hr 25	22 mins.
London–Cardiff	2hrs 16	1hr 45	31 mins.
London–Leeds	2hrs 31	2hrs 11	20 mins.
London–Newcastle	3hrs 33	2hrs 55	38 mins.
London–Edinburgh	5hrs 30	4hrs 30	60 mins.
London–Exeter	2hrs 34	1hr 58	36 mins.
London–Plymouth	3hrs 42	2hrs 59	43 mins.
Newcastle–Bristol	5hrs 27	4hrs 27	60 mins.
Liverpool–Southampton	5hrs	5hrs 33	27 mins.
Manchester–Plymouth	6hrs 02	5hrs 24	38 mins.
Leeds–Cardiff	4hrs 37	3hrs 44	53 mins.

ADVANCED PASSENGER TRAIN

The High Speed Train raises average speeds to 90 m.p.h., but it is on the straighter routes where the train is at its best. On the routes where there are a large number of curves, such as the West Coast Main Line, only new technology can achieve further large reductions in journey time.

This will be fulfilled in the '80's by the Advanced Passenger Train (APT), which is built with tilting bodies to the coaches, enabling them to take curves significantly faster than existing trains, without any discomfort to the passenger. With APT, the throughout time between London and Glasgow will be reduced from 5 hours to just over 4, and significant journey time reductions will also be achieved between London, Liverpool and Manchester. Average speeds will then be raised to 100 m.p.h., due to the need for less braking and acceleration into and out of tight curves.

Figure 11.6. Mock-up of interior of APT coach showing toilet facilities and vestibule.

Figure 11.7. Interior of second class APT coach.

Figure 11.8. Internal view of driver's cab of electric Advanced Passenger Train(1978).

Part 4 Discussion:

Case Studies — Vehicle Design

Chairman: H. G. Conway

D.R. VERNON (Greater Manchester Transport) There are one or two points on which I would ask Mr. Burnicle to comment.

In previous rear-engined buses the lower deck rear seat has been uncomfortable and often very hot. I wonder if you will be able to do anything about this on the new Titan bus.

Secondly, heaters and demisters have been an emotive issue with our staffs. I wonder whether this equipment has been tested rigorously enough on the Titan to avoid this problem. The main complaints seem to involve the driving position and you might consider placing a heater under the driver's seat.

D.S. BURNICLE (Leyland Vehicles Limited) In previous double deck vehicles the heater has been situated under the rear seat, and of course there is bound to be a concentration of heat around the unit. In the Titan it is placed under the staircase, and there is very little equipment emitting heat under the rear seat box. In addition, there is much noise insulating – and therefore heat insulating–material between engine compartment and lower saloon, so that the problem is solved.

With reference to the driver's compartment, there is a separate heating and demisting unit under the driver's control. You will notice that the driver's compartment door extends down to the floor, so that he can generate any required environment in his little cubicle.

MIRIAM HOWITT (Architect and Designer) Having appreciated greatly the mechanical qualities of the Titan, I was jolted rudely by Mr. Burnicle's questions which referred to an illustration of a plushy interior extravaganza: "Is that how you want the bus to look, or do you want it to arrive on time and not care how the interior looks?" he asked. Those just did not seem to be the only two alternatives available. There seemed to be a third - that the bus not only could have an interior as handsome as the Advanced Passenger Train or the latest aircraft, but also could function efficiently. I know that you will probably respond that these options cost more, but I feel that design also plays a part in this.

D.S. BURNICLE (Leyland Vehicles Limited) I am very pleased to hear that, because I feel that the design features incorporated will guarantee both reliability in service - arriving on time - and an attractive interior appearance.

I was, I suppose, asking whether we should go any further, or has the law of diminishing returns set in.

MIRIAM HOWITT (Architect and Designer) My feeling is that, in interior design, buses are where the railways were twenty years ago.

D.S. BURNICLE (Leyland Vehicles Limited) When comparing interior design features of the British Rail Mk III coach, the Boeing JETFOIL and the Leyland Titan bus one must remember the wide gulf in prices of these vehicles, and the levels of passenger carrying markets at which they are aimed.

H.G. CONWAY (Deputy Chairman, Engineering Design Advisory Committee, Design Council) Both the aircraft and the railway industries utilise industrial engineers, while the automobile industry employs stylists. Is there a point perhaps there?

M. HEATH (Leyland Vehicles Limited) The main difference between designing cars and buses is that cars tend to follow fashion while buses, due to their 15 – 20 year lifespan, demand a style which will not age too rapidly.

The "stylists" involved in the Titan project recognised this and restricted their ideas. It would be interesting to define fully the terms "stylist" and "industrial designer".

K. GRANGE (Pentagram Design) I am very concerned about passenger comfort in aircraft. My concern is strictly not connected with the way you detail the aircraft, but relates more to the general level of hysteria generated by the whole travel system.

For instance, the very simple ticket purchase system by rail compares so favourably with the complications of multiple tickets and documentation at airports.

It also concerns me greatly that discussion of passenger comfort always seems to focus on the seat and interior decor; rather it should be concerned with the apparent tendency of the system to produce lack of peace of mind on boarding the aircraft. I consider that this is a very important point.

Mr. Molony omitted a feature which I consider to be one of the most important for air passengers - namely the fitting of lockable overhead luggage compartments. That is one of those little benefits which do so much to make a flight more comfortable.

G. MOLONY (British Airways) We have introduced luggage lockers, albeit not lockable since they need to be opened and shut rather quickly. We have these in most of our aircraft now and are introducing compartment doors on some of our earlier aircraft.

With regard to the tickets, I can only thoroughly agree with you. The computer systems now being used will tend to reduce the workload, but the majority of information on the ticket is required for international accounting and legal

requirements, the ticket being used in many countries.
There is little scope for reducing the size further.

H.G. CONWAY (Deputy Chairman, Engineering Design
Advisory Committee, Design Council) I suspect that at least
you can buy an airline ticket with a Diners or an American
Express Card.   But try and buy a British Rail ticket with
one!. It cannot be done, except with an Access or Barclay-
card.

J.A. NISBET (Greater Glasgow Passenger Transport
Executive) With reference to Mr. Burnicle's point about buses
arriving on time, I wonder whether all the design effort
invested in the Titan really will make buses arrive on time?
We have tended to overlook the development taking place in
area traffic control and in radio control for buses, which will
give the bus operator much better control.   It will also ease
the bus industry's difficulties in communicating with
passengers in the event of service disruptions.

   Does Mr. Burnicle think the Titan is the full answer?

D.S. BURNICLE (Leyland Vehicles Limited) Well, of course,
it is not.   It is only one part of a whole transport system,
indeed quite a minor part when it comes to making a bus
arrive on time.

   I am very pleased to hear of the other activities which are
going to help.

RACHEL WATERHOUSE (Loughborough University of
Technology, Institute of Consumer Ergonomics) The luggage
area in the Titan, which covers the heating element, is in
fact very small.   In the buses which I know, the luggage
area stretches right down to the floor, and this is important
for example if you have a folding push chair.   In addition,
the sideways seats at the front of the staircase have foot
rests, because they are too high.   This reduces the area for
people walking into the bus.   Presumably here is another
conflict between the 'guts' of the bus and the passenger
seating area.

   Were both of these problems unavoidable?

D.S. BURNICLE (Leyland Vehicles Limited) The two-door
Titan described has a front entrance and centre exit.   The
single-door versions have a much larger luggage compartment
instead of the longitudinal seating beside the front door.

   You are right that the luggage compartment does not extend
to the floor on the Titan.   But it is not very high.   It is
quite possible to have an alternative luggage compartment on
the other side, but this means a loss of seats, of course.
This is one of the problems of that particular layout.   There
is an alternative forward position for the staircase.

   There are several variations on this layout, one of which
completely eliminates the footstools, but then of course you
cannot have seats there.

Conclusions

Roy Cresswell

"Design for Passenger Transport" explored the ways in which the design of passenger transport systems might be improved to enhance, in particular, their attractiveness to existing and potential users.

Six main themes emerged from the Conference:

1. INTERCHANGE DESIGN

There were pleas for passenger transport interchanges to be of better quality in design, and to be more exciting, perhaps incorporating some of the better concepts of present-day architecture and urban design. It was suggested that more entertainment facilities might be provided at airports and other major interchanges. At a more mundane level, higher standards must also be set for smaller bus stations and other elements of transport infrastructure.

2. INFORMATION SYSTEMS

The provision of adequate and well-designed information systems was considered to be a great necessity for transport operators and passengers alike. For the operator such a system provides an extension of his advertising media for the services available, and for the passenger, helps in promoting his well-being and eliminating the sense of worry or anxiety on a journey. Well designed information systems should range from time-tables to information at the entrances of the vehicles themselves. It was felt that the information systems of certain bus undertakings left something to be desired, particularly the information at bus stops and the provision of adequate indicators on the buses themselves.

3. CORPORATE IDENTITY SCHEMES

The advantages of a good corporate identity scheme for a transport undertaking were expressed. Such a scheme, covering design policy from tickets and time-tables to buses, aircraft, trains and buildings, helped to create an air of purpose, well-being and sense of caring on the part of the operator. It was shown that such programmes justified the modest financial outlay which was marginal compared with the total revenue of most transport undertakings. A good corporate identity programme helped to promote confidence in passengers and boosted morale amongst the staff.

4. OBSOLESCENCE OF EQUIPMENT

The life of transport vehicles varies from some twelve years for a bus to over thirty years for a railway coach. With these life spans, it is inevitable that a large proportion of the passengers of any transport undertaking will be travelling in vehicles which do not come up to the standards of the latest equipment. Because of this, it is necessary to adopt good design principles which do not date, and to maintain vehicles in first-class condition through regular programmes of maintenance and refurbishment.

5. SUSPENSION SYSTEMS

Case studies of trains and buses clearly showed the awareness of higher standards of passenger comfort which are now demanded. These case studies showed that the development of advanced suspension systems played an important role in the drive towards improving passenger comfort.

6. VEHICLE INTERIORS

Over recent years there has been a merging of design thought on the interiors of passenger transport vehicles. New types of seating, seat cover materials and interior lining materials have been adopted for aircraft, trains, buses (especially long-distance coaches), and sea-going vehicles. At one time the interiors of these vehicles developed along many separate lines resulting in a difference of interior environment. Today there are fundamental similarities in the interior designs of these various types of passenger vehicle. It is perhaps in this field that the greatest exchange of ideas between one mode and another has so far taken place.

As indicated by Kenneth Robinson in his Introduction, the phrase "Fitness for Purpose" pinpoints the objective for good design in passenger transport. Such good design can reduce boredom and frustration and bring a delight and enhancement to travelling. It can lead to efficiency, cleanliness and boost morale by creating an "esprit de corps" amongst the transport operators' staff. It is hoped that "Design for Passenger Transport" will inspire those concerned with passenger transport operation in all its forms to seek improvements in transport design, perhaps using techniques developed for one mode, which can be carried over successfully to another.

Index

FASHION SOURCE BOOK

FASHION
SOURCE
BOOK

AMY DE LA HAYE

A Macdonald Orbis Book

Copyright © 1988 Quarto Publishing plc

First published in Great Britain in 1988
by Macdonald & Co (Publishers) Ltd
London and Sydney

A member of Maxwell Pergamon Publishing Corporation plc

British Library Cataloguing in Publication Data
Haye, Amy de la
    Fashion sourcebook.
    1. Fashion, 1900-1987
    I. Title
    746.9'2

ISBN 0-356-15928-0

This book was designed and produced by
Quarto Publishing plc
The Old Brewery, 6 Blundell Street
London N7 9BH

Senior editor   Henrietta Wilkinson
Designer   John Grain
Picture researchers   Jan Croot, Cindy Greenslade, Joanna Wiese

Art director   Moira Clinch
Editorial director   Carolyn King

Typeset by Burbeck Associates Ltd
Manufactured in Hong Kong by Regent Publishing Services Ltd
Printed by Leefung-Asco Printers Ltd, Hong Kong

Macdonald & Co (Publishers) Ltd
Greater London House
Hampstead Road
London NW1 9QX

FOREWORD

"The glass of fashion and the
mould of form,
The observ'd of all the
observers."
— HAMLET, ACT III, SCENE 1, LINE 161

This book has aimed, within the brevity of its text, to discuss the consumption, production and retailing of fashion, and ultimately to consider garment design itself. Although the century's leading couturiers do appear, a broader analysis has also been made of the dress available to all social classes. This is in stark contrast to the majority of dress histories, which almost exclusively focus upon haute couture, and the collection policy of most museums with their emphasis on the rare and precious. This selection of the superlative too often distorts our view of history, so that we inevitably accept the images of Schiaparelli and Dior as representative of their time. In reality, couture is available to a minority only, and thus to gain a truer perspective we should also look at everyday clothing. The methods of design dissemination, from the most luxurious couture dress to the cheapest rayon one, have been discussed in the main introduction.

The bulk of this book is pictorial. While the glossy photographs of couture garments on mannequins epitomise an ideal, everyday photographs have also been used extensively to provide a balanced view. Few, if any, of these have appeared in other books. Thus they provide vital source material for the dress historian or designer and are a delight to the interested fashion consumer.

Amy de la Haye

MA (RCA)

INTRODUCTION

The Paris couture industry was founded by Charles Frederick Worth, who opened his premises at 7, rue de la Paix, Paris, in 1858. In succeeding from the generally anonymous dressmaker and tailor of the time, he was to become the first highly acclaimed designer, who dictated what his customers wore. He started his career as an apprentice to the drapery trade in London, moving to Paris at the age of 22, where he dressed his wife in clothes that he designed and made himself. His opening came when he persuaded the rich and influential Princess Pauline de Metternich, wife of the Austrian ambassador, to wear one of his garments to a ball at the Court of Napoleon III. It was much admired, and Worth was soon dressing the Empress Eugénie, Napoleon III's wife, her ladies-in-waiting and visiting members of the foreign aristocracy. He was also patronised by women of the demi-monde and the new industrial millionaires' wives, who clamoured to live and dress in the same style as those with landed wealth; the elaborate crinolines that Worth designed for these women are inseparable from the luxury and extravagance associated with the Second Empire. It is interesting, however, that although Worth became the great arbiter of

Punch cartoon, July 4, 1863, The Haunted Lady, or The Ghost in the Looking Glass. *Madame La Modiste: "We would not have disappointed your ladyship, at any sacrifice, and the robe is finished." The woman in the mirror is the exhausted dressmaker. Punch regularly highlighted the plight of clothing workers during these years.*

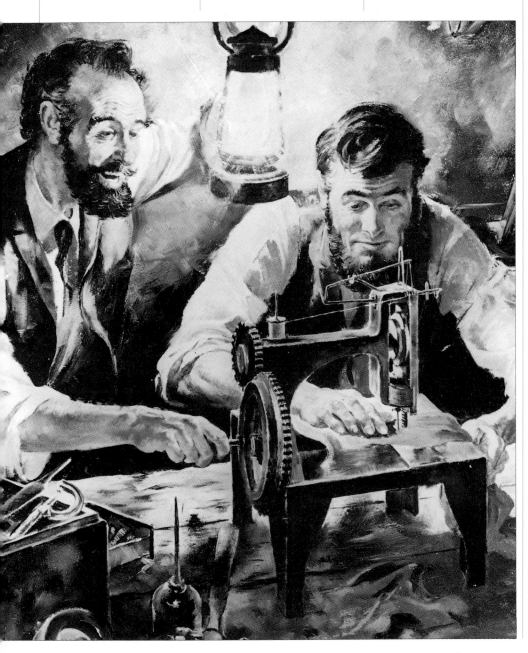

Romanticised painting of two tailors working with a Singer sewing machine. Singer became the major manufacturer of sewing machines from the mid nineteenth century onwards. The reality was appalling working conditions, long hours and pathetically low wages.

taste in dress, he did not enjoy the high social status which leading designers enjoy today. Despite the fact that fashion was widely accepted to be an art, its makers were regarded as tradespeople and did not mix socially with their customers.

Couture for the rich

The Parisian couture industry became established around Worth's premises and the neighbouring Place Vendôme (where it is located to this day), and many subsidiary but vitally important trades — such as specialist beading and embroidery workshops, and luxury ribbon- and button-makers — also surfaced to feed the burgeoning couture houses. By 1900, the most successful of these were employing up to 1,000 workers and exporting nearly two-thirds of all their model gowns. Creative talent in the form of fine artists, writers and designers had always flocked to Paris, and throughout the nineteenth and twentieth-centuries, artists and fashion designers often combined forces to achieve the most spectacular results. Among the many twentieth-century examples are the heads with long wispy hair drawn by Jean Cocteau for Schiaparelli to have embroidered onto her garments, and the magnificent costumes which Chanel designed for the Ballets Russes performance of *Le Train Bleu* in 1924.

From the days of Worth until the 1930s, Paris and fashion became synonymous, its supremacy virtually unchallenged. In part, this was due to the French government, who always encouraged the arts (including fashion) which contributed considerably to their economy: in Britain and the United States, on the other hand, this support system never existed to the same extent. American haute couture was essentially a wholesale enterprise (while French and British couture houses were retail concerns) with many of their couturiers — including Hattie Carnegie and Nettie Rosenstein — selling their fashions through department stores, such as Lord and Taylor and Bergdorf Goodman, during the 1930s. The former of these stores was particularly progressive in 1932 when it advertised dresses that were designed and made in the United States. Although many American couturiers were immensely successful, their clothes often bore the name of the store through which they were sold and the designers themselves remained anonymous. As the department stores had always promoted their allegiance with Paris, it was often implied that the designers of their clothes were all of French origin, thus reinforcing Paris's grip on fashion.

During the 1930s, Hollywood did exert some influence upon popular fashion and British couturier Norman Hartnell's clothing for royalty was widely admired. Generally, however, what was created in Paris remained the last word in fashion. Wealthy women from all over the world bought their garments from Paris, and the middle

Left
Luxurious ball gown by the House of Worth, c. 1900.

Right
Fashion plate from the American magazine Godey's, c. 1870. Bustles were very fashionable during the 1870s and 80s — although Flora Thompson's poor community did not adopt them until the 1880s, when they were considered the very latest in style.

Far right
Expensive visiting costume, 1902. At this date fashion revelled in luxury.

GODEY'S FASHIONS.

FOR DESCRIPTION SEE FASHION DEPARTMENT.

classes, unable to afford couture clothes, patronised dressmakers and department stores where they could obtain cheaper versions. Couture garments were — and indeed are today — available to only a tiny fraction of the population, perhaps less than one per cent, but while the number of these fashions was not significant, they were most important stylistically. From the 1920s onwards, their designs disseminated down to the cheapest levels of clothing.

Dress for the poor

Up until that time, fashion had been the prerogative of the rich and leisured. The limited income of, and hard daily work undertaken by, working-class women meant that their clothing had to be comfortable and durable. High fashion fulfilled neither of these requirements. Apart from the financial restrictions, a crinoline or hobble skirt would have been utterly impractical. Thus, the rather shapeless garments made from humble fabrics which these women wore clearly reflected their financial constraints. A

fashionable appearance could sometimes be achieved within communities, but these were markedly behind the styles displayed by high society. In her memoirs, Flora Thompson[1] describes how the agricultural women in the isolated hamlet in Oxfordshire, where she was brought up during the 1880s, used to roll up pieces of fabric like cushions and wear them under their frocks to give the impression of bustles — which were high fashion during the 1870s. These women were aware of fashion — albeit slightly out of date — and made what concessions they could to achieve it.

Working-class men's and children's clothing could be bought ready-made from the mid-nineteenth century, following the advent of the sewing machine, invented in the United States by Elias Howe in 1846. There had been many attempts to design a sewing machine since the middle of the eighteenth century, but Howe was the first to produce a working model. Due to the standardised nature of men's and children's clothes, manufacturers could produce them in bulk without worrying about fashion changes.

Below
A selection of particularly decorative stockings from 1880 until 1910.

Right
Fashionable woman, c. 1926. By this date the loose-fitting and simple style of fashionable clothing could be cheaply translated for the mass market.

1880 1890 1895 1900 1910

Furthermore, they had a large and assured market as few women could tailor a man's suit, although they could often make many of their children's clothes. In general, from 1900 onwards, men had just one suit which was worn for "best" and at weekends, the design of which was fairly static until after World War II. Indeed, it was not until the 1950s that the majority of men's clothing was truly influenced by fashion.

Ready-made fashion for all

The single most important development in twentieth-century dress was that fashion became widely available in the form of ready-made clothes. From the 1920s onwards many couturiers designed styles which could be worn by active, hard-working women as well as by a rich elite. In contrast to the production of men's and children's clothing, however, women's off-the-peg wear was produced on a small scale, providing both individuality of design and insurance against fashion misjudgements.

Then, as now, manufacturers of women's fashion clothing obtained their designs from two sources. The first was the purchase of fashion forecasts, which illustrated the forthcoming season's designs, textiles and colours; and the second and most widely used method was the direct copying of couture or *prêt-à-porter* garments, which were then adapted for the mass market. This practice reached its peak during the inter-war years, when fashion was more rigid than it is today and designs came almost exclusively from Paris.

The direct copying of couture models was undertaken by the top end of the clothing trade — that is, at department store level. Although store representatives did visit Paris with the express intention of purchasing prototypes and buying models or toiles for this purpose, most copying was unofficial. Lillian Farley, a mannequin for the couturier Patou during the 1920s, describes how his models were copied: "They bought little and would ask to see a model over and over again: always in a group of four or five. It was well known that each one would memorise a certain part of the dress, one studying the sleeve details, another the skirt and still another the trimmings. Back at the hotel they would make an accurate sketch of the model to be copied at home"[2]. These were then sent by ship or plane to the East End of London or to Seventh Avenue in New York and within days replica dresses would appear in all the shops. The cheaper end of the trade, unable to visit Paris themselves, would in turn copy the top end's version. By these means, the design of the most luxurious couture model eventually filtered down to the cheapest rayon dress.

Edna Woolman Chase, a leading American couturier and editor of American *Vogue* from 1914-1952, went so far as to state that this was "... an international spy system to turn the military green with envy". Some manufacturers even sewed facsimile labels of leading Paris houses into their garments

13

to give the impression that they were originals. This association with Paris imbued a garment with added desirability and could often command a higher price than the same garment without one. The copying and diluting of couture garments for the mass market has continued to this day, only now New York, London and Milan are also recognised capitals of fashion.

Retail outlets

An inevitable consequence of the off-the-peg mass market was the development of the retail clothing outlet. Ready-made clothing for men, women and children is available from three types of outlet: the department store, the small-scale unit retailer and multiple stores. Department stores have always stocked top-quality items, and during the nineteenth century were exclusively patronised by the middle and upper classes. As the twentieth century progressed, they recognised and responded to the changing and broadening nature of the market. In the 1920s, for example, Selfridges opened an immensely successful bargain basement, and during the 1960s introduced Miss Selfridge to entice the fashion-conscious teenager to spend her earnings.

Top left
Marks & Spencer gaberdine suit, summer 1988.

Above
Mary Quant has generally been credited for opening the first "boutique", Bazaar, in Great Britain in 1955. Here is the new footwear she launched in the 1960s.

Above

Marks & Spencer's "inexpensive frocks", c. 1933. This shows a trial window display, copies of which were sent to all branches of the store to ensure identical displays. Priced at 2s/11d, these were amongst the cheapest ready-made dresses available. The basic design is the same, but they are differentiated by the use of different fabrics, collar shapes, belts and buttons.

But it has been the small-scale unit retailer that has dominated the fashion market throughout most of this century. Their strength lies in the personal contact between the customer and the owner, and in the limited quantity of merchandise on display, which implies an exclusive design. The small retailer flourished during the inter-war years, providing an outlet for the flood of fashion clothing which swamped the market, and reached its peak again during the 1960s with the "boutique revolution".

The late 1920s and early 1930s saw multiple stores, such as Marks & Spencer in Great Britain, introduce ready-made clothing to their stocks of household goods. The design of their garments was "safe", neither in the forefront nor lagging behind contemporary fashion. Marks & Spencer achieved commercial success by defining an area of the market which did not seek high fashion, but preferred to benefit instead from good-value, quality garments which their large-scale production made possible. The 1980s are witnessing the rise of a new type of multiple, such as the Next chain of stores, which sells limited quantities of fashionable, quality garments. They have also revitalised and upgraded the mail order business.

[1](*Lark Rise to Candleford,* London, Oxford University Press, 1945, p94.)
[2](Chase, Edna Woolman and Chase, Ilka, *Always in Vogue,* Victor Gollancz Ltd, London, 1954, pp166-7.)

Camille Clifford, 1906. Her hour-glass curves epitomized the fashionable ideal

CHAPTER·ONE
1900
TO
1908

"The Edwardian age was a period of gaiety, when life was so inexpensive that a dandy with four hundred pounds a year could go out dancing most nights of the week, wearing lavender gloves and a wired button-hole in the lapel of his tail-coat."[1]

From 1900-1907 rich men and women dressed in a tremendous variety of clothing for different occasions —at great expense. For example, a weekend away involved as many as 16 complete changes of outfit, including hats, gloves, shoes and jewellery. Separate ensembles were worn during the morning, afternoon and evening, and likewise for specific occasions and activities, such as garden parties and balls, walking, riding, golf and motoring. Completely different sets were also required for town and country wear. Numerous books on etiquette appeared on the market to guide the uncertain on the correct modes of behaviour and dress for these myriad social events. The author of *Etiquette for Men* advised those who were in the city out of season that, "In August and September society people are not supposed to be in town, you can wear country clothes — a light thin lounge suit and a straw hat. If you are in town in August and September, you are supposed to be there only because you are passing through on your way to the country."[2]

Throughout this period the restrictive and elaborate clothing that rich women wore signified their wealth and leisure. In his famous sociological survey *The Theory of the Leisure Class* (1899), Thorstein Veblen stressed that couture clothing was the most blatant form of conspicuous consumption, and that body-compressing corsets were worn for the purpose of lowering the subject's vitality and rendering her completely unfit for any strenuous activity: "It is true, the corset impairs the personal attraction of the wearer, but the loss suffered on that score is offset by the gain in reputability which comes from her visibly increased expensiveness and infirmity."[3]

At the other end of society, Robert Roberts describes his memories of growing up amidst a poor background at the

Left
The Edwardian S-bend corset achieved the desirable shape shown here by distorting the spine and compressing the waist and abdomen. Padding often assisted the fashionably top-heavy silhouette.

Right
Queen Alexandra was noted for the promotion of pearl chokers; they emphasized her elegant long neck, and also disguised a birthmark that was said to embarrass her.

beginning of the century, shrewdly observing that prestige was not automatically inflated by proofs of affluence. "Nelly," he writes, "for all her fancy boa, frocks and jewellery, stayed 'ruined' while the temporary flushes of thieves served only to lower their status further."[4]

The back room of Roberts' family shop was used as a depot for goods under the custody of the pawnbroker. In poor Edwardian society, position was not judged solely by what one possessed, but also by what one pawned. Roberts describes how people were thankful to have spare clothing to pledge in return for cash for food so that they could avoid pawning goods from the home, such as bed-linen and kitchen utensils.

During the early years of the twentieth century the Parisian couture houses of Paquin, Callot Soeurs, Drecoll, Doucet and Worth led international fashion. The prestigious house of Worth was run by Jean Philippe and Gaston, the two sons of the founder, who had died in 1895. The daughters and wives of wealthy American plutocrats were great customers of the Paris couture trade and between 1879 and 1914 American society, which worshipped European culture, increasingly married into the British aristocracy. In 1907, *The Gentlewoman* magazine announced the marriage of Miss Padelford and the Hon Bertie Grosvenor, stating that this added "...yet another American-born lady to the ranks of future English peeresses". These women, who became known as the Dollar Princesses, gained a highly-sought-after title and the families received a fortune in the form of a dowry.

The fashions designed by Lady Duff-Gordon, under the trade-name of Lucille, were immensely popular in Great Britain. In the mid 1890s she was the first couturier to hold an entertaining fashion parade in the vein that we are accustomed to today. Live models had only just been introduced at this date, replacing sawdust and wax dummies.

As no society women would consider modelling gowns, Lucille sought six young girls from the middle and lower-middle classes of South London to perform this role. Lucille is an isolated example of a British dressmaker who created individual styles, whereas most, such as Jays and Redfern, adhered strictly to Paris dictates. Rumour had it that the 17-year-old Lady Clarendon had secured her marriage to a very eligible husband by wearing a grey satin Lucille dress. As a result, Lucille, who was already highly successful, became considered lucky and was widely patronised by debutantes. She was also the pioneer of glamorous underwear.

For those who could not afford, but had aspirations to possess, Paris couture, Kate Newton of Great Portland Street, London, advertised that her establishment regularly received consignments of "exhibited" gowns from the leading aforementioned houses at just one-fifth of the original price. The cost of a couture garment is the private

Above
It became the vogue in the 1900s for women to take up sports with a vengeance. They still had to contend with long and heavy skirts and restrictive corseting, however.

Left
An extravagant design of 1902, trimmed with chinchilla fur and lace.

agreement between the maker and customer, and is rarely divulged. Women's magazines often incuded a "Private Exchange" section, through which women could sell and buy slightly worn garments. This was particularly useful for mourning dress, generally worn for a brief period only.

Vogue has become the dominant fashion magazine of the twentieth century. This was founded in 1892 and bought by the publisher Condé Nast in 1909. During the 1900s, 10s and 20s fashion was photographed, but this was considered to be an inferior medium to drawing: *Vogue* did not use a photograph on its cover until 1932. Actors, actresses, dancers and society women frequently modelled clothing, whereas since World War II *Vogue* has almost exclusively used professional models.

From the 1890s to 1914 the American illustrator Charles Dana Gibson exerted a tremendous influence upon women's dress. His "Gibson Girl" character first appeared on the pages of *Life* and *Colliers,* and did much to aid women's emancipation during the period. The Gibson Girl was illustrated playing golf, swimming, riding and bicycling; she was independent and stood tall and proud, often overwhelming the presence of any men she was drawn with; she wore long, tailored skirts and blouses with an S-bend corset, which thrust the top half of her body forward (giving women the tightly upholstered-looking mono-bosom which characterised these years); and so popular was she, that by the turn of the century, wallpaper covered with Gibson Girl heads was marketed for bachelors. Because she was always illustrated with clean-shaven men moustaches went out of fashion. Whereas maturity was the keynote of most Edwardian fashion, the Gibson Girl was youthful, and the blouses which she popularised (intricately embroidered, faggoted, pintucked and often with a lace insert) introduced separates into women's wardrobes.

However, these items were frequently made by sweated labour in Europe and America, and factory conditions were often appalling, as were those of home — and outwork. In Great Britain the *Daily News* Sweated Trades Exhibition of 1906 highlighted the plight of many of the trade's home-workers, among the lowest-paid of whom were the shirt- and blouse-makers. White flannel shirts were made for 1d. each, and a dozen of these took 14-15 hours to make. Throughout the twentieth century, out- and home-workers have co-existed with, and complemented, factory production, and foreign immigrants and women have always provided a pool of cheap and largely unorganised labour.

Above

This magazine advertisement, c.1900, depicts the popular activity of cycling. However, it also hints at a dilemma for the 1900s woman — what to wear on the bicycle? Bloomers or Rational Dress were considered rather racy, and only the more daring wore them.

[1](Beaton, Cecil, *The Glass of Fashion,* Weidenfeld and Nicolson, London, 1954, p6.)
[2](As quoted by Thompson, Paul, *The Edwardians,* Weidenfeld and Nicolson, London, 1975, p20.)
[3](Veblen, Thorstein, *The Theory of the Leisure Class,* Allen & Unwin, London, 1954, p121.)
[4](Roberts, Robert, *The Classic Slum,* Manchester University Press, 1972, p11.)

COATS AND SUITS

Opposite page Tailor-made suits and a coat, illustrated in The Gentlewoman, 1907. Note the great variety of detailing on these garments and the women's highly-decorated wide-brimmed hats. All wear high collars, and muffs were also very fashionable.

Far left Decorative tailored costume in mauve and yellow for the races, with extravagant hat. **Far left** (bottom) Tailored suits, 1902. **Above** Illustration of women enjoying skating in their wide-skirted suits. Hats were always worn out of doors. **Left** Beautifully detailed pale blue suit with fur muff by Paquin, 1907.

DAY DRESS

IM SOMMERKLEIDE   Paul Haustein (München)

Above Art Nouveau fashion drawing, 1903. Art Nouveau, very fashionable between 1890 and 1910, was an international movement within the decorative arts and architecture. This illustration was taken from the Viennese magazine Jugend.

Northern European Art Nouveau was less exuberant and made more use of rectilinear motifs than that from the South. Art Nouveau was an exclusive style, and did not filter down-market.

Right Liberty silk and velvet day dress, 1905. This London department store was famous for its aesthetic dress based on classical lines, of which this is an example.

Top left These walking costumes of 1903 emphasize the fashionable S-bend and mono-bosom of the period.

Bottom left Photograph of a woman wearing the characteristic blouse and skirt, c.1903.

Above Elaborate day dress with high-necked collar, 1903, illustrated with a decorative Art Nouveau border. These costumes clearly signified the wearer's wealth.

EVENING DRESS

Left *Reception gown with fur wrap, 1902. Note the elaborate neckline worn with a flower, unusual shoulder straps and choker necklace. Beneath this outer spendour, the Edwardians were often quite dirty and perfumed themselves heavily to mask body-odour. Hair was carefully back-combed, and hair pieces often supplemented existing growth to achieve the fashionable piled effect on the top of the head.*

Above *Ornate evening gowns, 1902. These are heavily decorated with lace, ribbon and embroidery.*
Right *The wrap, designed for theatre or restaurant wear, was made of faced cloth and trimmed with silk braid. It was available in ivory, biscuit, helio and pale blue. The Empire evening gown, designed for young ladies, came in white, sky, pink, mauve and black. Both are from 1907.*

SPORTSWEAR AND ACCESSORIES

Above Spring hats, liberally decorated with flowers and fruit, and ornate blouses, 1902.

Top Heavy travelling coat, 1907.
Above left Mrs Hillyard in a long-skirted tennis outfit, 1900. Tennis attracted widespread female participation from the 1870s when women played in bustles.

Above right The famous S-bend corset, enforced with whalebone, 1908.

MEN AND CHILDREN

Left An English country gentleman, 1901. **Right** Young man dressed for sport, 1907. His functional garments are no different from those worn today — and a great contrast to the bulky clothing women were compelled to wear for modesty's sake at the same date. **Below** The fun-loving King Edward VII at Windsor.

Opposite page. Left Gentleman dressed formally for the races, 1906. **Top centre** Dress suit, Eton suit and Dress Carlton suits for privileged young men and boys, 1907. **Far right** (top) Naval-style costumes to be made at home for children of both sexes, 1907. Note the emphasis on royal endorsement. **Bottom** Silk party dresses for young girls, 1907. The older girls are acquiring the same S-bend silhouette as their mothers.

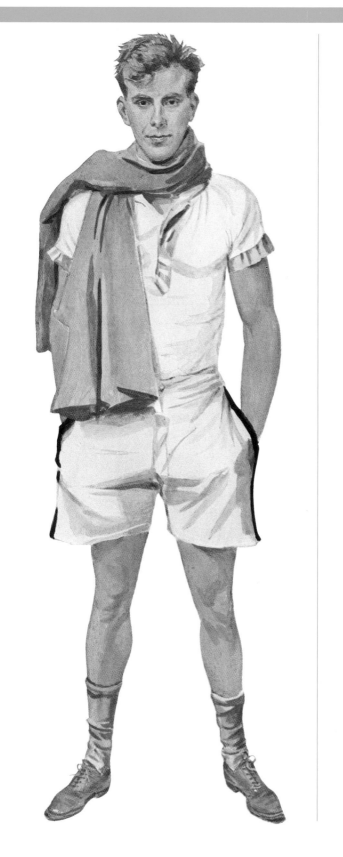

Fashion drawing by Georges Barbier, 1912.

CHAPTER·TWO
1909
TO
1919

From 1908 until the advent of World War I, Paul Poiret was one of the most influential and publicised of Paris couturiers. He worked for the House of Worth and for Jacques Doucet before setting up his own couture house in 1904. Three years later he took the radical step of freeing women of fashion from corsets, although it took many of them several years to adjust, and it was not the first time. The English Rational and Aesthetic dress movements of the 1880s and 90s had abandoned corsets in the belief that women's clothing should not be restrictive, but had few followers. However, the Paris Chamber of Commerce were so alarmed about the repercussions that this change in fashion would have upon the corset industry that they sent a delegate to beg Poiret to reverse this trend, which he flatly refused to do.

In complete contrast to the styles worn during the early years of the century, Poiret dressed his daring customers in harem pantaloons and lampshade tunics, and wrapped their heads in turbans decorated with extravagant plumes. These oriental styles emerged in conjunction with the first performance of the Ballets Russes in Paris in 1909. In stark contrast to the pastel-coloured scenery and traditional costumes of classical ballet, the Ballets Russes founder, Serge Diaghilev, employed Benois and Bakst to create vibrant and rich oriental designs. The results dazzled audiences and greatly influenced the decorative arts of the day. Poiret always maintained that he created his styles independently from those seen in the Russian Ballets. Cecil Beaton described him as an egocentric genius, who had no respect for good taste: "He forced his victims to wear chin straps of pearls, slung them with white foxes, stabbed them with fantastic ospreys, imprisoned them (as one hobbles the forelegs of a horse to prevent him from running away) in harem skirts. Wired tunics like lampshades were hung around the ladies' hips, heavy capes enveloped them, and they were laden with tassels and barbaric jewells."[1]

Poiret loved the rich and exotic, and his costume balls, where the guests dressed in oriental costumes or as mythological creatures, became legendary. Although his harem pantaloons were not widely adopted, oriental styles of dress and accessories were. The immensely impractical hobble skirt, which he introduced in 1913, was worn by leisured women to whom mobility was of little concern. Most women continued to wear long, narrow skirts, which were not quite so restrictive.

Poiret was a great showman and travelled round Europe with nine mannequins, publicising his fashion. In 1914 he went on a lecture tour of the United States and was enraged to discover that replicas of his models, complete with labels, were selling in the shops for as little as $15. This sum was nonetheless too expensive for working- and many middle-class women. With reference to American *Vogue*, Edna Woolman Chase states that at this time, "...wanting, yet fearing, publicity the couture tried to palm off on us

LASSITUDE

Robe de dîner, de Paul Poiret

Left
Design by Paul Poiret, 1912,
illustrated by Georges Lepape.

Above
Illustration by Valentine Gross for
La Gazette du Bon Ton, 1915.
Gross also painted scenery for the
Ballets Russes. This plate, entitled
Il Pleut Encore, shows suits with
bulbous skirts by (from left to
right) Paquin, Lanvin and
Doeuillet, and a coat by Paquin.

Top right
Controversial exotic dancer and
World War I spy, Mata Hari.

Below right
This American girl, pictured in
1917, is a young war worker,
repairing army uniforms.

Costume design by Leon Bakst, for Serge Diaghilev's influential Ballets Russes, 1912.

Below
Illustration by SEM, 1914, emphasizing the discomfort of the hobble skirt.

amateur sketches of their inferior designs instead of allowing us to make good drawings or photographs of their best."[2]

The Protective Association of French Dressmakers, formed by Poiret in 1914, aimed to clamp down on this style piracy. The *Chambre Syndicale de la Couture Parisienne,* which dated back to 1868, also tried to do this; but it is an inevitable consequence of couture that its designs are copied. Poiret was an important figure not only for his fashion designs, but also for the influence he had upon fashion presentation and for the foundation of a decorative arts school, the Ecole Martine, in 1912.

In 1908 Poiret commissioned a young illustrator, Paul Iribe, to draw his costumes, which were to be reproduced in an album. Like many fashion drawings today, they did not accurately delineate the styles, but created a stylistic impression. Although this album appeared in a small, limited edition, it greatly publicised his couture house and in 1911 he employed Georges Lepape to produce another. The style of these illustrations reached a wider audience, although still a minority, through *La Gazette du Bon Ton,* founded in 1912. This exclusive magazine, published quarterly on handmade paper with hand-coloured plates, reflected mainstream art movements. The heavily stylistic drawings of regular contributors Iribe, Lepape, Georges Barbier, Valentine Gross and Charles Marty introduced a fresh and influential approach to portraying fashion. In 1925, *La Gazette du Bon Ton* merged with *Vogue*.

The work of the Ecole Martine gained an international reputation during these years. Poiret sought out 12-year old working-class girls who had left school but had no formal art training or pre-conceived ideas about drawing, and paid them a wage to work at the Martine. He took these girls to parks and zoos and told them to draw whatever they saw. He then applied their magical and naïve images to designs for carpets (which they made themselves), furnishings, wallpapers, ceramics and wall murals. He also used their images for textile and embroidery designs. An exhibition of their work was held at the important Salon d'Automne in 1912.

Mariano Fortuny was another highly creative designer of the period. Born in Spain, Fortuny lived in Venice and was entirely self-taught. He was a talented painter and primarily saw himself as an artist rather than a dressmaker. Fortuny's garments were timeless: their design hardly changed during his working life, from 1900-49, and as a result he rarely appeared in the fashion magazines of the period. His clothing had a renaissance elegance and often used classical draping; and the fabric designs were greatly influenced by those from the fifteenth and sixteenth centuries. He may have been influenced by the Pre-Raphaelite paintings of Rosetti and Burne-Jones, which portrayed women wearing renaissance styles of clothing. Fortuny, who had studied mechanics and chemistry, had his own secret methods of printing and embossing fabric so that they resembled ancient brocades. He tended to use faded-looking rich colours and often worked with gold and silver threads. In the tradition of William Morris, he believed that the designer and maker should be one.

His most famous garments were his Delphos dresses. To prevent these pleated sheaths from being copied he took out a patent on their design in 1909. The fabric for these dresses was so light that their hems had to be weighted with tiny metal beads. When they were not being worn they could be stored tied in a knot, and miraculously retained their pleats.

During World War I, daytime dress was dominated by uniforms and utilitarian wear. The sudden demand for female labour occasioned by the war drew an additional 1.7 million women into the labour force in Great Britain alone. Before 1914, women in the West represented approximately one-third of the total labour force, and married women represented just one-tenth of these. This was, however, the first time that many middle- and upper-class women had ever earned a living, let alone performed routine factory jobs or heavy farm work. Women munitions

workers wore trousers and overalls, and nurses and ambulance drivers wore uniforms. Most women dressed in ankle-length skirts, wide at the bottom, with loose jackets tied in the middle with a broad belt. Although materials were hard to obtain and labour scarce, many of the couture houses remained open during the hostilities. In 1915, the international San Francisco exhibition provided an outlet for the Paris couturiers to display their models to an American audience.

Poiret refused to surrender to the economies necessitated by the war and continued to create extravagant garments such as shortened crinoline styles with pagoda hips. Fashion responded gradually to wartime changes in society but these did not reach a peak until the mid 1920s; since Poiret did not fit in with these changes, his popularity died.

[1](Beaton, Cecil *The Glass of Fashion*, Weidenfeld and Nicolson, London, 1954, p17.)
[2](Already cited p98)

Left
An evening coat for the theatre by Paquin, 1912. Madame Paquin founded her fashion house in 1891, and at the height of her career employed over one thousand people.

Above
Suffragettes, c.1910. Organised campaigns for women's suffrage had existed in Britain since 1865, but only hit the headlines when the Women's Social and Political Union decided to take militant action in 1906, with suffragette women deliberately courting arrest. Militancy was stepped up in 1909, with campaigns of organised vandalism — window breaking, arson — and hunger striking on imprisonment.

LES DESSOUS
A
LA MODE

La mode actuelle impose des dessous légers.

Sur la chemise courte, en fin tissu de soie, une combinaison de soie également, à mailles serrées. Chemise et combinaisons ne sont retenues sur l'épaule que par des faveurs étroites.

C'est chez Lemaître, qu'il convient de choisir ces frivolités. Il vend aussi les seuls bas de soie élégants.

Left *Fashionable outfit trimmed with fox fur, 1913.*

Above *Fashion drawings for underwear by Marty, for La Gazette du Bon Ton, 1912. This shows the choice of summer and winter underwear.*

Left Visiting robe by Paquin, drawn by Barbier for La Gazette du Bon Ton, 1912. Note the Art Deco-style fabric. **Above** Costume worn at Longchamp Races, 1910. The cut and draped detailing on the dress accentuated the woman's fashionable hour-glass figure.

COATS AND SUITS

Below *Studio photograph of a woman wearing a fashionable but cheap (note the rough hemlines and stitching) suit, c.1912.* **Right** *Burberry coat, 1917. Burberry and Aquascutum were the leading makers of protective outer coats for men and women. Their garments were widely worn for motoring.* **Far right** *Women wearing expensive fur coats, 1914.*

Left Woman wearing a heavily embroidered and fringed evening coat, 1909; it is a good example of the very elaborate clothing that the rich wore during the early years of the twentieth century. **Below** Studio photograph of a woman wearing a typical, wide-belted suit with a three-quarter length jacket, 1915.

EVENING DRESS

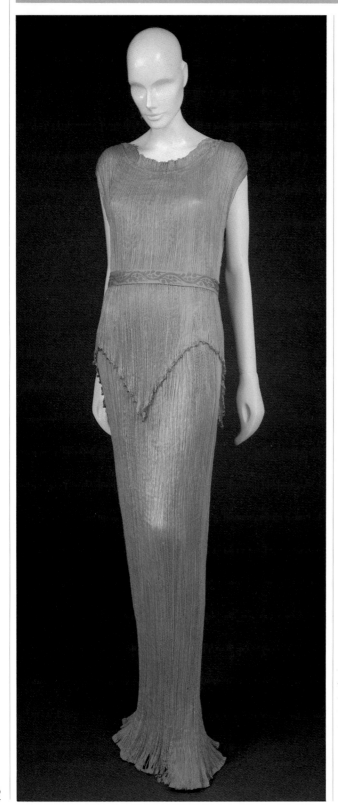

L'ADIEU DANS LA NUIT

Robe du soir de Paquin

Left *Fortuny's pleated sheath Delphos dress, 1912. The intricacy of this garment clearly could not be translated for the mass market.*

Above *Elaborate, oriental evening dress designed by Paquin, 1913, and drawn by Marty for* La Gazette du Bon Ton — *another style reserved for the rich.*

Above Evening robe by Talbot of Paris, 1913. Note the oriental head-dress.

Right Evening gown by the English dressmaking establishment, Jays Ltd, 1908. The exquisite hand embroidery must have taken hundreds of hours to work.

WARTIME CLOTHING

Top left Women serving in the Land Army being presented to the Queen. Their practical uniforms consisted of coats, knee breeches and leggings. **Far left** (bottom) Snapshot, 1919. Note the young boys' Norfolk jackets, knee length shorts and black wool stockings. **Middle** (bottom) Snapshot, 1916. This relatively functional and comfortable style of dress was widely worn by women during the war. **Below** Snapshot 1916. Typical of clothing widely worn by women during the period, the older woman's clothes seem almost Victorian, whilst the younger woman wears a casual style which looks ahead to the 1920s. **Right** American magazine advertisement, 1914-15. **Far right** Woman's suit, 1919, with shortened skirt and spats.

THE all wool English gabardine cloth used in making up this 1915 advanced model is greatly in demand this season. This garment has wonderful style. It has been copied from a very expensive model and makes a serviceable and rich looking dress. The vestee, round collar and cuffs are made of good quality satin. Yoke and collar are of Oriental top embroidered net, collar being wired to stand up. Loose hanging waist in coatee or jacket effect, high waisted and button trimmed both front and back. Long flaring Russian tunic skirt, with fine quality silk satin flounce on underskirt. Dress closes invisibly in front. Women's sizes only. *Give measurements.* Average shipping weight, 2½ pounds.

No. 31A4460½
Navy blue; black satin bottom.

No. 31A4461½
Navy blue; navy blue satin bottom.
Price,
each.................. $16.50

SIZES—These Dresses will be furnished in the following sizes only: From 32 up to and including 44 inches bust measure; waist measure up to and including 33 inches, and front skirt length of 39 or 42 inches, with wide basted hem. See page 499 for simple measuring instructions.

THE very newest style is portrayed in this elegant garment. The material used is an all silk satin which will be extremely popular this fall and winter. A most stunning and easily becoming style. The bodice of dress is made in semi-fitting modified basque effect shirred in front. Cuffs and standing collar of fine quality organdy, trimmed with silk embroidered paon velvet which makes a very handsome trimming. Waist in back extends slightly below girdle in coatee effect and is trimmed with self covered buttons. Underwaist is lace trimmed. Handsome plaited Russian tunic skirt. Dress fastens in front. A dress that is popular both for afternoon and evening wear. Women's sizes only. *Give measurements.* Avg. shpg. wt., 2¾ lbs.

No. 31A4465½
Amethyst.

No. 31A4466½
Russian green.

No. 31A4467½
Black.
Price,
each.................. $19.95

SIZES—These Dresses will be furnished in the following sizes only: From 32 up to and including 44 inches bust measure; waist measure up to and including 33 inches, and front skirt length of 39 or 42 inches, with wide basted hem. See page 499 for simple measuring instructions.

Sears, Roebuck and Co., Chicago, Ill.

The cover of a sheet music collection of songs from the 1920s musical Wonder Bar.

CHAPTER THREE

1920
TO
1929

In the post-war years, the idea that a woman would give up "gainful" employment upon marriage continued to be accepted, with the exception of the very poor. Women did, however, enjoy a greater variety of leisure activities outside of the home, the most significant of which was the growth of paid annual holidays, often spent at seaside resorts; and on a more regular basis, public dancing, taboo in Victorian times, became immensely popular among all classes.

Art Deco — influenced by Egyptian and African art, Cubism, Fauvism, Expressionism and European Purism — was the dominant decorative style of the 1920s and 30s. The 1925 Paris *Exposition des Arts Décoratifs et Industriels Modernes* acted as a showcase for this movement, which embraced the Modern Age and largely rejected historical reference. The first decorative style which did not remain exclusive, and seized upon by manufacturers, Art Deco's abstract and geometrical motifs were liberally applied to a vast range of goods, from garden gates to cosmetic compacts, and greatly influenced textile design. Avidly consumed by the fashion-hungry post-war market, dress also became widely available in the form of ready-made clothes; but although many women wore garments of a similar design, the wealth of the wearer was only slightly less obvious than in pre-war years. Social status continued to be indicated by sartorial superiority and the two remained inextricably entwined.

The fashions of the 1920s were dominated by what became known as the "Garçonne Look", which had reached its peak by 1926. Cecil Beaton describes how the fashion illustrators drew "... those longer-than-life ladies who, with their short, tubular dresses, cigarettes in long holders, cloche hats, bobbed hair, plucked eyebrows, bands of diamond bracelets from wrist to elbow and earrings hanging like fuchsias symbolised the visual aspect of the period."[1] As its name suggests, the "Garçonne Look" was boyish in comparison with the accentuated feminine curves so desirable in previous decades. Hemlines had crept up from the beginning of the 1920s to reach just above the knee in 1926. Never before had a woman revealed so much of her legs. In contrast, waistlines dropped from their natural position to the hips.

It was the Parisian couturiers Gabrielle Chanel and Jean Patou who were largely responsible for creating this dramatic new style. They recognised that the post-war women would no longer accept being immobilised and contorted into unnatural shapes in the name of fashion. Although for some the new styles involved dieting, wearing breast-flattening bras and narrow, elastic, boneless corsets, these were relatively light concessions to make in comparison to the constriction of Edwardian profiles. Chanel and Patou dressed the modern woman in loose-fitting, comfortable and functional garments, many of which were based along the lines of sportswear and the

Above
Noel Coward pictured at home in
1927. Note the Art Deco
headboard and bedspread.

Left
Film star Clara Bow was dubbed
the "It" Girl by popular novelist
Elinor Glynn.

clothing of working people. Indeed, they were often credited with creating a *poverty-de-luxe*.

The couture industry had traditionally used the finest and most expensive silks for its garments. Chanel therefore created quite a furore when she introduced what had always been regarded as rather humble fabrics — such as knitted jersey — in simply cut suits and dresses for society women, while still designing the most luxurious bead-encrusted evening dresses and trenchcoats with sable linings. Chanel was only too delighted when her clothing was widely copied, aware that the quality and cut of the original would always stand out. She promoted an understated elegance, believing that women rather than their clothing should be highlighted. Indeed, her own appearance epitomised the fashions she created. The perfume Chanel No 5 was introduced in 1921 and from that date onwards its sales helped to support the house of Chanel. Patou designed styles akin to those of Chanel, and the two remained great rivals throughout the 1920s. Wealthy, fashion-conscious men of the period sported Oxford bags, Fair Isle jumpers (as popularised by the Prince of Wales), plus-fours and two-tone shoes.

The "Roaring Twenties" automatically conjures up images of these "Bright Young Things" clad in their adventurous clothing, sipping cocktails and dancing the Charleston until the early hours. While this exhilarating experience was enjoyed by a few, hunger marches and long-term unemployment were the stark reality for a great many people. In between these polarised socio-economic extremes there existed a large section of the population in Britain and the United States who experienced a decrease in the cost of living and an increase in real earnings. This group formed the mass market for women's fashionable ready-to-wear clothing, which became available during this decade.

For the first time, the essence of couture could be adapted and translated for mass production. The small quantity of fabric required for, and, the simplicity of, the loose-fitting fashionable tubular shapes enabled manufacturers to copy the styles of high fashion. Ultimately, they were suitable for the lifestyle of working women and housewives as well as the patrons of couture.

The introduction of rayon was, in design and manufacturing terms, one of the most significant textile developments of the twentieth century and was a great boon to the production of ready-to-wear clothes. Attempts had been made to perfect a synthetic fibre since the 1880s, but these had met with little success. In the immediate post-war years rayon (or artificial silk as it was known before 1926) was used to line the cheaper ranges of menswear. Its breakthrough, however, lay in the manufacture of stockings, the demand for which was stimulated by the fashion for shorter skirts. Rayon stockings laddered easily, but they cost a quarter of the price of silk ones. Women sometimes wore them inside out and powdered their legs to subdue the shine. Dyeing and production methods were improved during the late 1920s and rayon became increasingly used as dress fabric. As it superficially resembled the feel and appearance of natural silk, rayon enabled manufacturers to emulate top-quality knitwear and silk garments at a fraction of the cost.

In spite of the availability of ready-made fashions, most working- and many middle-class women made a great deal of their own, and their children's, clothing at home. This was for financial reasons and, for a proficient dressmaker, to obtain individual and perfectly-fitting garments. Down-market fashion magazines — such as *Mab's* in Great Britain — illustrated fashionable garments which could be made at home and often included a free paper pattern. In the United States, where many families lived a considerable distance from the nearest town, such magazines and mail-order catalogues — of which Sears Roebuck was among

the largest — were invaluable for keeping in touch with the latest trends.

In 1929 the hemline dropped, the waistline returned to its natural position and the bosom was emphasised once more, these realignments signalling a change to the more figure-moulding styles of the 1930s. In 1929, the 20s came to a dramatic climax when the American Stock Exchange collapsed with devastating financial repercussions around the world.

[1](Beaton, Cecil, *The Glass of Fashion,* Weidenfeld & Nicolson, London, 1954, p.133.)

Above
Funeral procession for Emmeline Pankhurst. Mrs Pankhurst died at the age of 69 in 1928 — the year that women were given the vote on an equal footing with men — having actively campaigned for women's suffrage since 1903.

Right
*The discovery of Tutankhamen's
tomb in 1923 popularized the use
of Egyptian motifs in all branches
of the decorative arts and formed a
considerable part of the Art Deco
style.*

DAY DRESS

LA BAGUE NEUVE
OU
LA JALOUSIE DISSIMULÉE
ROBES. DE PAUL POIRET

Far left Fashionable woman at Ascot, 1925. **Above left** Egyptian-inspired dress by Vionnet, after the opening of Tutankhamen's tomb, c.1922. **Left** Snapshot, c.1928. Note how similar the women's dress and shoe designs are. Fashion during the 20s was much more rigid than it is today. **Above** These dresses of 1924 are among Poiret's most simple designs.

Unusual Values

16 X 220
Crepe
$4.98

16 X 225
Embroidered
"Hard Twist"
Voile
$8.98

Stylish
Dresses
at
Moderate Prices

16 X 221
Embroidered
Voile
$5.98

16 X 224
Imported
Ratine
$6.98

22 X 3091
Hand-
Embroidered
Voile
$2.79

16 X 223
Pure
Linen
$7.49

16 X 222
Figured
Crepe
$2.98

Left American ready-to-wear, medium-priced dresses of 1924.

Below Photographs of a fashionable woman, c.1926. By this date the design of women's dress was simple and often based on sportswear.

53

COATS AND SUITS

Left Photograph of Sir
Winston Churchill, 1927.
Bottom left Snapshot showing
women wearing fur coats with big
collars and cloche hats, c.1926.
Around this date, cloches were
worn deep over the brow. *Right*
Tailored suit by Beer, 1922. The
waisted jacket is reminiscent of the
Edwardian era and the shorter skirt
of the 1920s.
Above The couturier Chanel,
1928, wearing one of her classic,
understated outfits.

EVENING WEAR

Far left *Evening dress, c.1926. During the 20s it was often only the use of richer fabrics and decorative detailing which differentiated day from evening dress.* **Above** *A fashion drawing of elegant evening dresses with trains, pictured in a classical setting, House of Worth, 1924. Illustration, La Gazette du Bon Ton.* **Left** *Dress by Jeanne Lanvin, worn with an ornate bandeau around the hips, c.1928.*

Right *Evening dress with plunging backline and uneven hem, 1924. Uneven hemlines appear where there is uncertainty as to whether the hem will rise or fall. Illustration, La Gazette du Bon Ton.* **Far right** *Beaded evening dress, c.1926. These beads were individually applied with a tambour hook, and such dresses often weighed up to 9lbs. This weight helped them to hang in the fashionable straight style from the shoulders.*

SPORTSWEAR AND ACCESSORIES

Above Beachwear drawn by René Vincent, 1927. **Left** Bathing, 1926. This style of bathing suit, made of wool or cotton, was worn by men, women and children throughout the 1920s. Never before had women exposed so much of their bodies in public and never before had they been able to swim unencumbered by bulky swimming costumes.

Above Chemise c. 1926. By the 1920s most women did not wear corsets, although some bound their hips and wore breast-flattening bras to achieve the fashionable boyish figure. Chemises like this one were widely worn throughout the decade.

Above Women's golf outfit. Jeanne Lanvin, 1925. Drawn by George Lepape for La Gazette du Bon Ton. During the 1920s women enjoyed a greater variety of sports activities than ever before. By this date there was little difference between the design of sports and everyday dress. **Top right** Bathing costumes and beach pyjamas, 1928. Beach pyjamas were the only trousers which most women wore during the 1920s.

Right Susanne Lenglen, the French tennis champion, c. 1922. Lenglen, who was dressed by Patou, personified the 1920s "New Woman". Her sleeveless tennis dresses were worn daringly short, revealing the top of her stockings.

MEN AND CHILDREN

Left These 1927 drawings of coat styles for young girls aged 4-10 years reveal how similar their design was to womenswear. **Bottom left** This photograph, c.1923, represents the plain style of suits that most men wore. **Below** Photograph of two young girls, c.1924, the one on the left wearing a knitted dress and the other a velvet one.

Above The Prince of Wales wearing a Fair Isle jumper, c.1925. Many men, copying the royal example, adopted these jumpers during the 1920s.

DANSONS LA CAPUCINE

ROBE D'ÉTÉ ET ROBES D'ENFANTS, DE JEANNE LANVIN

Gazette du Bon Ton. Année 1921.—

"J'AI FAILLI ATTENDRE"
COSTUME VESTON, DE LUS ET BEFVE

Année 1922.— Plancke

Left Illustration of children's
dresses by Jeanne Lanvin, 1921.
Pierre Brissaud for La Gazette du
Bon Ton. ***Above*** Fashionable man
wearing double-breasted suit,
1922. Rejelan for La Gazette du
Bon Ton. ***Right*** Heart-throb film
star Ronald Colman, c.1928.

HAIR, HATS AND ACCESSORIES

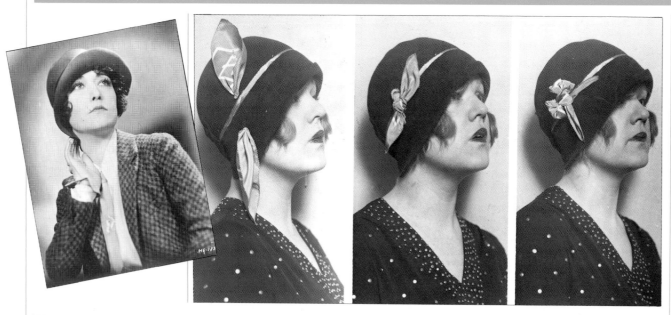

Far left (top) Film star Dorothy Sebastian wearing rolled-felt cloche hat, c.1926. **Left** Taken from an unspecified newspaper, the caption to these photographs describes the "love symbol" hats: "By varying the position of the ribbon, the wearer signifies her status as regards matrimony. When she wears it 'arrow-like'…she is single, but her promise has been given. Tied in a bow [centre] she is married. The arrangement on the right signifies single-blessedness, widowed or divorced, which is to say "fancy free". Now the young man has but to study the symbols of the hat to discover where he stands." **Far left** (bottom) Jean Grangier illustration of shoes for La Gazette du Bon Ton, 1924.
Bottom left Film star Anita Page wearing pale blue cloche hat c.1926.

Right Art Deco-style evening purse studded with diamanté, and with lipstick concealed in the tassles, c.1925. **Far right** Fashion illustration of Camille Roger's wide-brimmed hats for La Gazette du Bon Ton, 1921.

Evening dress c.1932.

CHAPTER·FOUR
1930
TO
1939

Throughout the Depression, the luxury trades in Paris — supported by the French government — remained intact. The couture industry did, however, lose much of its lucrative export trade in its fall in sales to the United States. As a result, many houses introduced top-quality ready-to-wear lines to supplement their continuing sales of individually made items; there remained a body of rich patrons who were either unaffected by, or who had profited from, the economic crises.

Fashion in the 1930s rejected the angular severity of the previous decade and replaced it with a sleek, streamlined look, achieved by bias-cutting of materials and the use of smooth fabrics. The new silhouette, which followed the line of the figure, closely hugged the waist and hips and then fell into a soft, flared skirt. Daytime hemlines reached mid-calf length and often dropped to the ankle for evening wear. In contrast to the rather uniform styles of the 1920s, fashion during the 30s succumbed to many influences, all of which shared an element of escapism and fantasy.

During this decade the Parisian couturiers Madeleine Vionnet and Madame Grès became famous for their intricately bias-cut and pleated dresses. Madame Grès, who worked under the name of Alix during the 1930s, had a passion for classical sculpture and sought to recapture some of its timeless elegance in her clothing. The fluid garments that these two women created were invariably photographed in a neo-classical setting; themes from Greek legends, classically draped figures and pillars were used as backdrops for the statuesque models who displayed these garments. Paris-based Hoyningen Heune was one of the leading fashion photographers who worked in this vein.

The surreal art movement also exerted some influence on fashions during the 1930s. In 1936 — 10 years after the surrealist manifesto was written — the first exhibition of surrealism was held in England, at Burlington House. This attracted some 20,000 people and enticed even larger audiences when it transferred to New York afterwards. Fashion illustrators for *Vogue* — such as Christian Berard — adopted the style of surrealism and drew women carrying their heads under their arms. Horst photographed models coiled in rope, which hurtled into oblivion, or posed next to cracked mirrors. With the exception of the Parisian couturier Elsa Schiaparelli, surrealism showed its influence upon the presentation of fashion, rather than upon garment design. Many of the more decorative aspects of the movement filtered down-market, as it was easy to copy the imagery without understanding the ideology.

Schiaparelli loved the bizarre and turned to the artists of surrealism — and particularly Salvador Dali — to assist her in her search for novelty. Schiaparelli dressed Dali's wife free of charge and he in turn provided the inspiration for many of her designs. Dali dyed an enormous stuffed bear shocking pink (the name and use of the colour was

Schiaparelli's trademark), put drawers in its stomach, and then dressed it in an orchid-coloured satin jacket and adorned it with jewels for her salon.

Many of her designs were outrageously daring, such as the 1936 black hat shaped like a shoe with shocking pink heel which Mrs Reginald Fellowes had the courage to wear. Another hat, which Schiaparelli herself wore, resembled a lamb cutlet with a frill on the bone. Even her classically draped evening dresses were decorated with the most unusual motifs — such as a large red lobster splattered across the front — and she was also famous for her unusual accessories (bags which looked like bird cages, buttons in the shapes of lips and lollipops, and the use of zips on couture garments). But even though Schiaparelli dressed the most adventurous society women of this period, she also had a large conservative clientele, for whom she designed more subdued classical garments.

Throughout the 1930s the clothing worn by Hollywood's stars provided a major new fashion focus. Joan Crawford, Greta Garbo, Ginger Rogers, Marlene Dietrich and Jean Harlow were among the many glamorous actresses whose hairstyles, make-up and clothing were avidly copied by European and American women. The

Above
Jeanne Lanvin's Surreal haute couture display for the 1937 Paris Exhibition.

Right
Joan Crawford in lounging pyjamas.

Far right
Adrian's design for the film Letty Lynton, *worn here by Joan Crawford in the title role, 1932.*

actresses received much greater exposure than the mannequins on the catwalks of Paris. Each week some twenty million people in Great Britain and eighty-five million in the United States packed the picture palaces to soak up the escapist world of Hollywood.

During the 1920s, Hollywood aimed to dress the stars in the very latest styles, and sent scores of stylists to Paris to keep them informed of fashion changes. On occasion, the studios commissioned the great dictators of style to design garments for the films, but the crunch came in 1929, when thousands of feet of film were discarded because Patou had

unexpectedly lowered his hemline, and this footage had been shot showing garments with shorter lengths. In an attempt to overcome such problems the studios began to promote the talents of their own designers, such as Adrian, Travis Banton, Walter Plunkett and Edith Head. Although their designs varied little from those created in Paris, the studio designers made their garments more elaborate. The fashion elite often condemned the stars for being too "showy", but to many of the less well-off fashion-hungry

Above
Vivien Leigh as Scarlett O'Hara in Gone with the Wind, *1939.*

women who worked long hours in dull jobs they represented the ultimate in style and beauty.

The stars did become associated with, and promote, certain styles, such as Greta Garbo's trenchcoats and berets, and perhaps the most famous example of all, the dress with large ruffled sleeves which Adrian designed for Joan Crawford to wear as Letty Lynton in the film of the same name (1932). This has frequently been credited with instigating the fashion for padded shoulders, although Schiaparelli and Marcel Rochas had included them in their collections the previous year. It was not, however, until a Hollywood star wore them in a screen hit that they became widely adopted and invariably associated with this actress. In spite of the fact that *Letty Lynton* was withdrawn soon after general release (as a result of a copyright infringement), Macy's in New York is reputed to have sold over 500,000 copies of this dress. Many department stores had "Cinema Departments", which sold reproductions of garments from specific films at low prices, and fan magazines — such as *Filmfair* in Great Britain and *Photoplay* in the United States — further promoted the styles worn by the queens of Hollywood.

Male stars provided their own contemporary wardrobes and just had to ensure that their clothing was in harmony with that worn by the leading lady. The double-breasted suits with wide lapels and turn-up trousers which Robert Taylor, Clark Gable, Spencer Tracy and Tyrone Power wore were widely copied by the male audience, as were their mannerisms, moustaches and hairstyles.

During the inter-war years fashion went full circle. In great contrast to the "Garçonne Look", by the mid-1930s Norman Hartnell was designing evening dresses in Great Britain inspired by the painter Winterhalter, for Queen Elizabeth II among many patrons. Winterhalter was famous for his portraits of aristocratic and society women — notably for the painting of the Empress Eugénie and ladies of the court *c.*1860. Balenciaga and Vionnet also featured this type of dress between 1937-39. Only the wealthiest women could ultimately afford and enjoy a social life which made wearing a crinoline possible and they were often seen at debutante balls. These crinolines were made in whalebone instead of steel. Alternatively, a similar effect was obtained by sewing whalebone hoops into a detachable skirt, or even by using stiff horse hair and taffeta petticoats under a very full skirt. In keeping with this romantic revival, many designers added a bustle to the back of their dresses, while this vogue for Victoriana was also witnessed in interior design and the literature of the period.

On September 3, 1939 war in Europe was declared. For the next seven years a wartime style of dress was created and fashion remained static until Christian Dior presented his Corole line in 1947, evolved from these fashions created before the World War II.

Above
A novelty design for stockings to celebrate an impending visit to Paris from British Royalty, 1938.

Left
Punch *cartoon, November 27, 1935, captioned: "Now let me see — it 'appened just when I was changing from the Marlene to the Greta accent".*

DRESSES AND SUITS

Very tailored— with Soft Necklines

The delightful beige suit above has a very new story to tell—it is the line, which shows fullness in the skirt at the back, and an almost straight front.

Note, too, the brown scarf looped into a bow. The careless-looking cravat bow in a contrasting colour is the vogue with suits, as is also shown in the navy costume of woollen bouclé. The jacket of this last model is cut rather on the waisted lines of the suits in the "naughty 'nineties." So, too, is the street frock on the right of black marocain, with the short full basque at the back, and green cravat tie.

Models — AUGUSTA BERNARD

47

Left The original caption to this picture, taken in 1933, stated: "The latest Marlene Dietrich fashion has crossed the Atlantic. A mannequin appeared at a dress show this week wearing a perfectly tailored man's lounge suit and it looks as if an attempt is being made to popularise this Hollywood craze in this country." Suit from Harvey Nichols of Regent Street, London.

Above Tailored suits featured in Woman's Journal, 1932.

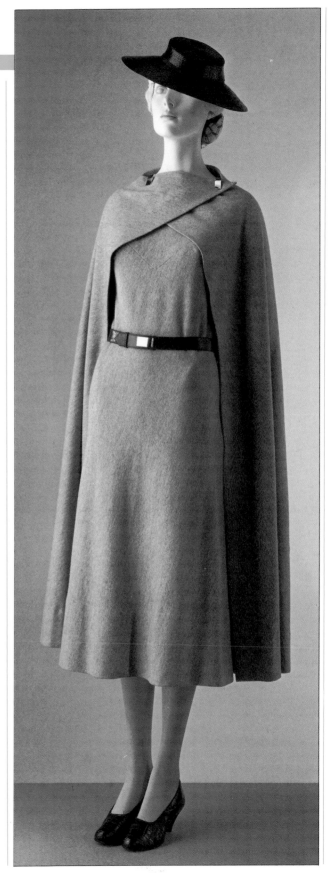

Above Coat and suit, 1935. Both of these women are wearing sailor-style straw hats at a jaunty angle.

Right Classical and beautifully-cut Vionnet suit, 1933.

The Interest Begins at the Top!

In this charming dinner frock of satin and lace, it is the amusing and attractive sleeves which lift it to stardom. The next frock is of the same *genre* with a contrasting top, and uncommon sleeves, but it makes its contrast with pink ninon and Seville blue chiffon. Very delightful is the evening frock— its back view shows the low cartridge pleating on either side of the skirt, and the front shows the careless cowl bodice and fascinating little taffetas coatee which accompanies the model.

Muslin models cut in Paris, as well as hand-cut paper patterns are obtainable of these designs. For particulars see page 106.

Opposite page. Left *Satin dress by Charles James, 1934, and fur coat by Vionnet c.1936.* **Centre** *Evening dress called "Tears" by Schiaparelli, 1938.* **Right** *Striking Chanel evening dress, 1937.*

Left *Feature on evening dresses, Women's Journal, 1932. This middle-market magazine is displaying fashionable garments which readers can make from paper patterns. Note the emphasis on muslin models "cut in Paris".* **Above** *Evening outfit by French couturier Nina Ricci, 1937.*

MEN AND CHILDREN

Below Men wearing boater hats, 1934. **Bottom** The Duke of Windsor, then Prince of Wales, with his brother, Prince George, 1931. **Right** Working men at a fishing port, 1936.

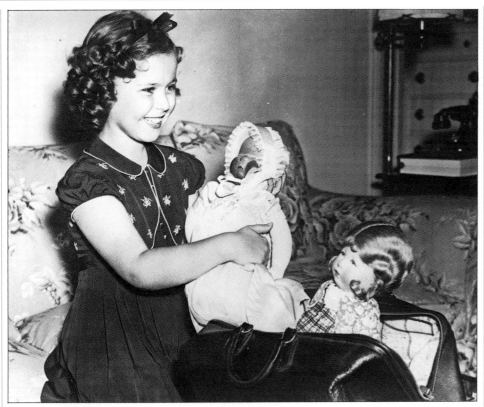

Far left (top) Shirley Temple, c.1934, exerted a great influence upon children's dress and hairstyles. **Far left** (bottom) A poor mining community, 1935. **Left** Young girl in Shirley Temple-style frock and curls. **Below** Young girl with pram, 1933.

75

BEACHWEAR AND UNDERWEAR

Above These women, wearing beach trousers over swimming costumes and trousers with halter neck fronts and straps at the back, are from c.1935. During the 1930s swimming costumes became tighter and more revealing, and in 1935 two-piece suits were shown on Vogue's pages for the first time, although they were not worn until the 1940s. **Right** Carefree models walking along the promenade, c.1935.

Left Tailored navy linen beach suit with large patch pockets and striped shorts-suit from c.1937.

Right Girl wearing shorts at an outdoor public swimming pool. *Below* This pair of cami-knickers was made in Courtaulds' printed rayon crepe, 1938.

Above Night- and underwear as shown in the Woman's Journal, 1932. *Left* This photograph shows typical 1930s stockings and shoes.

HAIR, HATS AND ACCESSORIES

Left and **below** These two hats designed for Ascot 1939 by top society milliner Aage Thaarup show the extreme variety of shape that could be worn in any one particular season.

Below A Victor Stiebel design of 1939, perched forward on the head, with the very popular veil.
Bottom Contrasting wide-brimmed and pill-box straw hats as they were worn at Newbury Races, 1939.

Left Thousands of women aspiring to Hollywood glamour at a low cost bleached their hair with cheap peroxides to imitate screen stars like Jean Harlow, the archetypal platinum blonde, seen here in an MGM publicity photo of 1933.

Left These four models at a hairdressing fair of 1932 demonstrate the popularity of softly-waved hair in the 1930s. This was a reaction to the severe bobs, crops and shingles that had seemed so daring in the 20s.

Above This magazine advertisement of 1936 for Dolcis shoes shows feminine, strappy styles and hints at luxurious living and cruise-liner trips – a popular setting for Hollywood films.

Christian Dior's "New Look" suit, 1947.

CHAPTER FIVE

1940
TO
1949

During World War II many of the Paris couture houses remained open. Madame Grès infuriated the Germans by designing her first collection under Occupation in the colours of the French flag — and as a result of this defiance was closed for one year. But the couturiers remained open to clothe a small Franco-German set who enjoyed a glittering social life and luxurious couture clothing, existing alongside the devastating poverty that most French people suffered. There were also a few wealthy Frenchwomen who glided through the period dressing and living according to pre-war standards, as if oblivious to the hostilities.

Great Britain and the United States, cut off from Paris until October 1944, had to rely upon the talents of their own designers to create wartime dress. In Britain there emerged a wartime socialism which promoted the belief that what few resources there were should be evenly distributed among the population. Clothing was put on a points system and weighted according to the quantity of fabric used and the amount of labour involved in its production. The famous *CC41* (civilian clothing 1941) utility label was introduced and became recognised as a guarantee of quality. This stylishly-cut clothing was designed by the Incorporated Society of London Fashion Designers, whose members included Digby Morton, Norman Hartnell and Victor Stiebel, with the leading British couturiers conforming to a strict design brief imposed by the government. This stressed that a minimum quantity of fabric should be used and that there should be no unnecessary decorative detailing. In response to these economical requirements, hemlines were raised to just below the knee, waists were nipped-in and collars, belts and lapels, if used, were small. As silk stockings were banned, ankle socks became widely worn, and snoods, turbans and head-scarves became very popular, although hats were not rationed. Elaborately-waved hairstyles and the use of facial cosmetics were highlighted to compensate for the rather austere clothing designs.

As the design of women's clothing was restricted during the utility period, manufacturers were encouraged to experiment with large-scale production. The Eastman cutter, for example, enabled a hundred or more garments to be graded and cut in one lay, which greatly increased the production process.

Initially 20 coupons were allocated to each person bi-annually — and a woman's coat alone consumed 14 of these. As the war progressed this allowance was reduced and reached its lowest level in the acute economic crisis which Britain experienced after the war. To supplement this meagre allowance women were encouraged to "Make do and Mend", which became the Board of Trade's wartime slogan. The women's press provided advice on how to remake old clothing, unravel discarded jumpers and reknit new ones, and make patchwork items out of scraps of

fabric. As clothing rationing often did not keep pace with the rate that children grew, the Women's Voluntary Service opened clothing exchanges for women to swop their offsprings' outgrown garments. For the one-third of the British population undernourished in 1938, wartime socialism provided their first wholesome diet and decent set of clothing. And although the design of clothing was restricted, the rich could still buy top-quality items and owned large pre-war wardrobes.

In the United States the War Production Board did impose restrictions upon the quantity of fabric which could be used for clothing, but these were moderate in comparison with Britain. This period gained many American designers the public recognition they had long deserved, of whom Claire McCardell was one. Her designs epitomised what became known as the "American Look", created during the years that native designers were cut off from Paris, and in the immediate post-war period; these distinctly American garments included loose-fitting trousers, pulled in at the waist with wide belts and worn with flat shoes, and jersey dresses worn during the day or evening. From 1940 onwards, Claire McCardell designed under her own name for Townley, the New York ready-to-wear manufacturer, and sold her medium-priced, ready-to-wear clothing in the department store Lord and Taylor. She was the first designer to use denim for dresses and made a feature of double rows of stitching and fastenings, such as hooks and eyes. Her clothing, always smart, invariably included deep side pockets, which gave a casual appearance. As footwear in the United States was strictly

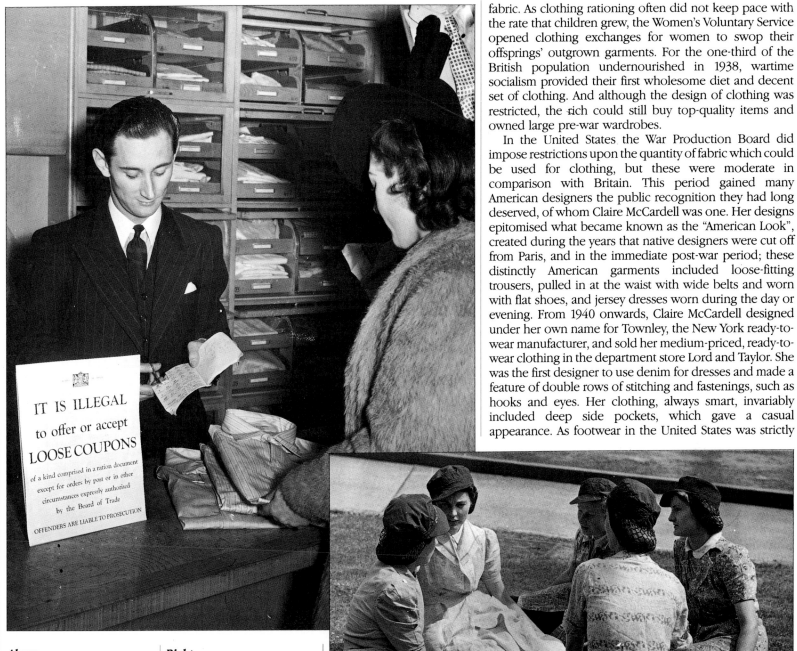

Above

A shopper of 1941 presents her ration book when buying shirts. The notice on the sales counter hints at attempts to control the black market trade in coupons.

Left

One solution to the problem of the shortage of stockings.

Right

These factory-workers, seen here enjoying a lunch-break, are wearing the typical protective caps, hair nets and printed cotton overalls of the time.

83

Top and left
Two American hat designs in straw, trimmed with flowers.

Right
Accessories such as scarves became very important when new clothes were so rare. The morale-boosting print by textile company Jacqmar depicts "The American Forces in London". Note also the lady on the right, who is wearing the "Stars and Stripes" tied round her hair.

rationed but ballet shoes were not, McCardell encouraged manufacturers to produce them with sturdier soles and retain the soft uppers. These became very popular with American women, who wore them with dresses and trousers. From this period onwards the fashion press, from *Vogue* down to the cheaper magazines such as *Seventeen* and *Mademoiselle*, included American designers in their fashion pages.

On February 12, 1947, Christian Dior shocked the world with his collection, which almost instantly became dubbed the "New Look". Dior's designs were a great contrast to wartime styles and created much controversy. His dresses had narrow shoulders, exaggerated busts, tiny waists, padded hips and very full skirts which reached just 12 inches from the ground. In Great Britain, there was an outcry about the extravagance of these dresses, which required up to 25 yards of material and would represent many years' worth of accumulated coupons. *Picture Post* angrily exclaimed that the "New Look" was "... launched upon a world which had not the material to copy them — and whose women have neither the money to buy, the leisure to enjoy, nor in some designs even the strength to support these masses of material."[1]

Paris had clearly re-established her position as world leader of fashion. Indeed Britain responded as if she were obliged to copy the "New Look". By launching styles which Europeans could clearly not afford, Paris must have had her eye on recapturing the American market, where fabric restrictions had been lifted in 1946.

Initially, both Great Britain and the United States mocked the "New Look" and stressed its impracticalities for the housewife and typist in an age when fashion was no longer the prerogative of the rich. Against all the odds, however, women soon yearned to throw away their wartime clothes and associated memories, and adopt this new outline for the post-war era. This was harder to achieve in Europe than in the United States as rationing was not lifted until 1949 and many utility clothes remained in the shops until 1951. During this intermediary period English women did pay lip-service to the "New Look" by adding a band of material to the bottom of their utility skirts to lengthen them. Even so, by 1948 wholesale versions of Christian Dior's fashion were available in many shops for those women prepared to spend many of their treasured coupons.

[1](*Picture Post* 27.9.47, p26.)

UTILITY CLOTHING

Turned out nice again

Find time to be gay—even this busy Spring—in 'Viyella.' It'll keep you on good terms with your purse, for in spite of its soft texture and lighthearted colours 'Viyella' wears tirelessly and washes like a kitten's ear. Digby Morton—famous fashion designer—shows one way to be clever with 'Viyella'—and there are plenty more.

Fancy Woven Designs, Checks, Stripes, Plain Shades and Marls from 6/8 yard, including Tax.

Viyella REGD.
FROCK DESIGNS

WILLIAM HOLLINS & COMPANY LIMITED · VIYELLA HOUSE · NOTTINGHAM

Left *Viyella frock, 1941.* **Below** *This photograph displays a new woollen stocking compared to a silk one. Manufacturers and designers combined forces to create alternatives to silk; the production of silk for clothing was banned during WWII.*

Top *A display of Utility cotton and rayon frocks. The basic design of all these garments is very similar, although some differentiation was achieved by the use of a variety of patterned fabrics.*

Top A customer makes her selection from the collection of Utility suits available, 1942.
Below A variety of Utility spring fashions worn by mannequins in Selfridges, 1945.

Top right The first "demobbed" men from the RAF received civilian clothing, May 1945. Note the generous cut of these pinstriped suits, the wider lapels and turnups on the trousers.

Far right Civilian suit designed by Major Morris May, President of the Leeds Wholesale Clothiers Federation, 1941. This had eight pockets and used only three yards of cloth, which represented a saving of 16in (40.5cm) on the average lounge suit. This alternative was not very widely worn, however.

AMERICAN WARTIME AND POSTWAR DRESS

Left Denim dress by Claire McCardell, 1942. This was initially intended for house and garden wear, but became so popular that its design was used for both day and evening dresses. All these photographs were taken by Louise Dahl-Wolfe for the American Harper's Bazaar, and all the clothes are by McCardell.

Top left Full circle skirt and knitted circlet shoulder wrap, 1947. Both McCardell and Dior recognised that after the war women would welcome a complete change of style. McCardell's garments, however, were much simpler than Dior's corsetted, stiff fashions. **Bottom left** Wool-jersey sleeveless top and long shorts for cycling, 1949. **Right** Timeless grey jersey, halter swimming costume, 1945. **Above** Comfortable and classic, cotton calico summer dress, 1945.

EVENING DRESS

Left Evening dress by Paquin, 1946. This dress, made in off-white slipper satin with unusual panier draperies on a sheath skirt, develops into a voluminous fantail train. **Bottom** Black crepe two-piece dress worn by Joan Crawford in the film Humoresque (1946).

Right Black evening gown of Chantilly lace, designed by Peggy Hunt of California, c.1947. **Far right** Evening dress made from Eastman acetate rayon, 1947.

THE "NEW LOOK"

Left A London dress manufacturer produced this dress, called "Midway", as a compromise between the old, short skirts and the new full-lengths which were causing so much controversy. This dress retailed at 79s.11d — the equivalent in rationing terms of seven clothing coupons.

Right "New Look" suit, c.1947.

Above The Duke and Duchess of Windsor, 1947. The fashion-conscious Duchess is wearing the nipped-in-waist and full-skirted "New Look". **Right** At the same time that Christian Dior launched the "New Look", Jacques Fath introduced a long, lean, hobble-skirted design which was also fashionable. This garment was created by an American desginer, Paul Parnes, in 1947. **Far right** The "New Look" at its most extreme, Christian Dior, 1947.

SWIMWEAR

Jantzen

makes the whole
world swim

You too can be a 'danger' in one of the
new Jantzens. They're specially cut and coloured to make
you and everyone else think you're just wonderful — Knit to fit
like skin they'll help you to swim like a mermaid. The two-piece
is Rayon/Lastex with a bra adjustable in three fascinating
ways, and the one-piece is wool Jacquard/Lastex with thrilling back
exposure. The mesmerised male is wearing wool/Lastex
trunks with tunnel belt and zipp coin pocket.

JANTZEN KNITTING MILLS LTD · BRENTFORD · ENGLAND

Above *Magazine advert, 1948, for
swimwear in synthetic fibres.*

Right *Printed separates for
American beachwear.*

Left *Ruched swimsuits and extra-large straw hats, 1947.*

Below *Mother and daughter in matching two-pieces at an American beauty parade. Note the little girl's Shirley Temple curls.*

Left A simple turban-style hat decorated with a sword-shaped pin. **Right** Black felt turban with Bird of Paradise feathers, 1946.

Left A simple pill-box shape is adorned with spotted net, fake flowers and butterfly in this American design. **Right** An ensemble by Digby Morton for 1948. This version of the "New Look" suit is in rayon, and the extreme femininity of the style is set off with a "Dolly Varden" bonnet, giving a nostalgic feel. **Below left** Spectators at the first horseracing meeting in Paris after Liberation, in 1944, show the eccentricity that French fashion indulged in during the Occupation. **Below right** In contrast, a smart and simple American design in grey felt for 1947.

Typical fifties patterned fabrics.

CHAPTER·SIX
1950
TO
1959

During the 1950s and 60s many areas of art and design — including fashion — rejected war-time values of quality and permanence. Pop Art emerged during the early 1950s and Richard Hamilton, a leading exponent, summarised this movement in 1957 when he stated that, "Pop Art is Popular, Transient, Expendable, Low Cost, Mass Produced, Young, Witty, Sexy, Gimmicky, Glamorous, Big Business."[1]

Pop artists wholeheartedly embraced commercial — and particularly American — culture, and promoted the idea that comic and packaging art was as valid as traditional fine art forms. Rock 'n 'Roll, which started in the United States, hit the world by the mid-1950s and was enthusiastically consumed by the relatively affluent and increasingly visible teenage market. Audrey Hepburn, Marilyn Monroe and, by the late 1950s, Brigitte Bardot were the most popular and widely copied film stars of the period. Lana Turner also influenced dress. She became known as the "Sweater Girl" for the tight-fitting jumpers she wore over bras which were reinforced with stiffening points, and helped to create the vogue for knitwear. James Dean's and Marlon Brando's denim and leather clothing became almost universally adopted by young men. The United States economy had been thriving since the war, and by the mid 1950s the United Kingdom, too, was enjoying a period of full employment. Between 1945 and 1958 world manufacturers of consumer goods increased by 60 per cent. The dual-income family became increasingly common and this rise in income, coupled with the rapid extension in credit and hire-purchase facilities, greatly expanded the market for consumer goods and clothing.

Technology became a dominant force throughout the 1950s and 60s and was seen to symbolise the modern world. Technological developments were welcomed with excitement as they optimistically promised to transform lives, and consumer durables in particular promised to liberate the busy woman from housework. Many major strides were also made in the production of synthetic fibres, which became a great asset to the 1950s wardrobe. Nylon, which arrived from the United States after the war, was invaluable for the manufacture of tights and underwear. Other trademarked fabrics included Aurilan, Banlon and Orlon, all of which were easily washed, dripped dry and did not require ironing. As a result, thick synthetic jumpers and suits manufactured in light colours became very popular, although a later return to natural fibres made them redundant by the 1970s.

In Paris, Dior designed a variety of intricately cut and highly sophisticated couture garments. In 1951 he created the Princess line, in 1954 the long-waisted H line, and the A and Y lines in 1957, when he also designed the first chemise dresses. These began the long fashion for loose-fitting clothing which Yves Saint Laurent, Dior's assistant, designed after his death in the same year. Chanel, who had

closed her doors in 1939, reopened her salon in 1954, and continued to design classical, comfortable clothing for her customers, in contrast to Dior's garments, which quickly dated. During this period, she designed the famous Chanel suit — just-below-the-knee length skirt, and round-necked

Above left
Marilyn Monroe, the ultimate sex symbol, was as well loved by women as she was by men. Both during her lifetime and after her death, hundreds of women have copied her style. She's pictured here in 1954.

Above right
Jayne Mansfield was a "dumb blonde" in the Monroe mould, who successfully parodied Hollywood's depiction of women whilst being a part of the system. This photo is from 1957.

Left
Richard Hamilton compiled this collage, entitled Just What Is It That Makes Today's Homes So Different, So Appealing? *from American advertisements in 1956.*

Right
London Teddy Boy, 1954.

jacket trimmed in a contrasting colour braid. As in the 1920s, her clothing was widely copied by all grades of manufacturer. Balenciaga, Fath, Rochas and Balmain were also among the leading couturiers of the period, all of whom depended on the talents of Irving Penn, John French and Richard Avedon, top fashion photographers who captured the elegance of their clothes for *Vogue* and *Harpers*. In Great Britain, the fashions of Norman Hartnell, Hardy Amies and Victor Stiebel were internationally admired, as were the exquisite sculptural evening gowns of New York designer Charles James.

During the 1950s the couture trade began to decline as top-quality, ready-to-wear clothing became increasingly available. For financial reasons, many couturiers designed for multiple stores and manufacturers: Amies designed prototypes for Hepworths and Debenhams; Hartnell designed for Berkertex. The couture industry has always dressed large numbers of influential women free of charge, and therefore spin-offs such as the sale of perfumes and accessories have boosted their profits and often kept them in business.

The style of men's clothing changed dramatically during the 1950s. After an initially formal start, men's dress relaxed considerably as the conventional shirt and tie was sometimes replaced with a sweater, and separates became widely worn. Savile Row and Jermyn Street in London had always led the world in menswear, but in 1957, when John Stephen opened his first shop in Carnaby Street, this too became internationally established for its cheaper high-fashion clothing.

In 1950, British *Vogue* reported that, "There is a new almost Edwardian formality in men's London clothes, which is reminiscent of the pre-1914 period."[2] This had been a glorious period for the English upper class and one which many undoubtedly wished to revive. The "New Edwardians", as they became known, adopted stove-pipe trousers, high, stiff white collars, and patterned waistcoats, but by 1954 the term "Teddy Boy" was interchangeable with "New Edwardian": a group of working-class youths had adopted cheaper and more elaborate versions of the style. *Punch* stated that, "Crimes are now committed, on fashionable commons, by young gentlemen in the velvet collars and fancy waistcoats, the turned-up cuffs and buttoned-down pockets of the Edwardian masher."[3]

According to many people, "Teds" were involved in racist attacks and petty larceny, and their clothes became synonymous with their crimes: they wore their collars turned up or tied down with boot-lace ties, tight draped trousers and heavy crepe-soled "brothel creepers" on their feet; their hair was long, and they used grease to style variously shaped quiffs. Although Teddy Boys consisted of only a minority of individuals, they reflected the increasing confidence and financial independence that enabled young people to express themselves through their dress

during the 1950s. For the first time, teenagers donned different clothing from that worn by their parents and fashion became a youthful phenomenon.

In great contrast to the stylised artificiality of the Teds, most young men and women adopted more casual clothing. Many teenage girls wore drainpipe trousers, big jumpers and flat pumps and for evening a full circle skirt with a turtle-neck sweater. It was jeans, however, which transformed the appearance of the 1950s teenager. Denim was first used for trousers by Levi Strauss, when it provided hard-wearing and cheap work clothing for American gold miners during the mid-nineteenth century. From then onwards it was used to make men's and boy's bib overalls for work, and was used by the American armed forces throughout World War II. However, the huge demand for jeans and dungarees which emerged from men, women and children, but mainly from teenagers, during the 1950s was sparked off by film when James Dean wore jeans in *Rebel without a Cause* (1955), and Elvis Presley wore a denim suit in *Jailhouse Rock* (1957). Although jeans have often been credited as being truly democratic clothing, they have, like other fashion garments, always had to be of

Above
Working-class teenagers at a dance-hall.

Left
Teddy Boy in Bristol, 1955.

Right
Audrey Hepburn epitomized a chic, gamine style. She was frequently dressed by Givenchy, who also designed the costumes for her best known film, Funny Face.

Far right
This stand at the Ideal Home Exhibition of 1956 represented the designers' predictions for furnishings and fashions of 1980.

the "right" brand and style.

In 1955 Bazaar was opened on the Kings Road, London, by Mary Quant and her husband Alexander Plunket Green and heralded the dominance of the British boutique. Quant went on to become one of the many art school-trained designers who radically changed the face of fashion and established London as a major fashion centre. As she could not find the fashions she wanted to retail, Quant designed and, initially, made her stock. She and her husband already mixed socially with the much spotlighted "Chelsea Set", who formed a large part of their initial clientele and helped to publicise her garments: within one week of opening, Bazaar took more than five times the amount of money anticipated. Mary Quant and Alexander Plunket Green proved both to themselves and the clothing trades at large that there existed a huge demand for fashionable clothing from the young which reached its peak in the 1960s.

[1](Hamilton, Richard, *Collected Works 1953-77*, Thames & Hudson, London, 1982, p28.)
[2](*Vogue*, April 1950, p109.)
[3](*Punch*, February 24, 1954, p268.)

SUITS AND COATS

Left Suit, Nina Ricci, 1951. Black and white hounds-tooth suit with astrakan cuffs, developing into a muff. **Top left** Suit, Jacques Fath, 1951. Black wool suit trimmed with mink. **Top** Wool suits, 1957, showing the popular "stand away" neckline.

Above Duster-style coat, designed by Adele of California c.1955. **Right** Coat by Pierre Balmain, 1951. This full-skirted coat had a hemline with a circumference of 12ft. The waistline silhouette is formed by a series of darts that throw pleats above and below the waistline.

Left A two-piece grey silk suit from the House of Christian Dior, 1957.

105

DRESSES

Right *American debutantes on being presented to the Queen in 1955. The last presentation of debs was in 1958.* **Below** *Afternoon dresses by Yves Saint Laurent for Christian Dior, 1958. The two dresses on the left are in printed silk, the one on the right in fine black wool.*

Left *Printed cotton summer dress, 1956.*

Left A dress in coral pink wool by the House of Worth, 1956. **Right** A spotted sundress.

EVENING DRESS

Left Green swathed evening dress by Christian Dior, 1959.

Left Off-white doeskin wool by the House of Worth, 1955. This earliest of fashion houses was controlled by members of the Worth family until 1954, when they were bought out by the House of Paquin.

Left *Ballgown in white tulle, scattered with yellow flowers and with large green bustle-bow, Norman Hartnell, 1954. Hartnell is best known for his designs for the Queen (particularly her wedding dress and coronation robe) and Winterhalter-inspired crinolines, like the one seen here, were his forte.* **Bottom left** *Evening dress and coat by Jacques Fath, 1956. Fath started his career in 1937, and was a key name in the immediate post-war period. After his death in 1954, his wife Genevieve kept the House open until 1957.* **Right** *Evening coat by top British ready-to-wear company, Berkertex, 1957, in a synthetic satin fabric.*

The teen-market became very important in the affluent environment of the late 1950s. **Far left** A 1957 collection showing the "acceptable" face of Rock'n'Roll styles, achieved with a liberal use of synthetic fibres such as nylon net and taffeta. **Left** This shows a more disreputable and down-market version — notice particularly the stiletto-heeled shoes. There were attempts made to ban these from public venues because of the damage they did to floor surfaces.

Centre The Beatniks of the late 50s mixed influences from the Left Bank Paris set and American jazz performers. Their dress reflected a deliberate rejection of consumer values, and the free-and-easy lifestyle documented by Allen Ginsburg and Jack Kerouac. Ironically, many of the styles they favoured have become fashion classics, such as the check shirt, "sloppy-joe" sweater, and black dirndl skirt. **Top left** Teddy Tinling separates of 1957. The girl's T-shirt cashes in on the popularity of British pop singer Tommy Steele. **Left** These jive fans wear practical clothes for dancing.

CASUAL WEAR

Peggy Page COTTON SUNDRESS
and button-to-waist jacket, in bright Mexican inspired print. The dress has detachable shoulder straps and its own underskirt.
Colours: **PINK/BLUE, RED/OLIVE.**
Sizes: 36", 38", 40", 42" hips.

B.624 **84/-** or 12/6 monthly

SAIL CLOTH DRESS
buttoned through, with white saddle stitching to match pearl effect buttons. Huge patch pockets.
Colours: **DEEP ROSE PINK, ATLANTIC BLUE.**
Sizes: 36", 38", 40" hips.

B.623 **£4.19.6** or 15/- monthly

Linzi SUNDRESS AND FITTED JACKET
Flower print cotton dress. Empire line bodice, full skirt. Midi jacket has detachable belt.
Colours: **WHITE/BLUE, WHITE/PINK.**
Sizes: 34", 36", 38", 40" hips.

B.625 **£6.16.6** or 21/- monthly

Page 9

Top left Skirts and sweaters, Autumn, 1954. **Bottom left** Teenage spectators at Wimbledon 1953 show aspirations of Hollywood glamour with their sunglasses, strapless bodices, waspie belts and bangles.

Above 1957 mail order printed cotton sundresses.

Right These separates combine a strange mix of space-age and ethnic themes by Teddy Tinling, 1958. **Far right** Italian separates in mohair, 1958.

MEN AND CHILDREN

Top left *1951 styles for teenagers in new synthetic fibres. The boy is wearing a terylene/wool blend suit, terylene shirt, socks and tie; and she is in all nylon: dress, socks, ballet pumps and fake fur wrap.*
Bottom left *A large family of 1955, the girls in typical cotton dresses.*
Above *An ensemble by Kay Lewis of California, but...* **right** *in reality, the crumpled cotton frock and battered sun hat was more common. This photo is from 1959.*

Right Designers attempted to ring the changes on the traditional theme with printed jacket linings, or cut-away jackets, 1957.

Above Menswear of 1959: single-breasted three-piece suits in check fabrics. **Right** Marlon Brando presented an alternative image for young men. Here, he is wearing the leather jacket and blue jeans he popularized in the film, The Wild One (1953).

SWIMWEAR AND UNDERWEAR

Exquisite Form

CIRCLOFORM BRA
Has the famous 4-section cups stitched round and round for perfect fit. **WHITE** only.
Cup sizes: A 30″ to 36″, B 32″ to 38″, C 32″ to 40″.

Superfine poplin D.855 **14/-**
Nylon D.856 **18/-**

EQUALIZER STRAPLESS BRA
The most comfortable strapless made, it never, never slips! **WHITE** only.
Cup sizes: A 30″ to 36″, B 32″ to 38″.

Glamorous art satin D.859 **29/-**

NG LINE Floating Action BRA
glamour and comfort of Floating Action combined
torso band for full figure control. **WHITE** only.
B 34″ to 42″, C 34″ to 44″.
oplin. D.860 **27/-**

FLOATING ACTION BRA
Tangent straps give firm yet gentle support to the whole bra. **WHITE** only.
Cup sizes: A 30″ to 36″, B 32″ to 38″, C 32″ to 40″.

Superfine poplin D.857 **18/-**
Nylon D.858 **22/-**

EQUALIZER BRA
Designed for figure perfection. Its subtle contours give you complete figure confidence. **WHITE** only. Cup sizes: A 30″ to 36″, B 32″ to 38″.

Lustrous art satin D.861 **18/-**

Far left (top) Foundation garments by Sarong. **Above** Mail order underwear from 1957. Richard Hamilton parodied the whirlpool stitching of Exquisite Form bras in his painting Hommage à Chrysler Corp, 1957, representing the sex symbol. **Far left** (bottom) 1950s underwear could be very uncomfortable and restrictive. **Left** Cotton beachwear separates of 1955. **Right** A Hollywood style in black with white trim. **Far right** Printed swimsuit with plunging back, pictured in Florida.

HATS

Above Although fashion in the 1950s was becoming more informal, a social occasion still demanded a hat. This 1957 design is one of the more elegant and upmarket hats on offer.

Right Traditional milliners in the 1950s could still hold their own against the mass-manufactured hat, a situation that was soon to change. This showroom display of 1955 demonstrates a preponderance of small, mostly brimless, hats.

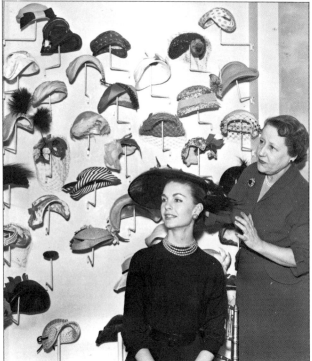

Above A 1955 design by society milliner Gina Davies is very characteristic of the period — small, smart and understated.

This black velvet hat with grosgrain trim shows one of the elegant and aristocratic styles popular in the 1950s. British models such as Barbara Goalen characterized this look.

"Is Paris dead?" design by Pierre Cardin.

CHAPTER·SEVEN
1960
TO
1969

During the 1960s the media played a major role in creating mass markets for goods and used fashion as a marketing device to redefine constantly consumer tastes. This built-in obsolescence reached its peak with the brief vogue for fashionably styled throw-away paper dresses and inflatable plastic furniture. Television and car ownership, which had increased during the 1950s, accelerated rapidly, greatly reducing variations within and between countries, and increasing personal mobility. Much has been made of the introduction of the contraceptive pill and the "permissive society", but a great deal of deep-rooted Victorian moralism also existed. This was highlighted by the much-publicised court case in 1963 concerning the explicitly sexual passages in D H Lawrence's novel, *Lady Chatterley's Lover.*

The dominant fashion retail outlet of the 1960s was the boutique, which provided a conducive selling environment for the young — gimmicky interiors, loud pop music and a self-service approach — but this decade also witnessed a rapid expansion in multiple-store trading for cheap- and medium-priced garments. Textile design was greatly influenced by Op Art between 1960 and 1967. Op — short for optical — Art played on visual responses to abstract paintings which appeared to ripple, project or recede, although the painting was static and the surface two-dimensional. These were often monochrome, but also juxtaposed coloured hues to achieve a similar effect. Bridget Riley, Richard Anuszkiewicz, Peter Sedgley and Piero Dorazio were the leading artists of this important, although marginal, art movement.

Fashion during the 1960s was mainly British-led, but the styles had repercussions around the world. In 1961 Mary Quant opened her second boutique in Knightsbridge, and a year later was designing garments for J C Penney's 1,700 American chain stores. Quant, Plunkett-Green and their financial advisor Archie McNair combined a great talent for design with outstanding business acumen. By 1964 Quant was designing paper patterns for Butterick, which made the styles of her medium-priced garments available to a wider market, 1966 saw the start of Quant's cosmetic empire, and by the 1970s her daisy logo promoted a huge range of items including stationery, bed-linen and toys. Quant designed mini-skirts, hipster flared trousers, gym slips and fun furs for the young. As hemlines rose — sometimes to thigh level — brightly coloured and textured tights became very fashionable, and were another area in which Quant designed under licence.

Barbara Hulanicki and her husband Stephen Fitz-Simon, who was her business manager, also made a significant contribution to 60s fashion. She started her career selling cheap, mail-order fashion clothes which she advertised in the press to the teenage market. The demand for these was phenomenal, and in 1963 she opened her first boutique, called Biba. In contrast to the many bright colours of the

60s, Biba clothes were made in muted mauves, prunes, blues, greys, pinks and black. Her high-fashion clothing cost a fraction of Quant's and was consumed within minutes of going on display. Far from looking sexually provocative in their skimpy clothing, Quant's and Hulanicki's customers often assumed a child-like appearance and by the late 60s Twiggy and Maddy Smith's

Above
Leading 1960s designer Ossie Clarke, with Chrissie Shrimpton modelling his 1965 Op-Art quilted-silk coat.

Above

Men's clothes in the 1960s demonstrated a freedom in the use of colours and fabrics never seen before or since in this century. The shirt here is of embroidered cotton voile from the London boutique, Mr Fish.

Top left

Coat by Biba, in characteristic dusky colours.

Bottom left

The music and appearance of the pop group, The Beatles, dominated the decade. In the early 1960s, their haircuts were considered to be daringly long and their Italian-inspired suits spawned numerous high-street copies.

Top right

Mary Quant launching a range of her shoe designs in the early 1960s.

Bottom right

Brightly coloured evening dress with label, "Light Years Ahead".

Above

The Mod style — Italian suits, parkas, short, sharp haircuts and the all-important Italian (Vespa) scooter — seen here at a rally. The violence that often accompanied such meetings kept the image of the Mods in the newspapers.

teenage figures became the fashionable ideal: a strong contrast to the shapely and more mature physique fashionable during the 1950s.

The Chelsea spirit was witnessed in Paris too — not in the quiet salons of Dior or Balenciaga, but from the new houses of André Courrèges and Paco Rabanne. The widespread interest in space throughout the decade was reflected in the garments of these designers. Paco Rabanne and Courrèges used unconventional materials, such as plastics and metals, and silver and white were

predominant. Andy Warhol, the American pop artist, loved Courrèges' clothes and proposed that everyone should look the same, dressed in silver, as that merged into a futuristic technological environment. The dictatorship of Parisian couture upon mass-clothing styles began to crumble as the new generation of young London designers largely dominated the field. Nina Ricci, Lanvin and Yves Saint Laurent opened ready-to-wear boutiques to broaden their market.

Men's clothing broke down barriers about what was

considered acceptable or effeminate, as designers challenged men to wear pink, flower-patterned shirts. Mick Jagger, lead singer of pop group The Rolling Stones, defied convention when he went on stage wearing a white organdie mini-dress over trousers. Teddy boys had largely died out (although small groups retained the style and are still evident today), and by 1963, Mods and Rockers became the dominant sub-cultural groups in Britain. Mods were acutely fashion conscious and adopted Parka coats, smart and fairly tight-fitting Italian suits, shirts with button-down collars and winklepicker or hushpuppy shoes. For casual clothes, Levi jeans, Fred Perry sports shirts and cardigans were worn, and Mod girls dressed in knitted twin-sets, shift dresses, ski-pants and suits with straight skirts which reached three inches below the knee. Much of the Mods' clothing was bought from boutiques in Carnaby Street. The Vespa motor scooter became central to their group identity and these, adorned with flags and mascots, provided the transport to seaside resorts where they fought bitter battles with their opponents, the Rockers. The latter, in complete contrast, were disinterested in fashion and wore old jeans and leathers and rode high-powered motor-bikes.

Hippies formed a radically different group in the 1960s. Self-contained, they rejected the commercialism of the 60s culture and were in sympathy with the rising peace movement. Their ethnic styles of clothing, such as Afghan coats, kaftans, Indian fringed belts, headbands and beads, were bought from the newly opened Indian boutiques; they wore their hair long, and often painted their bodies with flowers and psychedelic patterns. From 1967 until the early 70s, peasant styles became very fashionable among more conventional circles.

By 1969 the highly successful American designer Rudi Geinrich stated that, "Haute couture doesn't have the same meaning any more because money, status and power no longer have the same meaning. Now fashion starts in the streets. What I do is watch what kids are putting together for themselves. I formalize it, give it something of my own, perhaps, and then it is fashion."[1]

This filtering up, as opposed to down, of designs became a significant factor in 1970s dress.

[1] (*Fortune,* January 1969, p87.)

Above
Designs in black leather and printed silk by Pierre Cardin, 1969. Cardin presented his first collection in his own name in 1953 and became known for "unisex" designs. He has since become famous, if not notorious, for attaching his name to almost every conceivable consumer product – from towels to luggage and even furniture.

Top left
As those involved in the hippy subculture became increasingly interested in Eastern cultures and religions, and travelled to India to sit at the feet of gurus, they adopted textiles and jewellery from the Third World.

Left
The unorthodox materials that Paco Rabanne favoured for his clothes led to bizarre methods of manufacture. Here he is seen wielding a pair of pliers to construct a chain-mail dress – a process more akin to sculpture than dressmaking.

SUITS

Left *Woven Courtelle wool tweed suit by Alexon, 1962. Alexon, a British company still in existence, sells quality medium-priced garments to a largely middle-class market. Their clothes are sold in department stores.* **Bottom left** *Mrs Kennedy, wife of the then President of the United States, 1961. Jackie Kennedy was a highly visible and widely copied fashion consumer during the 1960s.*

Below *Stretch-towelling cat-suits, 1967. These hooded suits demonstrate an easily wearable example of the influence of space exploration on fashion.*

Right *Publicity shot for the London showing of Yves Saint Laurent's Spring Collection, 1963.*

Left Tweed suit by Marc Bohan, chief designer at Christian Dior, 1966. Photograph by Cecil Beaton.
Right White lace mini-skirted suit, photographed at Ascot, 1966. By this date the mini had become widely accepted, even in the conventional setting of Ascot. This woman's escort is dressed, in great contrast, in Edwardian attire.
Below Twiggy and Justin de Villeneuve at the Ritz Hotel, London, c. 1969.

DRESSES

Above Smart, geometric mid-1960s styles. **Top right** These designs are by John Bates for a popular television series, The Avengers, in 1965.

Right In 1963 Mary Quant launched her Ginger Group range of cheap, interchangeable pieces. This selection from 1965 shows mix-and-match red sweaters with camel and red pinafore dresses or skirts. **Far right** A 1966 white tabard dress with printed sleeves and tights (in Bri-Nylon).

Top left As designers became bored with the ubiquitous mini, they began to experiment with new lengths. These two "maxi" dresses are by Pierre Cardin, 1969.

Left Cotton lace by top British ready-to-wear company Frank Usher, 1968.

Above Barbara Hulanicki started designing and manufacturing under the name Biba in 1964. This is a later style made in printed Tricel.

COATS

Below In this 1962 design, Paco Rabanne demonstrates his experimental approach to materials and manufacturing. Made from small pieces of cut leather, it is joined together by studs to give a chain-mail effect.

Above In 1965 the Sunday Telegraph magazine asked, "Is Paris Dead?", reflecting the lessening influence of haute couture. But these smart and simple coats by Marc Bohan for Dior are classic, stylish design. **Left** This sunshine yellow design with contrasting black collar and button trim characterizes the bold use of colour that exemplified the best of 60s fashion.

Right A smart geometric design of 1965. **Far right** A glamorous (if impractical) suit by Biba, 1968, of white moire coat and trousers. **Below** The informality of the 60s allowed the winter coat to be abandoned for a more casual style, such as a long, knitted cardigan: this example, from 1969, is in Shetland wool.

CASUAL WEAR

Left Bowling outfits in stretch nylon by Teddy Tinling, 1962. **Bottom left** Knitted separates in Bri-Nylon yarns, 1963. **Below** Printed separates.

Right Audience at a late 1960s Pop Festival. **Far right** (top) The influence of the military theme as seen in London's Portobello Road. **Far right** (bottom) The blouse on the left, and both pairs of slacks, are made of synthetic Dacron/rayon fabrics. The tunic on the right is in screen-printed linen from 1966.

EVENING DRESS

Left *Classical ballgown by the House of Givenchy, which opened in 1952.* **Centre** *Op-Art designs in silk jersey, 1966.* **Bottom** *Balmain evening dresses, 1966. The House of Balmain opened in 1946 and was immensely popular throughout the 1950s and 60s.*

Right *The rainwear company Burberry launched its knitwear collection in 1966 with these see-through, hand-knitted designs in gold mesh.* **Far right** *A characteristically inventive design by Paco Rabanne, 1967, in silvered leather.*

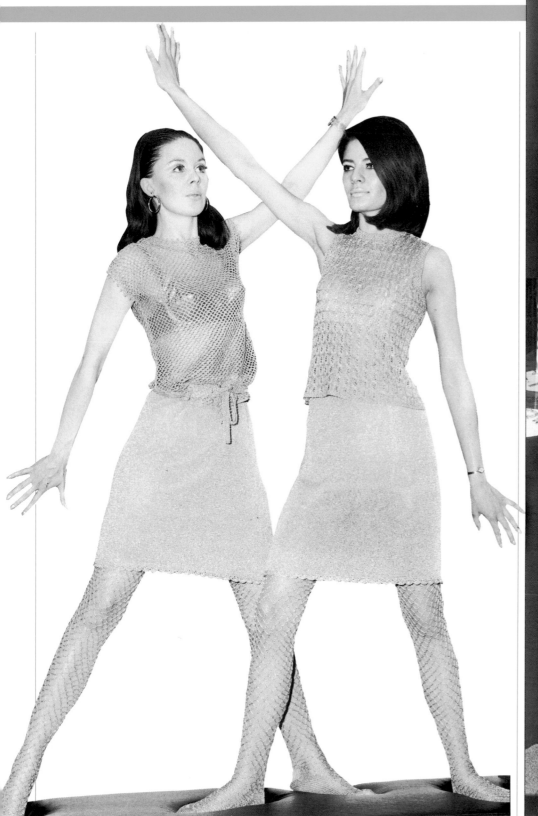

SWIMWEAR AND UNDERWEAR

Right *Underwear by Kayser Bondor for 1966. A bolder use of colour and pattern was made by this date than in the 1950s. These styles are for a slightly older woman, as by the mid 60s most young women would have preferred tights to stockings and suspenders.* **Below** *Nylon underwear, 1967, in "fun" styles made of synthetic fabrics.*

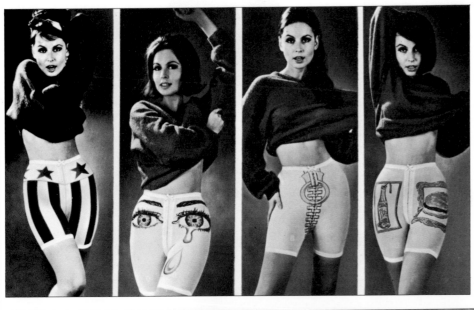

Far left These pantie-girdles may have "pop" motifs printed on them, but they demonstrate that even in the easy-going 1960s some women felt the need of "supportive" underwear to assist a fashionably stick-like look. **Left** A design for topless bathing by Rudi Geinrich. **Below** Swimwear suggesting the influence of the James Bond film, Dr No.

CHILDREN

Left A variety of styles from 1965. **Far left** (bottom) These boys' and girls' suits of 1968 were launched to introduce a new crease-resistant fabric by the Courtaulds company. **Below** Pierre Cardin repeated the space-age look for children's clothes in 1967.

Right These boys from the late 60s wear the fringed waistcoats and flares that were fashionable for men. **Far right** (top) Boys' and girls' party wear in black velvet from the Baby Dior range, 1968. **Far right** (bottom) Printed velvet maxi-length coats, 1969.

MEN

Top left Blazer by John Stephen, c.1965, worn with white shirt and flowery tie. Stephen, whose main shop was in Carnaby Street, became one of the leading fashion designers for men in the 1960s.
Above This photograph shows everyday, casual menswear, 1967.
Left The Beatles wearing hippy-style clothing, c. 1967.

Opposite page. Left Union Jack jacket, c.1965. **Top right** Fashions from Cecil Gee, one of Britain's high street retailers, 1966.
Bottom right Italian menswear, designed by the house of Ellesse, Perugia, 1969.

HAIR AND HATS

Left and **far left** Two designs from mass-manufacturer Edward Mann, 1966. **Bottom left** Hats for men and women, 1961.

Left Fun spectacle designs, 1964, in plastic and diamanté. **Bottom left** Caps of imitation flowers, 1963. **Bottom right** Victoriana styles by fashionable hairdresser Raymond "Mr Teasy-Weasy", 1969. False hairpieces were popular throughout the 60s.

143

Sequinned glamor by Bruce Oldfield, 1979.

CHAPTER·EIGHT
1970
TO
1979

The optimistic spirit of the 1960s began to fade in the 1970s with high inflation, rising unemployment and growing dissatisfaction with industrial life and technology. In his influential book *Design For the Real World* (1972), Victor Papanek stressed that the designer had a responsibility to provide for real human needs — particularly those of the disabled, and of under-developed countries — rather than to conceive trashy, ephemeral goods. Likewise, the Craft Revival in design, which emphasised the beauty of hand-made and individual items, rejected mass-produced popular culture. The great vogue for peasant styles of dress during the late 1960s and early 1970s was perhaps indicative of the growing interest in health foods, ecology and world peace. The carefully marketed goods from Body Shop International, whose beauty products have been made from natural substances and tested without cruelty to animals since the 1970s, commercially reiterate this mood. The women's movement also gained considerable momentum during this decade, fuelled by the publication of Germaine Greer's feminist book *The Female Eunuch* (1970).

1970 was a year of contradictory dress styles. Some women wore their hair in the mode of the Pre-Raphaelites and assumed long, ethereal dresses, while others shortened their mini-skirts even further. During the early years of the decade fashion did not change radically from that worn in the 60s. Shorts with bibs or straps, which became dubbed "hotpants", provided some variation to the ubiquitous mini-skirts, which were available in a variety of materials: cotton, satin, leather, suede, velvet, corduroy and sometimes knitted or crocheted. At the same time, and in great contrast, Laura Ashley designed her very popular cotton Edwardian-style dresses with high collars and puffed sleeves; many of her fabrics were printed from simple, floral motifs based upon eighteenth and nineteenth century designs.

The 1973 opening of the Biba emporium in Kensington High Street was to become the last symbol of London's swinging Sixties. A staggering £5 million were spent on re-building and decorating this store to Barbara Hulanicki's personal style, and the result was an eclectic combination of Victorian Art Nouveau and Art Deco mixed with Hollywood glamour. The woodwork was painted dark-brown, mirrors were peach-tinted, and peacock-backed basket chairs provided seating for the customers. Leopardskin rugs, feather boas and lilies created the store's decadent ambience, and Biba's reputation was such that it was the first boutique to risk mysterious blackened windows which did not promote the store's merchandise. Biba sold men's, women's and children's fashions, food, and objects for interiors.

Hulanicki sold a packaged lifestyle where wit and style took precedence over sales drives: her merchandise covered only 90,000 out of a possible 200,000 square feet.

Above

Hotpants were the favourite fashion for the young in 1971, but an impossible style for anyone out of their teens or not so slim.

Left

Interest in the cultures of developing countries continued to be a dominant theme throughout much of the 1970s.

Right and **Below**

The Biba premises in London, remarkable for — among other things — its dark, dramatic decor.

Shortly after the opening, Alistair Best was moved to remark in *Design* magazine that "...shopping is almost a fringe activity". In the food hall, dog food was stored in the belly of a giant Great Dane-shaped stand and yet there were only a couple of check-outs. It irked British Land, Biba's backers, to see that people were soaking up the environment without feeling any obligation to buy. Hulanicki was an enormously talented designer but she suffered from stock-control and security problems as well as from an urge to fulfil her own retailing ideals, even at the expense of lost profits. British Land tried to commercialize and functionalize Biba, but in so doing drained the store of its life and appreciative public. Biba closed its doors in 1975 with losses of £6 million and was taken over as premises for Marks & Spencer.

Throughout the 1970s jeans continued to be widely worn, as indeed they are to the present day, although their shape, colour depth and decoration has changed with fashion. During the early 1970s denims which flared from the knee down and became faded with age were the most desirable — so much so that a second-hand pair often cost

147

more than a new one. Embroidered and patched jeans were also very fashionable, and dungarees enjoyed popularity throughout the decade. Many of America's leading ready-to-wear designers, including Ralph Lauren, Calvin Klein and Perry Ellis, regularly included denim in their collections and produced status-loaded "designer jeans".

Punk, initially confined to a group of mainly unemployed youths, emerged in Great Britain in the summer of 1976. Their dispiritedness was heightened and excited by Malcolm McLaren who managed and hyped the Sex Pistols band. Punk aimed to shock, and defiantly contradicted accepted modes of beauty and behaviour. At its most extreme, black plastic bin liners parodied garments, toilet chains became necklaces, and razor blades and safety pins were worn as multiple earrings. Existing garments were made to look more fragmented with slashes and crudely and loosely knitted mohair jumpers were widely worn. Punks' acidic-coloured and carefully-spiked hair and their bizarre, dishevelled appearances highlighted their rebellion, poverty and leisure.

Vivienne Westwood, McLaren's partner, dressed the "well-off" punks and many art students. Their shop in the Kings Road assumed many names throughout the 1970s: in 1971, "Let It Rock" used styles based upon Teddy Boy clothes; in 1972 "Too Young To Live, Too Fast To Die" sold James Dean-inspired clothing; 1974's "Sex" sold fetishistic and rubber garments; in 1977, "Seditionaries: Clothes For Heroes" sold punk clothing; and in 1980 it was changed to "World's End". In 1977 the price of a pair of bondage trousers in black cotton, with a loin cloth or kilt, from "Seditionaries" was £30.00, more than one weeks' social security for many punks, and consequently completely out of reach. The punk image could be easily achieved, however, by buying second-hand garments and dyeing them black, dyeing and spiking the hair, and using black cosmetics. Period clothing and American surplus shops have enjoyed great patronage since the 1970s, especially from teenagers and students seeking a cheap and individual style.

As the decade progressed, the imagery of punk was commercialized, upgraded and filtered into mainstream fashion and couture. This took many forms, but the most noticeable were the widespread appearance of loosely-woven, unstructured garments, boiler suits, superfluous zips, and back-brushed and spiky hairstyles. Decorative safety pins and razor blades sold in boutiques as cheap fashion jewellery, and in high street jewellers fashioned in gold. Men and women also had numerous holes pierced in their ears.

Above

Managed by Malcolm McLaren and clothed by McLaren and Vivienne Westwood, punk band the Sex Pistols initiated a revolution in both the music and fashion industries.

Right

Many young women in Britain in the late 1970s adopted a style which showed the influence of the singer from the band, Siouxsie and the Banshees.

Far right

Zandra Rhodes has produced clothes of a unique glamour since 1968. Usually her designs proclaim her highly individual signature; in 1977, however, she used the imagery and motifs common to punk street fashion to produce hybrids such as this ripped-and-pinned silk jersey dress.

148

Fiorucci was one of the many fashion shops which sold punk-inspired clothing for the young. The first Fiorucci was opened in Milan, Italy, in the mid 1960s and came to London in 1968 where it stocked fashions by London's young designers; by the mid 1970s Fiorucci was selling many exciting garments which made much use of plastics and fluorescent colours, and others based upon 1950s styles. At the top level, Zandra Rhodes introduced and romanticized punk into the privileged world of couture.

During the 1970s Milan became a recognised new capital of fashion. Italian clothing designers, such as Simonetta, Fontana and Cappuci, had started to make a name for themselves from the mid 1950s, but with little impact internationally. Giorgio Armani, who has become one of Milan's leading ready-to-wear designers for men and women, set up his own company in 1975, having previously worked as a designer for the menswear manufacturer Nino Cerruti and as an independent fashion consultant. Armani has introduced ease and comfort into classic, tailored garments — favouring items which look a little worn or crumpled when new — and makes much use of linen.

149

DRESSES

Far left (top) Lee Bender designed young, cheap clothes for her chain of Bus Stop boutiques from 1968-1979. This purple printed crepe is from 1970. **Far left** (bottom) An ethnic-inspired outfit by Monsoon Fashions, 1974. **Left** Rust wool overdress worn with black pants, Dior Boutique, 1978. **Below** "Gipsy" style dress by Ossie Clark for Quorum, 1970. **Right** A characteristic design by Jean Muir in fluid printed chiffon. In 1962 Muir worked under the label "Jane and Jane" before launching her own company in 1966.

Above A puff-sleeved mini by Mary Quant's Ginger Group, 1972. **Below** Fabrics designed by Mary Quant in crimplene for ICI, 1975.

151

SUITS AND COATS

Right Knitted suit, maxi-length coat and cap, c.1974.

Right Mary Quant's Ginger Group suit, 1972.

152

Left Knitted jacket and wool coat worn with thigh-length boots, 1975.

Left Jeff Banks' "Punk Style" double-breasted Mitchum jacket and skirt, 1977. Jeff Banks' high fashion was, and is today, immensely popular. **Right** Top-quality knickerbocker suit, with waistcoat in wool and cashmere, 1978.

EVENING DRESS

Below *Mary Quant lurex and paper-taffeta mini-dress with double sleeves, 1972. This, like many 70s clothes, could have been worn during the day or evening.*

Top right *A fluid Jean Patou evening outfit, 1976.* **Bottom left** *Bill Gibb evening dress, c.1977.* **Bottom right** *Ossie Clarke tunic and trousers, c.1973, photographed by Helmut Newton.*

Far left Sculptured evening dress by the Japanese designer Yuki, c.1972. **Left** Yves Saint Laurent's ethnic styles, 1976. **Below** Halter-neck evening dress from Norman Hartnell's "Petit Salon", which was aimed at a younger clientele, 1972.

CASUAL WEAR

Left Hotpants suited the active, liberated, youthful image of women in the early 1970s. Photograph by David Bailey, 1971.
Above Another example of hotpants as witnessed in the Kings Road, Chelsea, 1971.

Above The ultra-wide flared trousers that epitomize the early part of the decade. **Left** Indian cotton dungarees were another 1970s favourite.

Left Vivienne Westwood with bleached, cropped hair and simple baggy T-shirt, 1977. This look was widely adopted by the young.
Right The influence of Ralph Lauren's designs for Woody Allen's film Annie Hall (1978) can be seen in this layered jacket and crumpled socks.

PUNK

Opposite page. Far left
Skinhead boy and punk girl wearing spider-knit jumper, leather mini, ripped fishnet stockings and heavy boots. **Top centre** *Punk girl with her cheek pierced, and chains hanging from ear to cheek.* **Bottom centre** *Half Mohican hairstyle and half skinhead.* **Left** *Punk couple, the boy wearing a Sex Pistols T-shirt.* **Right** *Punk girls posing for a photograph. Swastikas were used to shock, as were Nazi-looking leather caps. With the exception of skinheads, they rarely indicated an affiliation with extreme right-wing politics.* **Below** *Punks. These all date from c. 1976, but it is difficult to be precise as there are many punks still faithful to the original styles up to the present day.*

UNISEX AND MENSWEAR

Left Men wearing patterned jumpers, Oxford bags and platform-soled shoes, 1973. This fashion was widely worn by both men and women.

Above Unisex harlequin-patterned coats, designed by Jacques Esterl, Paris, 1970.

Left "His and Hers" V-necked woollen pullovers in green and beige, 1973. This style was also fashionable in the 1920s. **Above** Fashion clothing from the Chelsea boutique, Mr Freedom, the interior of which was based on the theme of a ritzy 1940s casino, 1973. **Right** Casual unisex-style clothing photographed at a fashion show, c.1976.

CHILDREN

Left *An example of the range for winter 1978 by high-street store Boots. This shows the sort of practical, reasonably-priced children's clothes that characterized the 70s.*

Above *These French designs of 1975 show how closely children's clothes and hairstyles follow adult fashion — flared trousers and open-neck shirts for the boys, frilled collars and natural fabrics for the girls.*

Right *The casual feel to children's clothing in the 1970s is seen here in the use of bright colours, appliquéd motifs and braided trims, and floral prints.*
Below *Denim dungarees and T-shirts were widely worn by men, women and children throughout the 1970s.* **Bottom right** *Girls' fashion of 1972. The sailor dress on the far right parodies Shirley Temple styles of the 1930s, just as Biba parodied Hollywood styles for adults.*

HAIR AND ACCESSORIES

Above *Skimpy lace underwear by Lejaby, 1975.* **Top right** *Short, bleached hairstyle, 1979.* **Right** *Thea Cadabra handmade shoes, 1979. Working full-time, this young shoe-maker made two pairs of shoes and one experimental prototype a month.*

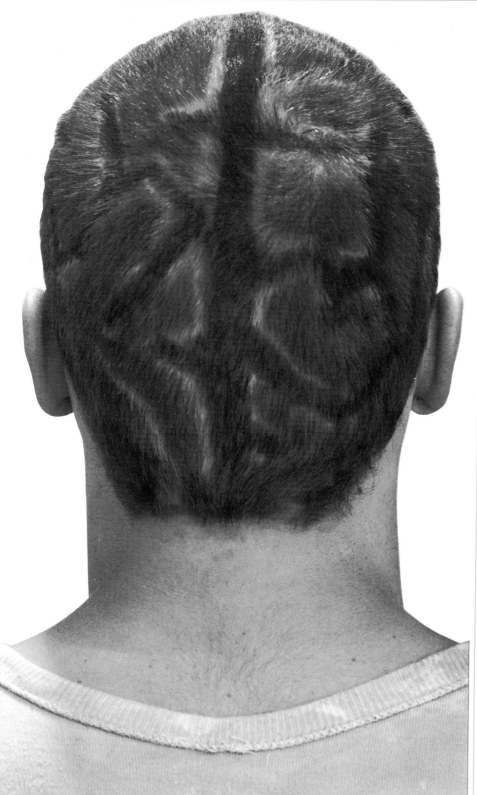

Left Elaborate skinhead hairstyle by Raymond Bird of Alan's in the Kings Road, Chelsea. The average price for such a cut was £30.00 for a seven-hour session. **Top right** Women's hats designed by Edward Mann, 1971. **Right** Cheap plastic fashion jewellery like this has been worn by many since the late 1970s. **Below** Punk-inspired haircut — known as The Brush — by top hairdresser, Vidal Sassoon, 1972

Women's suit by chain store Next, 1988.

CHAPTER·NINE
1980s

To date, fashion during the 1980s has been more pluralistic than ever before. The most noticeable shift in style is from the loose shapes favoured during the early 1980s to the more fitted and waist-accentuating designs currently in vogue. The most dramatic development in dress design this decade, however, has been made by the Japanese.

During the 1980s Japanese dress designers have introduced a startling and exciting new fashion force to the catwalks and greatly influenced everyday dress. Japan industrialised in the late nineteenth century and from this period onwards became increasingly receptive to European styles — be it of eating or dress — which were seen to represent progress. Although the Japanese welcomed aspects of Western culture, they have never discarded their own, and in fact have combined the best of both worlds. This trend is particularly evident in the clothing created by their fashion designers, who have repeatedly used the kimono as a starting point.

Japanese designers have rarely made a name for themselves in their own country, where the wealthy domestic consumer demands European — and particularly Parisian — labels. The Japanese did not propose Tokyo as a new fashion capital, but instead went to Paris to establish themselves, as so many designers had done before them. Indeed, as Peter Hillmore emphasized in *The Observer* in 1982, "Paris is an event, like Wimbledon or Henley. It matters not whether the fashion centre of the universe has moved on to Milan, New York or wherever; when people think of fashion they still think of Paris."[1]

Although Kenzo received some acclaim during the 1970s, his garments were largely designed along Western lines. Issey Miyake during the same period, however, injected radical new ideas into fashion having studied couture under Guy Laroche in 1968, the year of the Paris student uprisings. In 1970, Miyake independently created "Peeling Away to the Limit", which consisted of wrapping the figure in a long, narrow strip of fabric and then unwinding it until the naked body was revealed. By reducing body covering to its most basic, Miyake questioned the role of fashion and what exactly constituted acceptable modes of dress. By the early 1980s, a number of Japanese designers started to show their collections in Paris. Rei Kuwakubo, who had worked as a textile and freelance-fashion designer, formed the significantly French-named Comme des Garcons company in Japan in 1969. During the current decade Rei Kuwakubo, Yohji Yamamoto, Issey Miyake and Kansai Yamamoto are among the leading Japanese designers who have markedly changed the face of fashion.

These designers have created layered, loose-fitting and skilfully cut garments, which are predominantly made from wools, silks, cottons and linens in navy, grey, black, tan, and sometimes white and cream. These are often roughly

woven and while the colours are largely dull, the surface texture is not. Rei Kuwakubo, for example, uses exciting combinations of velvet mixed with hand-cut cord, or cotton woven with wool, and makes much use of crumpled fabrics. The skill of their cut is accentuated when the wearer moves and has, ironically, been carefully contrived to give a look of disarray. Many designs are influenced by traditional Eastern and Western working clothes and the garments worn by the poor. *Vogue* described Yohji Yamamoto's winter 1983 collection as reminiscent of, "...the ruched black and blue urchins, Artful Dodgers and twentieth-century waifs in stretched fisherman's jerseys, mixed-up T-shirts, Dickensian pinstripes and twisted stiff collars"[2]. While the intricacy of many Japanese designs is difficult to reproduce for the mass market, their choice of colours, fabrics and pyjama-shaped styles has been widely adopted.

In 1982 Rei Kuwakubo's post-Hiroshima look made a tremendous impact. Suzy Menkes, fashion editor of *The Times*, described this dramatic fashion show: "Down the catwalk, marching to a rhythmic beat like a race of warrior women, came models wearing ink black coat dresses, cut big, square, away from the body with no line, form or

Above

David Bowie has continued to be a fashion influence on the young throughout the 1970s and 80s. He is pictured here at the major cultural/media event of the decade, the fund-raising Live Aid concert of 1985.

Above right

Since Katherine Hamnett started her own company in 1979 she has produced designs aimed at active women. Her range of slogan T-shirts was extensively copied (as she intented it to be), proclaiming her views on political issues such as nuclear disarmament; here, "Stay Alive in '85".

Left
The Princess of Wales, in her
famous wedding dress, 1981, by
the Emmanuels.

Above
Joan Collins, star of American TV
soap opera, Dynasty, is pictured
attending a film première 1987.

recognisable silhouette...A skirt is a T-shirt, the dangling arms sashed around the hips. Over it goes a real T-shirt in wool jersey, cut asymmetrically, perhaps with a piece of splash printed black and white fabric tied to the shoulders. From the soles of her rice paddy slippers or square-toed rubber shoes to the top of her rag-tied hair (lower lip painted a bruised blue), this is a creature from a race apart."[3] The Japanese combine their flair for clothing design with great showmanship, which has assured them extensive press coverage.

In stark contrast to Japanese dress, the elaborate clothing worn in the internationally transmitted soap operas *Dynasty* and *Dallas* has had some impact upon dress in the 1980s. Their actresses, today's equivalent of the 1930s screen stars, promoted the fashion for exaggerated padded shoulders during the first half of the decade. The garments worn by the much publicized Princess of Wales have also had considerable influence upon conventional smart and evening wear; Elizabeth and David Emmanuel, who created the Princess's wedding dress in 1981, are among the many designers who are currently creating nostalgic evening dresses for the rich. Sarah Mower, associate editor of *Vogue*, described some of the most recent fashions which totally reject punk and Japanese styles (although these also remain very popular): "The current sexy-doll, high colour, very expensive fashion inspired by Christian Lacroix is almost certainly opposite in its insolent challenge to all the salient features of what went directly before. With the Right in power, this is the perfect right-wing look, revelling as it does in luxury, elitism and traditional versions of decorative femininity."[4] In 1986 Vivienne Westwood designed the eccentric mini-crini, which has since been taken into the realms of more conventional high fashion by Lacroix. These styles offer conspicuous, escapist and glamorous dress to a minority.

During this decade, wealth is increasingly being held in the hands of a few and as a consequence the couture and *prêt-à-porter* industries for both adults and children are flourishing, as are all the luxury trades. In spite of this, numerous leading designers are more than ever before licensing their names to enormous ranges of mass market goods. Many such items, like Dior stockings, retail at similar prices to those in the high-street shops. These goods have the advantage of prestigious connections — however far removed — to the luxury world of couture, and so the chain stores are being forced to upgrade their images. Furthermore, the high-fashion impetus of the very successful Next outlets has given the other multiple stores considerable competition. Next, whose clothing is targeted at the 25-45 age group, opened its womenswear shops in 1982, menswear in 1984 and introduced children's clothing in 1987. From the outset Next has placed great emphasis on clarity of display and colour-coordination, and has forced other manufacturers on to the defensive —

Above and ***Right***
Paul Smith's menswear features subtle variations on traditional shapes and colours to produce clothes that are interesting but never outrageous. He has exerted a major influence upon the design of all levels of menswear.

Left
Issey Miyake designs of 1984, featuring textured weaves; fabric textures are important in much of contemporary Japanese design.

Top right
In contrast to the sweetly feminine image of Princess Diana, or the sexily glamorous Joan Collins, a more active image of woman is seen at the Greenham Common US airbase which has been the scene of numerous demonstrations by women against the presence of nuclear weapons.

hence Marks and Spencer, in spite of the fact that their clothing sales represent one-fifth of the British total, are currently advertising in the society magazine *The Tatler*. Likewise Richard Shops, whose middle-range goods have recently been given a facelift by Conran Associates, are advertising in *Vogue*. This is a very new trend and one of major importance to the clothing industry.

In recent years a small section of the trade has begun undergoing a technological change as dramatic as the introduction of the sewing machine. Computer Aided Design (CAD) is being introduced into the design process, as both laying and cutting, the traditional skills of the pattern cutter, can now be worked by the computer. Cutting devices, such as the Eastman and the bandknife, can be programmed and the use of sewing machines can also be enhanced through microprocessor-based controls. These make high quality more easily and quickly obtainable. The industry's uptake of CAD will no doubt take many years and will only ever be introduced into the largest establishments. The vast majority of production units continue to employ less than 50 workers and rely heavily on homeworkers. The fashion industry has always been a labour, rather than capital, intensive industry and will doubtless remain so.

[1](Hillmore, Peter, *The Observer Review*, 24.10.82.)
[2](*Vogue*, 9.83.)
[3](Menkes, Suzy, *The Times*, 22.03.82.)
[4](*The Sunday Times Fashion Supplement*, 6.3.88.)

DRESSES

Above Dior dress with dropped waistline, summer 1980. **Top right** Jersey mini dress by Azzedine Alaia, summer 1987. This style has been very popular and widely copied. **Right** Half mini, half long dress by John Galliano, 1987.

Below Beige cotton and linen dress by Marks & Spencer, summer 1988. The choice of models and styles of garments that Marks & Spencer are currently retailing are aiming to entice a more discerning and fashion-conscious customer. The design of this garment is timeless, but more appealing than those of previous years.

Left Classic and very fashionable floral summer dress by Next, summer 1988.

SUITS

Left Neutral colours and simple shapes for 1987. **Below** Sophistication in black leather by Yves St. Laurent, 1984, whose career has hardly faltered since 1962.

Opposite page. Left Citrus colours for Jean Muir, 1986. **Top right** Guy Laroche started his own label in 1957. This 1982 style features an exaggerated shoulder line. **Far right** American designer Calvin Klein is known for his simple shapes which have been widely influential on chain stores such as Next. This suit is from 1984. **Bottom right** Karl Lagerfeld took the helm at Chanel in 1983. His witty interpretations of the classic Chanel suit are much copied: here it is in black denim for 1984.

COATS

Left Heavy coat designed by Jeff Banks for the Warehouse Utility Clothing Company, 1983. Ankle-length boots were widely worn during the early 1980s and these hairstyles have been fashionable throughout the decade. **Right** Winter coat by George Armani, for winter 1986-87.

Left Winter coat and classic, tailored trouser-suit by Ralph Lauren, winter 1984-85. **Top right** Mini-crini-style evening coat by Bill Blass, spring 1988. **Bottom right** Loose and unconventional coat-dress by Comme des Garçons, winter 1983-84.

177

EVENING DRESS

Left *Floral mini-crini dress with separate sleeves by Christian Lacroix, summer 1988.* **Above** *Princess of Wales, 1987.*

Opposite page. Top left *Egyptian-influenced dress by John Galliano, summer 1986.* **Bottom left** *Dress by Jean Paul Gaultier, summer 1987. Gaultier derives much of his inspiration from London street fashion, especially punk, which he glamorises for the Paris catwalks.* **Far right** *Turquoise and yellow evening outfit by Jasper Conran, summer 1987.*

CASUAL WEAR

Left Ralph Lauren is best known for his upmarket interpretations of classic American sports- and workwear, as in this stonewashed denim jacket. **Below** Black denim jeans and jacket by American designer Norma Kamali, 1986.

Right The re-emergence of the mini-skirt **Top right** Cotton and wool jersey leggings have provided a very popular and comfortable alternative to jeans. **Far right** (bottom) Blue denim jeans, in a baggy shape teamed with oversized jackets, London 1987. **Bottom right** 1980s street fashion, Parisian-style.

SEPARATES

Opposite. Left
Mixed check suit by Armani, summer 1987. Armani's garments are always beautifully cut and are often of a timeless design. **Top centre** *Casual London clothing, 1987.* **Bottom centre** *Perry Ellis, summer 1984.* **Right** *Thierry Mugler's padded-shouldered sports-style suits, winter 1984. As a result of the 1980s fitness craze, tracksuits and leggings have become widely worn for casual wear and have become an alternative to jeans. Mugler has exaggerated tracksuit styles, even to the point of aggression.*

Top left *Separates by Next, summer 1988.* **Bottom left** *Vivienne Westwood, 1983, controversially introduced underwear worn over outer garments.* **Right** *Marks & Spencer separates, summer 1988.*

183

MEN AND CHILDREN

Left Upmarket designs for children by Betty Jackson, 1987. **Bottom left** The popularity of hip-hop music in the late 80s has spawned its own style, based on American casualwear and sportswear. **Right** Polyester/cotton mix jacket for boys from high-street chain British Home Stores, 1984.

Left A simplified line for a two-piece suit by Issey Miyake, 1987.

HAIR AND ACCESSORIES

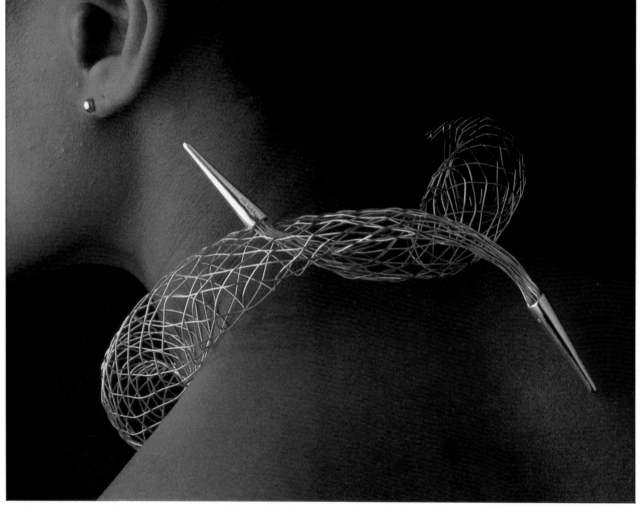

Top left Hairdressing photograph, 1987. Long and short hairstyles for men and women currently offer a great variety of choice. **Above** and **left** A selection of Paul Smith's shoes for men, and the interior of the Paul Smith shop in Covent Garden, London, 1988. Cheaper copies of these traditionally-styled cabinets have recently appeared in many men's clothing shops. Boxer shorts, which can be seen in the display case on the right, have been very fashionable in patterned fabrics for men throughout the decade. **Left** Experimental necklace, c. 1986.

Right and **Far right** These hairstyles have been fashionable in recent years. **Top left** Fashion earrings, c.1986. During the 1970s and 80s, many jewellery designers have adopted an exciting and experimental approach to their work.

5

INDEX

Page numbers in *italic* refer to the illustrations and captions

INDEX

Quarto would like to thank the
following for their help with this
publication and for permissions to
reproduce copyright material.
Key: t=top; b=bottom; r=right; l=left;
c=centre.

Cover: *c* Niall McInerney; *tl* Quarto; *tr*
BBC Hulton Picture Library; *bl,br*
The Telegraph Colour Library.

The Keystone Collection: **pp 9, 12, 13,
14**(*br*), **19, 28**(*bc*), **30**(*c*), **35**(*tr,br*),
37(*r*), **48, 49, 50, 52, 54**(*c*), **58**(*b*),
59(*tr,br*), **62**(*tl,tr,br*), **69**(*t*), **70**(*l*),
71(*l*), **74**(*tl,tr,r*), **75, 76**(*t, bl*),
77(*bl,tr*), **78, 79**(*tl,bl*), **82, 83**(*l,br*),
84(*l,r*), **85, 86**(*tr,br*), **87**(*tl,tc,b,r*), **90,
91, 92, 93**(*l,c*), **94**(*r*), **95, 96, 97, 98,
100**(*tr*), **102**(*r*), **103**(*r*), **104, 105, 106,
107, 108, 109, 110, 111, 112, 113, 114,
115, 116, 117, 118, 119, 123**(*bl,tr*), **124,
125**(*b*), **126, 127**(*tr,br*), **128**(*tr,bc,br*),
129(*tl,bl*), **130**(*bl,br*), **131**(*tl,bl*),
132(*tl,bl*), **133**(*tr,br*), **134**(*tr,br*), **135,
136, 138**(*bl,br*), **139, 140, 141**(*tr,br*),
142, 143, 147(*tl*), **148, 150**(*r*),
151(*tl,tr,br*), **152, 153, 154**(*l,tr*),
155(*tr,br*), **156**(*r*), **157**(*bc*), **158**(*tc*),
159(*tr*), **160, 161, 162, 163**(*br*),
164(*tl,tr*), **165, 168, 169**(*bl,r*), **171**(*tr*),
172(*l*), **175**(*tc*), **178**(*r*), **184**(*r*).

The Telegraph Colour Library: **pp2,
51, 120**(*c*), **123**(*tl,tc*), **125**(*tr*), **127**(*l*),
128(*l*), **129**(*r*), **130**(*tl*), **131**(*r*), **133**(*l*),
137(*b*), **138**(*tl*), **141**(*l*), **146, 147**(*tr*),
149(*l*), **150**(*tl,bl*), **151**(*c*), **154**(*br*),
155(*l*), **156**(*l*), **157**(*t,bl,br*),
158(*l,bc,r*), **159**(*t,bl*), **164**(*b*), **174**(*l*),
181(*l,tr*).

Mary Evans Picture Library:
pp10, 11(*r*), **16, 20, 21, 23**(*tl,bl,tr*),
24(*l*), **25**(*r*), **26, 28**(*l,br*), **30**(*l,r*),
31(*l*), **34, 35**(*l*), **36**(*r*), **37**(*l*), **38**(*r*),
39(*l*), **40, 41**(*c*), **42**(*r*), **43**(*l*), **45**(*l*),
52(*tc,tr*), **53**(*l*), **55**(*r*), **56**(*t*), **57**(*l*),
58(*t*), **59**(*tc*), **61**(*l,tr*), **62**(*bl*), **63**(*r*),
70(*r*), **73, 77**(*tl,br*), **79**(*tr*), **86**(*l*),
94(*l*).

Niall McInerney:
pp144, 154(*bc*), **169**(*tl*), **170,
172**(*tr,br*), **174**(*r*), **175**(*l,tr,br*), **176**(*r*),
177(*l,br*), **178**(*l*), **179**(*tl,bl,r*), **180**(*r*),
181(*bc,br*), **182, 183**(*bl*), **184**(*tl,bl*),
185.

The Victoria and Albert Museum:
pp23(*br*), **24**(*r*), **42**(*l*), **43**(*r*), **45**(*r*),
71(*r*), **72**(*l,c,r*), **93**(*r*), The Hearst
Corporation, courtesy of *Harper's
Bazaar:* **pp88**(*l,tr,br*), **89**(*l,r*). Next
Collection: **pp24**(*tr*), 166, **173**(*l*),
183(*tl*). The Marks & Spencer's
Archive: **p15** The Mansell Collection:
pp18, 25(*tl*), **38**(*l*), **39**(*r*), **44**(*tl*). The
Kobal Collection: **pp61**(*br*), **67**(*l*),
68(*t*), **103**(*l*). Barnaby's Picture
Library: **pp56**(*bl,br*), **57**(*r*), **59**(*tl*),
76(*br*). BBC Hulton Picture Library:
pp101, 102(*l*), *Christian Dior:* **p80.**
Elsie Clinch: **p63**(*l*). Punch: **69**(*b*),
Amy de La Haye: **pp41**(*r*),
44(*bl,bc,br*), **46, 52**(*br*), **53**(*r*),
54(*br*). John Grain: **pp25**(*bl*),
60(*bc,br*). Marks & Spencer:
pp173(*r*), **183**(*r*). Paul Smith:
p171(*tl,b*). Bill Blass Ltd: **p177**(*tr*).
Ralph Lauren: **p180**(*l*).

We would also like to thank John
Clancy and Michael Lowrie
Hairdressing, Brighton, for their help.
Every effort has been made to trace
and acknowledge all copyright
holders; Quarto would like to
apologise if any omissions have been
made.